COOK LIKE A PRO

COOK LIKE A PRO

A Complete Illustrated Course for Today's Cook

Eike Linnich

Christian Teubner

BARRON'S

Woodbury, New York · London · Toronto · Sydney

First English-language edition published 1985 by
Barron's Educational Series, Inc.

© 1983 by Teubner Edition, Germany

The title of the German edition is
Kochen Können Wie Ein Profi

All inquiries should be addressed to:
Barron's Educational Series, Inc.
113 Crossways Park Drive
Woodbury, New York 11797

International Standard Book No. 0-8120-5662-0

Library of Congress Catalog No. 85-13401

Library of Congress Cataloging-in-Publication Data
Linnich, Eike.
  Cook like a pro.
  Translation of: Kochen können wie ein Profi.
  "Translation from German: Susan Herrmann Loomis,
Irina E. Carrithers"—P.
  Includes index.
  1. Cookery.   I. Teubner, Christian.   II. Title.
TX651.L52413   1985   641.5   85-13401
ISBN 0-8120-5662-0

PRINTED IN WEST GERMANY

5 6 7 8 TBNR 9 8 7 6 5 4 3 2 1

Translation from German	Susan Herrmann Loomis
	Irina E. Carrithers
English edition editor	Pat Connell
Recipe test and text	Eike Linnich
Introductory chapters	Hannelore Blohm
Food Styling	Christine Reulan
	Walburga Streif
Photography	Christian Teubner
Photo Assistance	Walter Pfisterer
Design	Wolfgang Steger
Kitchen and Appliances	Robert Bosch, Munich
	WMF Württembergische Metallwarenfabrik Ag, Geislingen
	Christian Wagner Metallwarenfabrik GmbH and Co., Esslingen

INTRODUCTION

This book shows you how to cook well, and according to today's nutritional standards—today's art of cooking. In an easy-to-follow style, we offer food of superior quality while showing you how to achieve professional-level results in any standard home kitchen. We have chosen basic recipes which you can use to create even the most complex recipes of your choosing. With this basic knowledge we offer you ideas for developing your own creations, for enjoying and discovering new horizons in cooking, and for savoring meals in an entirely new way. **All recipes yield four servings, depending on the accompanying side dishes, unless otherwise stated.**

We have used color photographs to further illustrate important steps, and have shown entire preparation sequences to help you follow the recipes step by step. The photographs show the correct handling of ingredients and appliances, and the explanations of procedures help make for effortless cooking.

The art of cooking begins with shopping practices modeled after the French tradition of *la cuisine du marché*, or cooking according to what is available at the market. If quality and fresh ingredients are the basic requirements for good cooking, it follows that what is available at the market will determine what you cook. If you follow this premise, you'll have to say goodbye to routine cooking. You will need imagination, but that will make your shopping a pleasant experience. Always look for fresh, superior-quality ingredients—which may be a bit more costly than average ingredients, but good cooking is not necessarily expensive. Our selection of recipes shows that you can use common ingredients even for special meals and you may substitute less expensive ingredients, remembering always to keep quality and freshness in mind.

Cooking by the Seasons

You may think that using seasonal ingredients is no longer important since, thanks to today's transportation methods, almost any type of food is available year-round. Yet high prices and a lack of freshness and natural flavor, particularly in fruit and vegetables but also in fish and poultry, militate against this. Such foods simply taste better when they are in season, and that is also when they are least expensive.

Tools

Your tools have to be of professional quality, but don't rush out to buy a brand new kitchen. Just keep adding basic, reliable, functional professional tools to those you already have and you will accumulate a good, basic *batterie de cuisine*. Good equipment begins with knives and ends with reliable kitchen machines, which make many tasks easier. In particular, you will find most useful a good-quality food processor and an electric mixer that has a variety of attachments.

Cooking Essentials

It is not the quantity of appliances and serving dishes that guarantees success; it's the quality of the food. Here is a selection of essential appliances, dishes, and utensils.

● Top-of-the-line knives, which must always be kept sharp, are essential for cutting and peeling. You need a knife with a long, sturdy blade to slice, chop, and mince and another one with a thin, flexible blade to filet fish and bone meats. You also need a serrated knife and several smaller paring knives to clean, peel, and prepare fruits and vegetables.

5

Porcelain ovenware is the prettiest for soufflés, but the sides must be straight so the soufflé rises evenly. Use pots and pans made of heavy, top-quality materials such as cast iron and stainless steel. Since these materials conduct heat efficiently they will save you time and energy. They are easy to maintain and sturdy enough to take heavy use.

There are all kinds of useful kitchen gadgets, too, like cherry pitters, garlic presses, and egg slicers, and peppermills. You will also need ladles and scoops, as well as pastry brushes for greasing pans and molds. And for cooling freshly baked cakes you'll need a cooling rack.

Food Processors and Electric Mixers

The food processor is excellent for a variety of jobs. It has several attachments that can be added as desired. The body of the machine is compact enough to fit into the smallest kitchen, and the attachments can be easily stored in drawers and cabinets. The processor can grind meat, chop vegetables, purée fish, and blend liquids. The heavy-duty electric mixer performs other tasks, such as whipping cream, creaming butter, and kneading bread with perfect results. Yeast doughs are very smooth and satiny, whipping cream keeps its consistency even after several hours, and egg whites reach enormous volume with a mixer.

● A good kitchen scale and a standard set of measuring cups are the most reliable utensils for measuring and weighing. A glass measuring cup is useful for measuring liquids; a meat thermometer and a timer are helpful as well.

● A set of wire strainers and a colander are basic tools for sifting and straining. Very helpful too is a sturdy metal or plastic netting stretched over a wooden frame—like a *tamis*—for straining fillings, purées, fruits, or creams. And you should have cheesecloth on hand for straining clear stocks and juices.

● Plastic or metal bowls with rounded bottoms are handy for mixing. A stainless steel bowl can stand in for a double boiler top, since stainless steel conducts heat very efficiently. Wooden spoons and rubber spatulas are good for mixing and for cleaning bowls.

Tools for Turning and Basting Foods

Wooden or metal tools for turning roasts should have a handle bent at an angle so you avoid burning yourself. Narrow spatulas of various lengths are good for smoothing doughs, creams, and icings.

A rolling pin and a large, flat work surface are essential for rolling out dough evenly. For best results use a marble slab, which keeps the dough cool. To decorate and garnish foods, you need a pastry wheel, a decorating comb, and pastry bags with tips in various designs and sizes for making cream puffs and meringues.

Cake rings of various sizes, either aluminum, cardboard, or wax paper, are essential for baking, as are cake pans, cookie sheets, and molds. Cookie cutters are available in a multitude of shapes and sizes.

1 **A pro in the kitchen** uses a hand-held whisk to mix ingredients efficiently. The whisk is held at an angle to the bowl and moved in a circular motion to incorporate ingredients from the sides of the bowl. It is vigorous manual work but it guarantees optimum results.

2 **A rotary egg beater** makes beating a bit easie Be sure to move the bea around the bowl for thorough mixing. Also, altern beating with scraping the sides of the bowl with a rubber spatula.

4 **A heavy-duty electric mixer** with a rotating bowl guarantees professional results because the large whisk beats and blends while rotating around the sides of the bowl in an angled position so it can incorporate all the ingredients in the bowl.

The beaters of a portable electric mixer only rotate on one axis. They are small, so you must also move the beater around the bowl to thoroughly mix the ingredients. The technique is the same as with a rotary egg beater, but the motorized power of the electric mixer makes the work easier.

STOCKS AND SAUCES

We don't have to praise *nouvelle cuisine* to the sky, nor do we have to hide behind it any longer. But it must be admitted that the chefs of nouvelle cuisine have strongly influenced all kinds of cooking. From it we have rediscovered *la cuisine du marché*, or cooking according to what is available in the market. Using the freshest ingredients available gives the fullest flavor to good cooking—provided that the ingredients are prepared properly for delicate, fresh, light results.

This is true for all foods, including sauces, glazes, and soups made from rich, delicate stocks. These important sauces and stocks enable you to be creative in the kitchen and to perform delicious magic with meat, fish, poultry, and game. Forget thick, flour-based sauces, which are unfortunately still scooped by the gallon over roasts and potatoes. They no longer have a place in today's cooking, though a good velouté—a basic sauce made from a lightly flour-thickened mixture—is still indispensable. Velouté should be made with exquisite, flavorful stock, as should béchamel, Mornay, and velvety fish-based sauces. We show you how to prepare these sauces properly, and we send you to the kitchen with words from the French gourmand Gogue, who said in 1856, "Much sauce, bad cook; little sauce, good cook."

BROTH, BOUILLON, CONSOMMÉ

Broth is an appropriate but bland word for the delicious liquid that gains its flavor and richness from a variety of ingredients including meats, vegetables, and spices. "Clear soup" is correct, too, but the French *consommé* sounds much nicer. Consommé is a very flavorful, clear meat broth that becomes "double consommé" when it is clarified with extra beef.

The flavor and richness of a stock are determined by its ingredients. Beef and game make a very flavorful stock, chicken lends a mild flavor, and stock made from veal is very versatile.

A bouquet garni is a combination of herbs, usually thyme, parsley, and bay leaves, which adds a wonderful flavor to the stock. You can also add vegetables if you like, but too many can make the stock too sweet, and dark greens destroy its color. Light-colored vegetables give it a fresh flavor that is heightened if they are sautéed first.

Gelatin thickens stock. Use skin, tendons, gristle, and joint bones because they contain a lot of natural gelatin; beef shank and ribs work well, too. Veal also has a lot of natural gelatin, and stock made from chicken jells very well.

IMPORTANT

Stock can turn sour if stored uncovered. For best results, quickly cool the stock to room temperature by placing it in its container, uncovered, over a pot filled with cold water. When the stock is cool, cover it tightly and refrigerate or freeze it. Season the stock to taste before using. If you are storing stock in the refrigerator for several days, bring it back to a boil, then refrigerate again.

Trout, cod, sole, and tilefish are among the best choices for making fish stock. Bones, fins, and the head (with the gills removed) make the stock dark and cloudy, but highly flavorful. Clarifying the stock is necessary only if you want to make aspic.

The following recipe is a step-by-step explanation of how to prepare a basic clear stock. Follow it, too, for stock made from veal bones, beef, game, or poultry. Ham bones and bacon rinds also make a hearty broth.

For a basic veal stock, you will need: 3½ pounds (1½ k) veal bones; 1 pound (500 g) poultry parts; 1 pound (500 g) veal shank; 1 medium carrot, peeled;

the white part of 1 leek; a 2-ounce (50 g) piece of peeled celery root.

Prepare chicken stock according to the following recipe, substituting chicken parts and carcass for the beef and veal bones.

BASIC CLEAR STOCK

For about 2 quarts (2 L)
1 stewing fowl (with giblets), cut into 6 pieces
1 generous pound (500 g) beef shank
1 generous pound (500 g) veal bones
approximately 10 cups (2½ L) water
2 large carrots, peeled
1 medium celery root, peeled
2 firm leeks, with green tops
1 bunch fresh parsley stems
3 sprigs fresh thyme
1 clove garlic
1 bay leaf
2 whole cloves
2 yellow onions, unpeeled

Prepare stock following photographs and instructions. Depending on how you intend to use it, you may also clarify stock.

1 **Layer meat in the pot.** Layer chicken, beef, veal bones, and giblets loosely on a rack or strainer set in a large pot (rack will keep meat from sticking to the bottom and burning).

2 **Cover with water and bring to a boil.** Add enough cold water to reach 1 inch (2½ cm) above the meat and bones. Cover and set over low heat; bring to a slow boil. (This will take about 1 hour.)

3 **Skim off foam.** When the broth comes to a boil, carefully push the gray foam to the side of the pot and skim off with a ladle.

4 **Add cold water** and skim off foam periodically, until there is only clear white foam left, which will dissolve later.

5 **Tie bouquet garni.** Tie vegetables, fresh herbs, garlic, and bay leaf (bouquet garni) with string, leaving a loop in the end for handling.

6 **Add spices.** Stick whole cloves into onions (the onion skins will give the stock a nice golden color) and add to the stock with the bouquet garni. Cover with more water if necessary and simmer for about 5 hours. Remove meat after 1 hour, separate skin, tendons, and bones, and place them back into the pot to simmer in the stock.

7 **Strain broth.** Line a strainer or colander with cheesecloth. Pour the stock into it and let drain. Do not press on ingredients left in strainer.

8 **Remove fat from hot stock.** If you will be using the stock right away, carefully slide a strip of paper towel across its surface right to the edge of the pot; remove only fat, with as little broth as possible.

9 **Remove fat from cold stock.** If you have time to chill the stock this method works best; the fat is congealed and easily lifted off, resulting in a completely degreased stock. Reserve the fat for frying and sautéing.

HEARTY BEEF STOCK

For about 3 quarts (3 L)
1½ pounds (675 g) beef shank
1½ pounds (675 g) beef short ribs
1½ pounds (675 g) marrow bones
approximately 4 quarts (4 L) water
2 large carrots
1 celery root (reserve stalks)
3 medium onions
¼ cup (60 mL) oil
1 firm leek
1 bunch fresh parsley stems
2 sprigs fresh thyme
1 bay leaf

Place the meat and bones in a large pot and add enough water to cover well. Cover and bring to a boil over low heat. Skim off foam as shown in the recipe for basic stock. Meanwhile, peel and dice carrots, celery root, and onions and sauté in oil until they are golden brown and onions are transparent. Make a bouquet garni from the leek, reserved celery stalks, parsley stems, thyme, and bay leaf. Add with sautéed vegetables to the stock. Let the stock simmer slowly for 5 hours, half covered. Remove meat after 2 hours. Strain and season to taste.

Add sautéed vegetables to beef stock. During sautéing, the vegetables release flavors that will enhance this hearty stock. Add the vegetables and bouquet garni to the stock after the foam has been skimmed.

CLARIFYING STOCK

3 egg whites
1 medium carrot, diced
¼ celery root, diced
2 tablespoons oil
4 cups (1 L) stock made from beef, fish, game, or poultry

Clarify stock if you will be serving it as a garnished consommé or using it to make aspic, which is delicious with cold meats and which surrounds pâtés and mousses with a flavorful, protective covering.

1 **Beat egg whites.** In a bowl, beat egg whites with a whisk or beater until they form soft peaks. Sauté the carrot and celery root in oil until they are crisp-tender.

2 **Remove vegetables from heat** and let cool, then add them to the beaten egg whites. Stir lightly with a whisk until they are just mixed together.

3 **Pour the egg white and vegetable** mixture into the lukewarm stock. Turn heat to high and stir stock.

4 **Stir until egg whites have lost volume** and form a solid covering on the surface of the stock. Remove pot from heat and let egg whites set completely.

5 **Strain the clarified stock.** The egg whites will have absorbed all the cloudy impurities from the stock. Line a strainer or colander with cheesecloth and strain stock, letting it drain slowly.

FISH STOCK

For about 2 quarts (2 L)
3 tablespoons (40 g) butter
white parts of 4 leeks, cut into rounds
2 onions, diced
1 small carrot, cut into rounds
2¼ pounds (1 kg) bones, skin, fins, and heads from sole, bass, cod, and/or trout
approximately 2½ quarts (2½ L) water
½ fennel bulb, sliced, or 1 tablespoon fennel leaves
4 sprigs parsley
2 sprigs fresh thyme
1 bay leaf

Fins make stock bitter, so remove them by pulling them away from the head and cutting them off with scissors. Prepare the stock following the step-by-step photographs; clarify it if desired. Reduce stock to 2 cups (450 mL) for soups and 1 cup (225 mL) for sauces by simmering it gently. For a clear stock, skim off the foam periodically.

KEEPING STOCKS AND SAUCES

At first glance the quantities given for stocks and sauces in this book may seem very large. However, they work for small needs as well, because preparation time and effort are the same for large or for small quantities. And if you don't use stock within a couple of days, you can safely freeze it for up to a year. After they are cooked, let stocks and sauces cool down completely, uncovered. Then cover and store them in the refrigerator. Remove any fat after it has congealed. Place freezer bags inside freezer containers, fill with stock, and tie tightly to remove as much air as possible from around the stock. After the stock is frozen, you may remove the containers to use again. Ice cube trays also work well for freezing small portions.

1 **Sauté vegetables.** Melt butter in a large pot over medium heat, add vegetables, and sauté until onions are transparent. Rinse the fish pieces under cold water and add to vegetables.

2 **Add water** to cover all ingredients well. Add bouquet garni of fennel, parsley, thyme, and bay leaf and let simmer for 20 minutes.

3 **Skim foam from stock.** During cooking, skim off gray foam with a ladle, then strain stock through cheesecloth. Simmer stock for an additional 10 minutes, then skim off foam again.

13

1 **Making stock in the oven.** Combine ingredients in a large pot and place on center oven rack. Set the oven temperature to 400°F (205°C) and cook for about 15 minutes, or until fat collects on the bottom of the pot.

2 **Add water** to cover all the ingredients. Cover and cook for 30 minutes, or until stock starts to boil. Reduce heat to 250°F (125°C) and continue cooking for 5 hours.

3 **The golden stock is ready.** The flavors are concentrated in this hearty stock, which will be clear and pure.

LIGHT AND DARK SAUCE BASES

These light and dark bases are homemade "semi-finished" products. Usually used to create sauces for meats or to make aspics and glazes, they are prepared from beef, lamb, and pork. They keep for weeks in the refrigerator, provided that they are well reduced and covered with a layer of fat. Stocks and sauces from which the fat has been removed keep better if stored in the freezer. Stock frozen in an ice cube tray is very handy for use in small quantities.

Increased cooking time makes stock more concentrated. The more gelatin in the stock the sooner it jells, as shown in the light and brown glazes in the pans on this page. They were made from stock bases, described here, filtered through cheesecloth, then reduced to about one-quarter of their original volume.

LIGHT BASE

1 generous pound (500 g) veal shank
1 generous pound (500 g) veal rib
1 generous pound (500 g) chicken wings or backs
1 large celery root
2 leeks with tops
2 large carrots
2 yellow onions with only outermost skin removed
about 2½ quarts (2½ L) water

Place veal and chicken in a Dutch oven. Clean and coarsely chop vegetables, and place them around the veal and chicken. Follow photographs and instructions for clear stock. Strain through cheesecloth into a clean pot. Cool, chill, and remove fat after it has congealed. Over low heat, simmer skimmed stock until reduced to the desired strength. Cover lightly and let cool. Fill freezer containers with reduced stock and store in the refrigerator, or freeze for use up to 1 year later. Season to taste when using.

BROWN GAME BASE

6 tablespoons (75 mL) oil
2 large game bones (from venison, elk, boar)
1 generous pound (500 g) beef shank
1 large carrot
½ medium celery root
1 medium onion
1 tablespoon plus 1 teaspoon tomato paste
about 2½ quarts (2½ L) water
white parts of 2 leeks
5 sprigs parsley
1 sprig fresh thyme
1 bay leaf
2 shallots
2 cloves garlic
8 juniper berries

Have game bones and meat cut into 2-inch (5-cm) pieces. Heat oil in a Dutch oven or skillet as shown in the photographs and add the bones and meat. Peel and dice the carrot, celery root, and onion and add to meat with tomato paste. Continue cooking and pour cold water over all.

Cover and cook in 250°F (125°C) oven for 4 hours or simmer partially covered on top of the stove. Strain through cheesecloth, let cool, and remove congealed fat. Reduce stock to desired strength, fill storage containers, and let cool completely, uncovered. Close tightly and store in refrigerator for a few days or in the freezer for later use.

It is very easy to prepare a Bordelaise sauce from a reduced beef or game base. Separately reduce red wine and meat base to about one-third their original volume; mix together and reduce by about half. Season to taste with salt, pepper, and fresh lemon juice. Enjoy the sauce with game or beef.

2 **Add vegetables.** Dice carrot, celery root, and onion; add to meat with tomato paste and continue cooking for 20 more minutes, stirring occasionally.

1 **Browning the bones and meat.** Preheat oven to 475°F (250°C). Heat oil in a deep pot or Dutch oven, layer the bones and the meat in the pot, and brown in the oven for 20 minutes, turning frequently.

3 **Add water.** Add enough cold water to loosen any bits of meat stuck to the bottom of the pan. Turn off oven; after 10 minutes, transfer the contents of the pot to another large pot.

4 **Add water** until all the ingredients are well covered and "swimming" in the pot. Bring the stock slowly to the boil, partially covered.

5 **Skim off foam** when stock starts to simmer. Using a ladle, push foam to the side of the pot and skim it off. Continue skimming until the foam is light and clear.

6 **Add bouquet garni and spices.** Tie leeks, parsley, thyme, and bay leaf together and add to broth along with shallots, garlic, and juniper berries.

15

BASIC SAUCES

FRESH TOMATO SAUCE

For approximately 2 cups (450 mL)
1¼ pounds (525 g) fresh tomatoes
2 tablespoons (25 g) butter, or more
1 medium onion
1 small carrot, peeled
1 cup (240 mL) beef or chicken stock
white parts of 2 leeks
8 sprigs parsley
2 sprigs fresh basil
1 small bay leaf
salt and pepper
pinch of sugar

Prepare the tomato sauce following the photographs and instructions. If desired, add more butter to make it milder and more full-flavored. Or used fried bacon bits and onion instead of butter to make a heartier, more flavorful sauce; in this case, omit the basil and add a sprig of fresh thyme and a minced garlic clove. To make a very mild sauce with a delicate tomato flavor, stir in cream or crème fraîche, or finish the sauce with a few spoonfuls of velouté sauce (page 18).

Prepare a delicate, very quick tomato sauce by puréeing peeled, seeded, and quartered tomatoes in a blender. Pour into a pot and add 1 teaspoon Worcestershire sauce, 1 cup (240 mL) dry white wine, 1 teaspoon oregano, and 1 clove garlic, minced (optional). Bring to a boil and cook until thickened.

1 **Peel tomatoes.** Immerse briefly in boiling water and rinse under cold water to loosen the skin. With a pointed knife, start peeling from the stem end.

2 **Seed tomatoes.** Cut tomatoes into quarters and remove the seeds. Place the remaining tomato flesh in a strainer to drain. Peel and dice onion and carrot.

3 **Sauté vegetables.** Over medium heat, melt butter until it foams. Add onion and carrot and sauté until the onion is transparent, approximately 12 to 15 minutes.

4 **Add tomatoes,** stock, and a bouquet garni made from leeks, parsley, basil, and bay leaf; simmer for 25 minutes.

5 **Purée sauce.** Remove sauce from heat and let cool. Remove bouquet garni and pour sauce into blender. Beginning on low, purée sauce, increasing speed until blended.

6 **Pour sauce into a clean pot** and reheat over low heat to prevent sticking. Season to taste with salt, pepper, and sugar. If desired, add a little more butter.

SAUCE HOLLANDAISE

For about 1¼ cups (300 mL)
3 egg yolks
1 tablespoon water
1 teaspoon salt
¼ teaspoon white pepper
1 cup (250 g) butter
1 tablespoon fresh lemon juice

Hollandaise sauce must be prepared very carefully over low heat to prevent it from curdling. For the best results, use a double boiler top set over (not in) barely simmering water. Melt butter in a saucepan and set aside to cool. Clarify butter by carefully pouring off the yellow liquid into a small bowl, leaving the white milk solids behind; discard the solids. Prepare the hollandaise sauce according to the photographs and add lemon juice to taste. Leave in hot water bath, covered, until ready to use. Beat vigorously before serving.

1 **Beat egg yolks** in a bowl; add water, salt, and pepper. For best results use a stainless steel bowl, which is a good conductor of heat. Place over hot but not boiling water.

2 **Whisk sauce** until it is creamy. (Make sure you whisk all the sauce—not just from the center, but also from the bottom and sides of the bowl).

3 **Continue to whisk vigorously** until the ingredients are light and creamy. This step is completed when the sauce suddenly offers more resistance and thickens.

4 **Add clarified butter.** Add butter to egg mixture drop by drop, whisking constantly and being careful to incorporate butter completely before adding more.

Hollandaise is a very delicate sauce that goes well with meat, fish, and vegetables. It has a neutral flavor that complements foods without destroying their own flavors. We love it with vegetables like asparagus and artichokes, with poached fish, and with delicate shellfish. Hollandaise sauce is the base for several other sauces:

Prepare Béarnaise sauce as for hollandaise, but instead of water use a stock made from ⅔ cup (150 mL) white wine, ¼ cup (60 mL) white wine vinegar, 2 shallots, diced, and ½ cup (125 mL) each fresh chervil and fresh tarragon. Reduce mixture to 1 to 2 tablespoons of liquid, then season to taste with 1 teaspoon each chopped fresh chervil and tarragon leaves and a pinch of cayenne pepper. Enjoy this sauce with juicy beef or veal steaks.

Turn Béarnaise into Choron sauce by stirring 2 tablespoons tomato paste into the finished sauce, omitting the chervil and tarragon if desired. This pink variation tastes best over artichokes and poached eggs.

Prepare Maltaise sauce as for hollandaise, using fresh lemon juice instead of water and finishing the sauce with the juice of a blood orange, if available.

SAUCES WITH A ROUX BASE

These flour-and-butter-based sauces can be the foundation for several variations. They are incorrectly regarded as fattening or heavy, but need not be. It is important that these sauces be cooked well, that the ingredient combinations work, and that the stock, which determines the taste of the entire sauce, be of the highest quality.

BASIC WHITE SAUCE (VELOUTÉ)

For about 2¼ cups (600 mL)
1½ tablespoons (20 g) butter
1 small onion, finely chopped
3 tablespoons flour
3 cups (700 mL) cold stock, fat removed, made from veal, poultry, fish, or vegetables
1 cup (240 mL) heavy cream
1 teaspoon salt
½ teaspoon white pepper

A good sauce takes time, and so does the roux, which is prepared as follows:

Melt the butter over medium heat until it foams. Add flour and whisk vigorously to completely blend the flour and butter, but do not brown. After 5 minutes, pour in cold stock. For a velouté sauce, sauté chopped onion in the butter before adding flour, as shown in the photographs.

The most important variations of this basic sauce follow later.

1 **Sauté onion.** Melt the butter in a saucepan over medium heat until it foams. Add chopped onion and cook, stirring, until transparent.

2 **Add flour.** Sprinkle flour over sautéed onion and stir constantly over low heat for 10 to 15 minutes. Do not brown!

3 **Add stock.** Pour cold stock a bit at a time over roux, whisking constantly to prevent lumps.

4 **Skim foam.** While sauce simmers for 30 minutes over low heat, stir occasionally and skim off foam. Boil cream until reduced by half and stir into sauce. Cook gently for 15 more minutes.

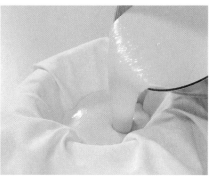

5 **Strain sauce** through cheesecloth, holding the corners of the cloth to form a bag and turning the bag to press sauce through. Season with salt and pepper.

6 **The basic white sauce is completed.** The French use the word *velouté*, which means "velvety," to describe this mild, creamy sauce, which pours easily from a spoon.

Here are some variations on the basic velouté:

Béchamel Sauce

Follow the recipe and directions for a basic white sauce; substitute 2 cups (450 mL) veal stock and 2 cups (450 mL) milk for 3 cups (700 mL) stock. Season to taste with pepper and freshly grated nutmeg. Béchamel is the basis for many other simple sauces.

Fish Sauce Bercy

For this delicate sauce, prepare a velouté using fish stock. Sauté 2 diced medium shallots in 1½ tablespoons (20 g) butter until transparent. Add ½ cup (125 mL) dry, white wine and reduce by one-third. Make a roux, stir in the fish stock, and continue as for basic white sauce. Season to taste with pepper and mix with 1 teaspoon finely chopped fresh parsley.

Onion Sauce

This sauce tastes superb over boiled beef or corned beef. Pour boiling water over 1 large sliced onion, place in a colander, rinse with cold water, and let drain. Sauté onion until soft but not brown in 2 tablespoons (25 g) butter, then purée in a blender. Add to velouté just after the stock (picture 3) and continue as shown. Strain through cheesecloth if a smoother sauce is desired.

Mornay Sauce

Mornay is a classic sauce, perfect for vegetables and ideal for browning under the broiler. It is made from Béchamel sauce; add ½ cup (50 g) grated Gruyère cheese, stirring constantly. Then add 1½ tablespoons (20 g) butter and 1 egg yolk, beaten with a little cream. Season to taste with freshly grated nutmeg and pepper.

Horseradish Sauce

Stir a generous amount of freshly grated horseradish into basic velouté sauce when it is completed. Season to taste with vinegar or fresh lemon juice and a pinch of sugar.

Browned Butter Sauce

This is very similar to basic white sauce; use with game or beef roast. Just cook the butter and flour mixture until light to medium brown. Continue as for a basic velouté.

Curry Sauce

Curry sauce tastes good with boiled fish, chicken, and lamb. Prepare as for basic white sauce, but remove finished roux from the heat and stir in 2 to 3 tablespoons curry powder. Return to heat, add fish or meat broth, and continue as for basic velouté. Strain through a strainer or cheesecloth.

Broccoli Mornay: pour Sauce Mornay over cooked broccoli and place under pre-heated broiler until lightly golden, about 2 to 3 minutes.

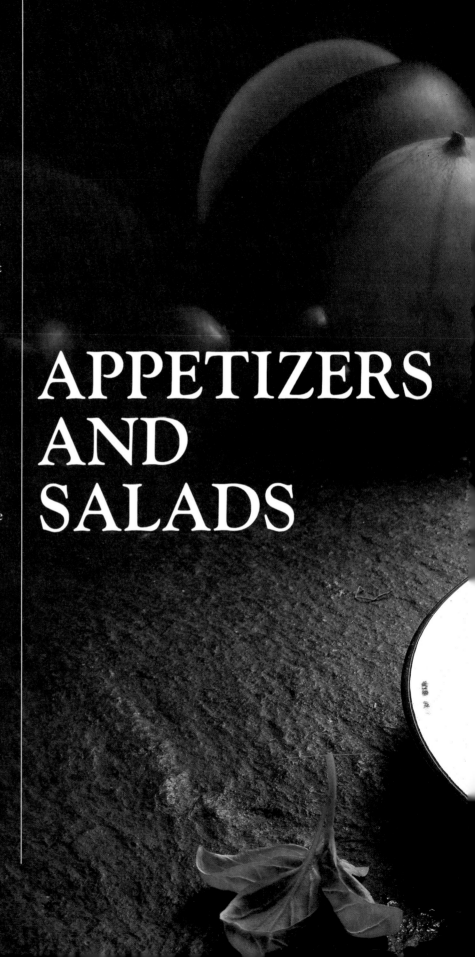

A well-prepared appetizer is a lovely addition to any meal. Consider an appealing salad like the one shown here, made with ruby-leaf lettuce enhanced by diced ripe tomatoes, orange sections, and butter-sautéed liver, all dressed with the best vinaigrette for zesty flavor and a soft, shimmer. Or how about a luscious Danish pâté? Or juicy, quickly sautéed scampi? Think of velvety sauces, and of scrambled eggs with caviar; the repertoire is infinite. Every day you can put a new creation on the table, as long as you have a vivid imagination and you know how to whip up good sauces and dressings. Salad can easily become a complete meal—a summer lunch or even dinner, if it is made not just with vegetables and fruit but also with high-protein ingredients like fish, cheese, poultry, game, red meat, or nuts. The most important thing for all salad dressings is to use only the best oils and vinegars and garden-fresh herbs. In addition to red and white wine vinegar there are also cider, sherry, and various fruit types.

Choose from vegetable oil, exquisite cold-pressed olive oil or flavorful walnut oil. Or liven up your salad with a tablespoon of hazelnut oil added to the dressing. Do as the Romans did: They asked a philosopher to add salt, a miser to add vinegar, a prodigal to add oil, and an artist to mix the salad. The salad chef can be all of those in one.

APPETIZERS AND SALADS

COLD APPETIZERS

Cold starters are both refreshing and convenient, because they can be prepared ahead of time. Some ingredients can be leftovers or purchased already prepared—for example, smoked eel with scrambled eggs on pumpernickel; slices of cold roast beef with garlic mayonnaise and mustard pickles; smoked salmon with toast and creamed horseradish; avocados stuffed with shrimp with salad; salami with olives; rolled roast beef with tartar sauce; artichoke bottoms with vegetable salad; hard-cooked eggs with anchovies; and beef tartare on bread with caviar.

The following appetizers are very delicate and don't require much preparation time; they are the perfect beginning for a festive meal.

Sweet and Sour Melon tastes wonderful with mild air-dried beef or prosciutto. Have the meat sliced as thinly as possible to enhance its flavor and texture. Serve with butter and toast.

ARTICHOKES WITH GARLIC SAUCE

4 large, firm artichokes
8 lemon slices
salt
1 tablespoon vinegar
1 small baking potato
3 cloves garlic
½ cup (125 mL) olive oil
juice of 1 lemon
about 1 cup (240 mL) beef stock

Place artichokes on their sides on a cutting board; hold them by their stem ends. With a sharp knife, cut about 3 inches (8 cm) off the tip. With scissors, cut ⅜ inch (1½ cm) off the tip of each leaf. Cut off stems. Immediately place lemon slices over tips and bottom and tie with string to keep cut surfaces from discoloring. Fill a large pot with 2 inches (5 cm) of water and bring to a boil over high heat. Add vinegar and 3 tablespoons salt. Place artichokes side by side in the boiling water. Boil for approximately 40 minutes, or until the leaves come off easily. Remove artichokes from water and turn upside down to drain and cool. Pull the small leaves from the center and remove the chokes.

To make the sauce, peel the potato, cook until tender, and mash. Sprinkle ½ teaspoon salt over the garlic and mash with the blade of a knife. Blend potato and garlic to make a paste, adding oil a spoonful at a time. Add lemon juice and enough stock to make a thick sauce. Pour sauce into individual bowls, then serve with cold artichokes.

To eat, dip the meaty end of each leaf into the sauce and pull it through your teeth to get just the tender, edible portion. Place a bowl for the discarded leaves at each place setting. Slice or quarter the artichoke bottom and eat with a knife and fork.

For a variation, serve the artichokes hot with Hollandaise sauce (see Index).

SWEET AND SOUR MELON

1 ripe honeydew melon
juice of 1 lemon
½ cup (125 mL) red wine vinegar
½ cup (100 g) sugar
3 to 4 ounces (100 g) air-dried beef or prosciutto, sliced paper thin

Cut melon into quarters, remove seeds, peel, and dice. Mix with the lemon juice and refrigerate. Cook the vinegar and sugar together for about 5 minutes, or until syrupy.

Pour hot syrup over melon pieces in individual dessert bowls. Arrange the beef or ham on a plate and decorate with parsley.

SEAFOOD SALAD

¼ head iceberg lettuce
1 large red bell pepper
1 small white onion
4 artichoke bottoms
6 ounces (150 g) cooked white fish
1 3½-ounce (100-g) can tuna
4 ounces (100 g) smoked salmon
1 3½-ounce (100-g) can crabmeat
1 hard-cooked egg, sliced
1 bunch watercress
2 green onions, diced
½ cup (125 mL) Vinaigrette dressing (see Index)

Tear the lettuce into small pieces, cut the red pepper into strips, and slice the onion. Cut the artichoke bottoms in half lengthwise. Cut the white fish into strips. Flake the tuna; cut salmon into strips and roll up. Decoratively arrange all of the ingredients on a plate. Add crabmeat, egg sections, watercress, and green onions. Serve the vinaigrette separately. Accompany with French bread and butter.

CRAB SALAD IN ASPIC

1 envelope unflavored gelatin
1⅔ cups (400 mL) fish stock
6 tablespoons (100 mL) dry white wine
1 tablespoon vinegar
salt and white pepper
3 cups (350 g) cooked vegetables
10 ounces (300 g) cooked crabmeat
2 cloves garlic
⅔ cup (150 g) crème fraîche
1 tablespoon chopped fresh parsley
1 ounce (30 g) red caviar

Soften gelatin in ½ cup (125 mL) stock for 5 minutes. Bring wine to a boil and add gelatin. Add gelatin mixture to remaining fish stock. Add vinegar and season with salt and pepper. Divide half the aspic among 4 chilled 2-cup (250 mL) molds and let cool until set. Layer with vegetables, add crabmeat, and fill with rest of aspic. Refrigerate until set, about 2 to 4 hours. Unmold onto plates. Mince garlic with ½ teaspoon salt, then stir in crème fraîche and parsley. Add caviar.

CHICKEN–FRUIT SALAD

⅔ cup (150 g) crème fraîche
2 tablespoons fresh lemon juice
salt and white pepper
1 tablespoon brandy
1 teaspoon sugar
¼ teaspoon ground ginger
2 cups (200 g) asparagus tips
4 slices pineapple
1½ pints (300 g) strawberries, hulled
1 ripe avocado
½ head Boston lettuce, separated
2 cups (200 g) cooked chicken
1 tablespoon chopped fresh parsley

Stir together the crème fraîche, 1 tablespoon lemon juice, ¼ teaspoon salt, pepper, brandy, sugar, and ginger. Cook the asparagus, separate the pineapple slices into small sections, and halve the strawberries lengthwise. Pit, peel, cut avocado into chunks, and toss in remaining lemon juice to keep it from discoloring. Cover individual serving plates with lettuce leaves and arrange chicken and fruit on each. Pour on dressing; sprinkle with parsley.

FISH PÂTÉS

These pâtés are culinary diamonds in the cuisine of the '80s. They melt on your tongue and have a tender, juicy texture. We want to whet your appetite with a salmon pâté, but you may use less expensive fish such as trout, pike, halibut, or flounder. Use only very fresh fish, which must be absolutely cold to ensure a successful, delicate pâté. If desired, use shellfish, smoked fish, or crisp vegetables in these pâtés. Tender fish quenelles are prepared from the same mixture—they taste superb with boiled potatoes which have been tossed in parsley, and topped with a fish-based velouté.

SALMON PÂTÉ

| 1 small onion |
| 2 tablespoons (25 g) butter |
| 1½ pounds (675 g) salmon filets |
| 6 slices white bread, crusts removed, diced |
| 1 egg |
| 1 teaspoon salt |
| ¼ teaspoon white pepper |
| ¼ teaspoon freshly grated nutmeg |
| 1⅓ cups (350 mL) heavy cream |
| 1 cup finely chopped fresh dill |

Dice the onion and sauté it in butter until transparent. Remove any remaining bones from the salmon using tweezers or the tip of a knife. Select the nicest pieces and cut them into strips as long as your 1-quart (1-L) loaf pan or baking dish. Dice the remaining salmon and place in a bowl. Continue according to the pictures and the directions; make sure you stir the puréed mixture (called a *mousseline*) over ice water until it is satiny smooth. To test, cook a teaspoonful in salted water; it should be resilient, but tender. If it is too tough, add an additional 1 to 2 tablespoons cream to the mixture. Butter the baking dish. If

you use a loaf pan, line it with parchment or wax paper. Pour half of the mousseline into the baking dish. Rap it a couple of times on your counter to remove excess air from the mixture. Continue as shown in photographs 7 and 8. Set the baking dish in a pan large enough to serve as a water bath. Fill the larger pan with water halfway up the sides of the baking dish. Bake 45 minutes, reducing heat if necessary to keep water from boiling. Remove pan from oven, remove baking dish from water bath, and let cool. Unmold pâté and let cool completely, covered with foil. Store in a cool place until ready to serve.

1 **Sauté onion until transparent.** Melt the butter over low heat. Sauté finely diced onion, stirring constantly, until transparent. Do not let it brown!

2 **Dice cleaned salmon pieces.** Carefully remove any remaining bones from the salmon filets. Set aside the nicest pieces and dice the remainder.

3 **Blend the mixture.** In a bowl combine all the ingredients for the *mousseline*: diced salmon, sautéed onion, bread, egg, and seasonings. Add cream. Cover and refrigerate until very cold.

4 **Purée mousseline ingredients.** Mix ingredients together in the bowl. Purée in a blender or food processor on high speed in small batches to prevent the mixture from getting warm.

5 **Beat mousseline in a bowl set over ice** until it is smooth and satiny. For the best results, use stainless steel bowls, which retain cold. Cook a teaspoonful of the mousseline to test the consistency.

Sprinkle finely chopped fresh dill over the Salmon Pâté before slicing it. Serve with lightly salted whipped cream and salmon roe. A crystal-clear white wine aspic made from clarified fish stock tastes particularly delicious with pâtés made from any variety of fish.

6 **Fill baking dish.** Butter the baking dish. Pour in half the mousseline, spread out evenly, and rap on counter to remove air.

7 **Layer with the strips of salmon,** which have been sprinkled with salt and pepper. Lay the strips just in the center so that they will be surrounded by the mousseline; if the salmon reaches the edges, the pâté will break when unmolded.

8 **Cook pâté.** Fill a roasting pan half full with water and heat to a simmer on top of the stove. Place the pâté in the roasting pan and bake in a 325°F (165°C) oven for 45 minutes, or until tester inserted in center comes out clean.

DANISH LIVER PÂTÉ

Pâté is a favorite in Denmark. It is usually part of a *smørrebrød* and is often enjoyed as a cold lunch. The fresh liver flavor blends well with crisp bacon and cranberries, with Cumberland sauce, and with a salad made from slightly bitter dandelion greens or radicchio.

1 pound 6 ounces (600 g) pork liver
12 ounces (350 g) unsmoked bacon, pancetta, or blanched smoked bacon
1 medium onion
2 eggs, 1 teaspoon salt
1 teaspoon minced green bell pepper
1 teaspoon minced pimento
¼ teaspoon ground cloves
¼ teaspoon ground ginger
2 anchovy filets, pressed through a strainer
For the Sauce Béchamel:
3 tablespoons (40 g) butter
5 tablespoons (40 g) flour
¾ cup (20 mL) heavy cream
⅔ cup (150 mL) beef stock
1 teaspoon salt
For the baking dish:
1 generous pound (500 g) salt pork, rinsed and thinly sliced

2 **Put the liver and bacon** through a meat grinder, using a blade with ¼-inch (¾-cm) holes. Repeat the process using a blade with the finest holes possible.

5 **Add Béchamel sauce.** Pour cold béchamel sauce, which is called a *panade* when used in making pâtés or stuffings, into egg mixture and mix well with a whisk.

3 **Grind meats a third time,** adding onion. Press wax paper through grinder to get all the meat from it.

6 **Line a 6-cup (1½-L) baking dish** with salt pork slices. Press salt pork tightly against the pan, allowing the ends to hang about 1½ inches (4 cm) over the rim.

1 **Prepare liver carefully.** Remove all the tendons and the skin from liver, using a sharp knife to waste as little liver as possible. Coarsely chop liver, bacon, and onion.

4 **Mix eggs and spices.** In a bowl, mix eggs, salt, green pepper, pimento, cloves, and ginger. Add anchovies and mix all ingredients well.

7 **Pour pâté mixture** into the baking dish, using a rubber spatula. Rap the dish a few times on a countertop to remove any air bubbles.

8 **Fold the salt pork** over the pâté, alternating strips as shown in the photograph and making sure the pâté is well covered to prevent it from drying out.

10 **Slice pâté** when firm; this will ensure even, smooth slices. Serve with Cumberland sauce.

CUMBERLAND SAUCE

½ cup (125 mL) dry red wine
2 shallots, finely diced
1 tablespoon finely grated orange peel
1 tablespoon finely grated lemon peel
3 tablespoons red currant jelly
3 tablespoons black currant jelly
2 tablespoons fresh orange juice
2 tablespoons fresh lemon juice
1 tablespoon Port
1 tablespoon medium-hot mustard
¼ teaspoon each cayenne pepper and ground ginger

Prepare pâté, following photographs and directions. First, make the Béchamel sauce. Melt butter over medium heat, add flour, and stir constantly for 5 minutes; do not brown. Slowly add cream and stock with salt and whisk to make a smooth sauce. Cook for several minutes, then let cool, stirring occasionally.

In a saucepan, simmer wine, shallots, and orange and lemon peels for 10 minutes over low heat. Add remaining ingredients and blend well. Cool sauce completely and season to taste before serving.

If desired, prepare Cumberland sauce without lemon and orange peel if you are not sure whether the peels have ben treated. Substitute ¼ cup (60 mL) cranberry sauce to get the same tart taste.

9 **Cover baking dish tightly with aluminum foil,** place in a hot water bath, and bake in a 350°F (180°C) oven for 1½ hours. Remove from oven and let cool, then refrigerate for several hours.

SMALL STEWS

Small stews (or ragoûts), are delicious warm appetizers or light suppers. You can offer individual bowls or serve from a large casserole. They are also very tasty baked in crisp, individual tart shells made from spicy pastry dough or in flaky, delicate puff pastry *vol-au-vents*, which are available ready-made in grocery stores.

Here we will concentrate on the quality of the ragoûts so that they turn out perfectly. Some ingredients, used here already cooked, are mentioned or described in detail in other chapters. For example, refer to the index to learn about preparing sweetbreads.

SWEETBREADS NANTUA

5 ounces (150 g) cooked sweetbreads (see Index)
3 to 4 tablespoons flour
1½ tablespoons (20 g) butter
1 cup (240 mL) Béchamel sauce (see Index)
5 ounces (150 g) shrimp, cooked, peeled, and finely chopped
2 tablespoons fresh lemon juice
salt and white pepper
¼ cup (30 g) grated Gouda cheese

Gently pull sweetbreads into small pieces and remover outer membrane. Coat pieces in flour, shake off excess, and brown in butter on both sides over high heat. Place on paper towels to drain; set aside. Heat the Béchamel sauce. Mash 3 tablespoons of the shrimp to a paste and add to the sauce; blend with a whisk. Add lemon juice and season with salt and pepper to taste. Heat the sweetbreads and remaining shrimp in the sauce, being careful not to boil sauce, which would toughen the shrimp.

Divide the ragoût among 4 individual coquille shells, sprinkle with grated cheese, and brown in a 400°F (200°C) oven for about 5 minutes, or broil in a toaster oven until cheese is melted and golden brown.

VEAL IN PUFF PASTRY SHELLS

4 ounces (100 g) fresh mushrooms
3 tablespoons fresh lemon juice
4 ounces (100 g) asparagus, blanched
6 ounces (175 g) cooked veal in 1 piece
¾ cup (100g) fresh or frozen peas, blanched
1 cup (240 mL) chicken velouté (see Index)
1 teaspoon Worcestershire sauce
salt and white pepper
4 prepared vol-au-vent or patty shells

Clean mushrooms and cook in boiling water with 2 tablespoons of lemon juice for 5 minutes. Drain and cut mushrooms in quarters. Cut asparagus and veal into ½-inch (1½-cm) pieces. If you use fresh peas, blanch and rinse under cold water (if using frozen peas, thaw them). Heat chicken velouté and add Worcestershire sauce, remaining lemon juice, and salt and pepper to taste. Add mushrooms, veal, and vegetables and heat in sauce but do not allow to boil. Serve veal ragoût in hot, freshly baked *vol-au-vents*; garnish with lemon wedges and fresh parsley.

ESCARGOTS IN RIESLING SAUCE

3 dozen canned escargots
4 ounces (100 g) fresh mushrooms
1 shallot
1½ tablespoons (20 g) butter
2 tablespoons Cognac or brandy
½ cup (125 mL) dry Riesling or other dry white wine
1 cup (240 mL) + 2 tablespoons heavy cream
1 clove garlic
1 teaspoon chopped fresh herbs (marjoram, thyme, basil)
1 egg yolk
salt and white pepper
1 teaspoon chopped fresh parsley

Drain escargots in strainer and reserve 2 tablespoons of liquid. Remove stems from mushrooms, then clean and finely chop mushroom stems and caps separately. Dice shallot. Over low heat melt butter until foamy, sauté escargots and mushrooms for 5 minutes, pour in Cognac or brandy and simmer for 1 minute. Remove escargots and mushrooms with a slotted spoon. Add shallot to butter and sauté until transparent; add mushroom stems and sauté until you can smell a mushroom scent. Add wine, escargot liquid, 1 cup cream, garlic, and herbs. Cook sauce until creamy, stirring constantly. Purée sauce in blender, strain through a fine sieve, and reheat. Beat egg yolk with remaining cream and stir into sauce, being careful not to boil, or it will curdle. Add escargots and mushroom caps; let stand for 5 minutes. Season to taste with salt and pepper and serve, garnished with chopped parsley.

Small ragoûts are a delicacy. They are light and are great as appetizers or light main courses. Front: Sweetbreads Nantua. Center: Veal in Puff Pastry Shells

CRÊPES

Crêpes taste great either prepared with bacon and served with a salad or made with apples and served with sugar and cinnamon. We love them with a refreshing compote or flambéed, with fruit and ice cream.

These crêpes may be varied with other ingredients as well; they are particularly light and airy when made with beer or cider. The thicker you make crêpes and the fewer eggs you use, however, the easier they are to cook.

CRÊPES

For about 18 crêpes

¾ cup (100 g) plus 2 tablespoons flour
¼ teaspoon salt
½ cup (125 mL) each milk and water
3 eggs
1 egg yolk
½ cup (115 g) butter

Sift flour into a bowl and add salt. Blend milk and water and pour slowly over flour, mixing constantly with a whisk. Whisk eggs into dough, cover, and set aside for at least 1 hour to allow the starch in the flour to swell completely.

Melt the butter, let cool, then pour off yellow liquid into another container, leaving the milk solids behind. Have clarified butter ready for frying crêpes.

Stir batter in bowl occasionally to keep the flour from sinking to the bottom. Heat a bit of the clarified butter in a 6-inch (15-cm) heavy skillet. Add batter in a very thin layer, swirling to coat the bottom of the skillet. Fry the crêpes until golden brown on each side, stack between two plates, and keep warm in a low oven until all are cooked. Fill crêpes with sweet or savory fillings.

To make the batter, mix all ingredients well with a whisk. If multiplying recipe, use an electric mixer. To cook crêpes, pour a little clarified butter into a skillet over medium heat, then pour out any excess; what remains is enough to fry 1 crêpe. Using very little batter, quickly turn pan in a circular motion to spread batter evenly and thinly across bottom of pan.

Stuffed crêpes are a delicious warm appetizer, easy to prepare ahead. Double the amount to serve as a main course. Serve with a clear consommé garnished with fresh chives for an appetizer, and with fresh fruit or compote as a dessert. Each filling is enough for 4 crêpes.

Crab Filling

Lightly brown 2½ tablespoons (40 g) butter, remove from heat, and toss with 6 ounces (200 g) crabmeat. Squeeze fresh lemon juice over to taste, sprinkle with pepper, and mix with 1 teaspoon finely chopped fresh dill. Spoon over crêpes and roll up.

Caviar Filling

Place crêpes on warm plates. Spread 1 tablespoon sour cream or crème fraîche on each crêpe and place 1 teaspoon of your favorite caviar in the center. Garnish with fresh dill.

Asparagus Filling

Spread herb butter or Béarnaise sauce (see Index) over crêpes and roll up with 3 asparagus stalks in each crêpe. Place in an ovenproof serving dish and sprinkle with about 4 tablespoons coarsely grated Emmenthal cheese. Broil until cheese is melted.

Tomato and Olive Filling

Thinly slice 2 onions and sauté them in ¼ cup (60 mL) olive oil until transparent. Add ½ cup (125 mL) beef stock and reduce by half. Season with salt, pepper, thyme, 1 tablespoon white wine vinegar, a pinch of sugar, and a dash of Worcestershire sauce. Slice 12 pimento-stuffed olives and quarter 8 cherry or plum tomatoes. Add to sauce and mix well, then heat over low heat. Spoon filling on half the crêpes and cover with the remaining crêpes.

Crêpes with Crab are ideal for Sunday brunch, but can be expanded to a full meal when accompanied by watercress salad with a mild yogurt dressing.

Crêpes with Asparagus taste best using freshly cooked asparagus. However, you could use canned imported asparagus. Serve with oak-leaf lettuce salad and French dressing.

Crêpes with Tomatoes and Olives are very flavorful. Serve them with salad made from Chinese cabbage and vinaigrette dressing. When served this way, they make a hearty appetizer.

Crêpes with Caviar are an especially delicate appetizer. Serve them with a tomato salad, as part of a champagne breakfast.

31

SALAD DRESSINGS

A good dressing makes the salad. It should cover crisp vegetables with a thin coating to keep them fresh and flavorful and to enhance their taste. People who enjoy salad may want to make a quantity of dressing which will keep, if refrigerated, for several days without losing its freshness. We will show you how to make a simple vinaigrette, a tomato-red French Dressing and several variations. Choose any of these dressings for a generous bowl of salad before each meal.

Sugar in your salad? Let the experts fight this one out. We are convinced that a pinch of sugar enhances flavor, but that more will destroy a salad's freshness.

VINAIGRETTE

For 8 to 12 servings

2 tablespoons white wine vinegar
1 teaspoon salt
¼ teaspoon freshly ground pepper
6 tablespoons (100 mL) olive oil

Mix vinegar, salt, and pepper in a bowl and whisk until salt is completely dissolved. Gradually add oil and blend until sauce thickens. You may choose different kinds of oils and vinegars for your vinaigrette, or you may change the flavor by adding herbs and spices.

Vinaigrette with Egg

Follow the recipe for basic vinaigrette above, but stir 1 raw egg yolk into the mixture before adding oil. Hard-cook the egg white, chop finely, and add to the dressing.

Vinaigrette with Herbs

Use fresh herbs such as dill, chives, parsley, basil, and/or mint. If desired, add finely chopped onion or shallots and season with finely grated horseradish.

FRENCH DRESSING

For 8 servings

1 egg yolk
2 tablespoons white wine vinegar
1 teaspoon salt
½ teaspoon tomato paste
¼ teaspoon paprika
¼ teaspoon grated onion
½ cup (125 mL) oil

Combine egg yolk, vinegar, salt, tomato paste, paprika, and onion in a small bowl. Mix well. Add oil slowly, whisking constantly.

Lemon-Cream Sauce

Combine ¼ cup (60 mL) fresh lemon juice with 1 teaspoon salt, ¼ teaspoon sugar, and ¼ teaspoon white pepper and stir until salt and sugar are completely dissolved. Slowly add ¾ cup (200 mL) heavy cream and whisk until sauce is smooth.

MAYONNAISE AND ITS VARIATIONS

Mayonnaises are creamy sauces used in appetizer cocktails or party salads and also served separately with cold meats and aspics. It takes time to prepare them by hand, but the reward is a dressing that's far better than the ready-made kind. Beat egg yolk; add oil drop by drop until it is blended with yolk and completely smooth. As the sauce thickens, add oil in a very thin stream. When it is soft and creamy, taste it. If too stiff, thin it with a few drops of lemon juice or vinegar. (NOTE: In the following variations, ingredients are given for half the amount of mayonnaise in the master recipe.) Each recipe is for 8 servings.

Garlic Mayonnaise

Force 2 or 3 cloves of garlic through a garlic press or sprinkle garlic with salt and pepper and mince it with a knife. Blend with beaten egg yolk before adding oil.

Remoulade Sauce

Finely chop or mince the following ingredients: 1 medium-size kosher pickle, 1 tablespoon capers, 3 anchovy filets, 1 tablespoon each chopped fresh chervil, tarragon, chives, and parsley. Combine all ingredients and stir into mayonnaise. Season with hot mustard to taste.

Cocktail Sauce

Combine 1 teaspoon Cumberland sauce, 2 tablespoons heavy cream, 1 teaspoon brandy, 3 drops hot pepper sauce, and 2 tablespoons catsup and stir into mayonnaise.

A QUICK MAYONNAISE

For 1⅔ cups (400 mL)

2 eggs
1 teaspoon salt
½ teaspoon finely ground white pepper
1 teaspoon white wine vinegar or fresh lemon juice
1⅓ (320 mL) cups of olive oil

Make sure all ingredients are at room temperature so they will thicken without curdling. You may substitute a neutral vegetable oil for the olive oil.

Preparing mayonnaise with whole eggs can only be done successfully in a blender. Place eggs in blender, add salt, pepper, and vinegar or lemon juice. Blend on lowest setting. Very slowly pour oil through opening in top of blender; the mayonnaise will be finished in seconds. Refrigerate in a tightly covered container until ready for use.

SIMPLE VEGETABLE SALADS

Raw vegetable salads are delicious, provided they are prepared with only the freshest ingredients. Delicate sauces and dressings enhance the flavors of fresh vegetables to make these salads a pure delight for your tastebuds. Raw vegetable salads are good for you. They are rich in vitamins, minerals and fiber—all essential to health. And these salads satisfy your hunger so you eat less during the main course.

Crisp salads are great for appetizers, snacks, and light suppers. You may wish to add nuts, which are rich in protein and can be quickly chopped in your processor, or to sprinkle your salad with wheat germ. And what would a salad be without herbs from your garden or windowsill? Cut them fresh so they release their fullest flavors.

All about Slicing and Grating

Chop raw vegetables finely or coarsely, depending on their consistency. For single servings, use a hand slicer and a metal grater. For larger amounts, and if you are a true salad fan, the slicer attachment for your processor is a good bet.

Cut firm vegetables to fit into the funnel opening. Place carrots inside in an upright position, fitting them tightly next to each other. Bundle soft vegetables, like leeks, celery stalks, and bell peppers, tightly together to get clean, even slices. Press each portion completely down with the pusher before adding the next bunch. If your machine has several speeds, use the low speed for most slicing, the high speed only when necessary. Thinly slice white and red cabbage, leeks, onion, bell peppers, radishes, and fennel.

Coarsely slice cauliflower, cucumber, zucchini, asparagus, mushrooms, celery stalks, green onions, and—if desired—any of the vegetables mentioned above for fine slicing.

Save time and energy by using the grater attachment of your processor to grate carrots, which are especially delicious in a dressing made from plain yogurt, fresh lemon juice, salt, pepper, sugar, and chopped parsley.

ITALIAN TOMATO SALAD

1 generous pound (500 g) fresh tomatoes
5 ounces (150 g) mozzarella cheese
1/2 teaspoon salt
1/4 teaspoon finely ground black pepper
1/4 cup (60 mL) olive oil
black olives (optional)
12 fresh basil leaves (optional)

Using a sharp knife, cut out the stem end of each tomato. Cut mozzarella and tomatoes crosswise into slices about 1/8 inch (1/2 cm) thick. Alternate slices on a plate, starting at the outside and ending in the center, making sure the slices overlap. Sprinkle evenly with salt, pepper, and finely chopped basil, and drizzle with olive oil. If desired, decorate with black olives and whole basil leaves. Serve as a side dish; if served as an appetizer, double the amount of mozzarella.

GREEN CABBAGE SALAD

Remove the core from 1 medium head of green cabbage. Cut cabbage into thin slices or feed through the processor, using the coarse slicing blade. Fry 3 ounces (100 g) diced smoked bacon in 1 tablespoon oil until crisp and golden. Remove from heat and stir in 1 more tablespoon oil, 1 tablespoon vinegar, 1 teaspoon caraway seed, ½ teaspoon salt, and ¼ teaspoon pepper. Pour hot sauce over cabbage and toss to mix well. Let stand for 20 to 30 minutes before serving.

MUSHROOM SALAD

In a small salad bowl, dissolve ¼ teaspoon salt in 1 tablespoon vinegar and 1 teaspoon water. Add 2 tablespoons oil and blend thoroughly. Grate 1 small onion into mixture and season with freshly ground pepper. Clean 12 ounces (300 g) fresh mushrooms and ½ bell pepper and grate both into dressing. Mix dressing with vegetables immediately and let it stand, covered, for 10 minutes. Add 1 tablespoon finely chopped fresh parsley, toss, and serve.

CARROT SALAD

Pour 1 teaspoon fresh lemon juic into salad bowl. Add ¼ teaspoon eac salt, sugar, and pepper. Mix in ½ cu (125 mL) plain yogurt and 1 tablespoo heavy cream. Add 1 tablespoon finel chopped fresh parsley. Finely grate large peeled carrots and 1 medium-siz unpeeled apple that has been cored an quartered. Toss with dressing and le stand for 30 minutes. Toss again an season to taste.

RED CABBAGE SALAD

In a salad bowl, dissolve ½ teaspoon salt and ½ teaspoon sugar in 2 tablespoons vinegar and 1 tablespoon water. Add 3 tablespoons oil and ¼ teaspoon finely ground white pepper and mix well. Grate 1 medium head of red cabbage (core removed) and 4 small unpeeled apples that have been cored and quartered. Add to dressing and toss. Let stand for 1 hour, covered, before serving.

WHITE RADISH SALAD

Coarsely grate 12 ounces (300 g) peeled white radishes. In a salad bowl dissolve ½ teaspoon salt in 1 tablespoon vinegar. Add ¼ teaspoon freshly ground white pepper, ¼ teaspoon paprika, 2 tablespoons oil, and 1 tablespoon water and mix well. Add grated radishes and toss. Finely chop 1 bunch chives and sprinkle over salad just before serving.

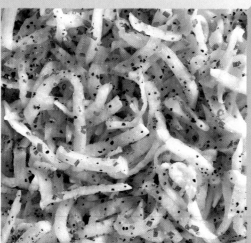

ZUCCHINI SALAD

In a salad bowl, prepare the vina grette: Dissolve ½ teaspoon salt in tablespoon vinegar and 1 tablespoo water. Add 2 tablespoons oil and tablespoon fresh thyme, mixing wel Thinly slice 1 pound (450 g) unpeele zucchini. Add to dressing, toss, and l stand for 10 to 20 minutes befor serving. Season with ¼ teaspoon fresh ground white pepper and add a pinch sugar if desired.

KOHLRABI SALAD

In a salad bowl dissolve ½ teaspoon salt in 1 tablespoon vinegar. Add 2 tablespoons oil and 1 tablespoon water and mix well. Coarsely grate 3 peeled kohlrabi right into bowl. Cut any tender leaves from the stems of the kohlrabi, chop finely, and toss with salad. Season to taste and let stand briefly. Garnish with fresh parsley.

RED RADISH SALAD

Wash 12 ounces (350 g) red radishes and pat dry. Thinly slice radishes using a knife or processor blade. Mix together 1 tablespoon vinegar, 1 tablespoon water and ½ teaspoon salt and blend with 2 tablespoons oil. Toss with sliced radishes and sprinkle with 1 bunch minced chives. Serve immediately.

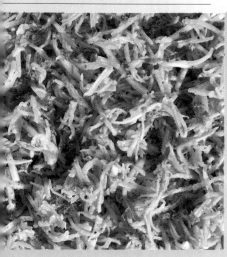

CUCUMBER SALAD

In a salad bowl, dissolve ½ teaspoon salt in 2 tablespoons vinegar. Add 3 tablespoons oil, ½ teaspoon finely ground white pepper and 2 tablespoons diced red bell pepper. Wash, dry, and thinly slice 3 unpeeled cucumbers. Immediately add dressing, toss and sprinkle with 2 tablespoon minced fresh dill.

FENNEL SALAD

In a salad bowl, dissolve ¼ teaspoon salt and a pinch of sugar in 2 tablespoons fresh lemon juice and 1 tablespoon vinegar. Add 2 tablespoons oil, ½ teaspoon prepared mustard, and 1 cup (240 mL) plain yogurt and mix well. Clean 2 medium fennel bulbs, slice them thinly by hand (or use the processor slicing blade) and add to the bowl. Toss thoroughly and let stand briefly. Season to taste, sprinkle with chopped fennel leaves, and serve.

CELERY ROOT SALAD

In a salad bowl, blend ⅔ cup (150 mL) crème fraîche with fresh lemon juice to taste and ¼ teaspoon salt. Finely grate 14 ounces (400 g) peeled celery root directly into bowl. Toss immediately to prevent celery root from discoloring. Coarsely chop ¼ cup walnuts and cut 2 pineapple slices into chunks. Mix walnuts and pineapple with salad. Let stand a few minutes, season with freshly ground black pepper, and serve.

LEEK SALAD

Clean 8 ounces (200 g) leeks and cut into 2 or 3 lengths. Slice them thinly, wash thoroughly, and drain. In a bowl blend 6 tablespoons (80 mL) crème fraîche, ¼ cup (60 mL) heavy cream, ¼ teaspoon salt, 1 teaspoon fresh lemon juice, and 3 to 4 drops Worcestershire sauce. Season with freshly ground white pepper. Toss with leeks and let stand for 30 minutes before serving.

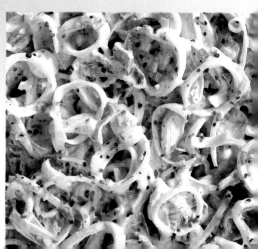

TOSSED SALADS

Salads using a large variety of ingredients can become fully balanced meals. Serve them with hearty bread to make a light supper or refreshing summer lunch.

GERMAN POTATO SALAD

For 2 servings
1 generous pound (500 g) russet potatoes
1 small onion
½ cup (125 mL) beef stock
½ teaspoon salt
¼ teaspoon sugar
5 tablespoons (75 mL) oil
2 tablespoons white wine vinegar
2 tablespoons chopped fresh chervil or borage
2 tablespoons chopped fresh salad burnet or dill
2 small pickles, cut into strips
2 hard-cooked eggs, chopped

The day before serving the salad, cook, rinse, and peel potatoes. Cover and refrigerate overnight; to keep slices from falling apart, do not cut until the next day. Dice onion and simmer in stock until tender. Season with salt and sugar and pour over potato slices. Toss gently but thoroughly and set aside. Just before serving, pour oil and vinegar over potatoes. Add herbs, pickles and eggs and toss gently but thoroughly. Garnish with edible blossoms (borage, violets, nasturtiums), if desired.

ROMAINE SALAD WITH FETA AND PECANS

1 head romaine
2 celery stalks
¼ teaspoon salt
¼ teaspoon black pepper
2 tablespoons red wine vinegar
2 tablespoons olive oil
8 ounces (200 g) feta cheese (preferably made with sheep's milk)
¼ cup shelled pecans

Wash romaine and celery pat dry, and cut into ¼-inch (¾-cm) strips. Combine salt and pepper with vinegar, blend with oil, and pour over vegetables. Toss, add feta cheese and pecans, and toss again. Serve within 10 minutes. This salad makes a light supper when served with whole-grain bread and butter.

WHEAT SPROUT SALAD

12 ounces (350 g) Chinese cabbage
1 apple
1 fresh pear
1 peach, fresh or canned
¾ cup (200 g) cottage cheese
4 ounces (100 g) wheat sprouts
scant ¼ cup chopped walnuts
¼ teaspoon salt
¼ teaspoon white pepper
2 tablespoons vinegar
2 tablespoons walnut oil

Clean and finely slice Chinese cabbage. Wash, core, and quarter apple and pear; thinly slice peach. Combine fruit in a large salad bowl. Add cottage cheese, wheat sprouts, and walnuts, and mix well. Mix salt and pepper with vinegar and blend with oil. Pour dressing over salad ingredients and toss. Serve immediately, with whole-wheat bread and butter.

GROWING YOUR OWN SPROUTS

Buy grains and seeds for sprouting in a health food store. Do not use seeds intended for use outdoors, because they are usually chemically treated.

Soak seeds in lukewarm water overnight; they will swell to double their original size. Rinse under cold water. Line a flat-bottomed strainer or colander with two layers of cheesecloth rinsed in warm water. Scatter seeds on cloth, making sure not to crowd them, and cover with another layer of cheesecloth which has also been rinsed in warm water. Place the colander on a plate and leave it in a dark place at room temperature. Spray with warm water twice a day to keep cloth and seeds moist; discard any liquid that accumulates on the plate. After a few days, tender, light-colored sprouts will appear: Wheat takes about 3 days, mung beans 4 to 5 days, soybeans 6 to 8 days. Store all sprouts in a cool, moist place to keep them crisp. They're a tasty, very healthy ingredient for salads.

German Potato Salad, Wheat Sprout Salad, and Romaine Salad with Feta not only taste good, they're good for you, since they contain essential minerals and vitamins.

MUSSEL SALAD

2¼ pounds (1 kg) fresh mussels
½ cup (125 mL) Sauternes
1 bunch fresh parsley
1 sprig fresh thyme
2 tablespoons diced onion
1 clove garlic
1 tablespoon butter
1 teaspoon peppercorns
For the dressing:
¼ cup (60 mL) mussel cooking liquid
¼ cup (60 mL) oil
2 tablespoons white wine vinegar
½ teaspoon fresh lemon juice
½ teaspoon finely chopped fresh tarragon
salt and pepper
To serve:
2 celery stalks
1 head chicory or Belgian endive

Under running water scrub individual mussels with a vegetable brush. Discard any mussels whose shells are open; they are not fresh. In a large saucepan, combine cleaned mussels with wine, parsley, thyme, onion, garlic, butter, peppercorns, and enough water to reach a depth of several inches. Cover and cook over high heat, tilting the saucepan a few times during cooking, just until the mussel shells open, about 5 to 10 minutes. Remove from heat and let mussels cool in broth. Discard any that do not open.

Mix all the dressing ingredients thoroughly. Remove mussels from their shells, add to sauce, and set aside. Slice celery stalks as thinly as possible. Clean and dry greens. Toss celery and greens with mussels just before serving. Use the mussel shells to decorate bowls or plates.

CHINESE CABBAGE WITH SEAFOOD

2 tablespoons fresh lemon or lime juice
½ teaspoon each salt and sugar
¼ teaspoon black pepper
2 tablespoons sesame oil
2 tablespoons finely chopped fresh dill
1 3½-ounce (100-g) can tuna, packed in oil
3½ ounces (100 g) smoked haddock filet
1 3½-ounce (100-g) can diced clams, drained
1 3½-ounce (100-g) can crabmeat, drained
1 large head Chinese cabbage

In a salad bowl combine lemon juice with salt, sugar, and pepper. Add sesame oil, dill, and chunked tuna, including any oil it was packed in; toss. Cut smoked haddock into ⅜-inch (1½-cm) strips and add to salad with clams and crab. Toss thoroughly and let stand, covered, for 15 minutes. Slice, wash, and dry the Chinese cabbage; add to salad just before serving. Toss and serve with freshly baked bread and chilled dry white wine.

GREEN BEAN SALAD WITH FLOUNDER

12 ounces (350 g) fresh green beans
salt
2 tablespoons finely chopped onion
1 tablespoon walnut oil
2 tablespoons dry white wine
1 bunch fresh parsley
10 ounces (300 g) small flounder filets
For the dressing:
6 tablespoons (80 mL) low-fat yogurt
3 tablespoons mayonnaise
1 teaspoon paprika
¼ teaspoon salt
¼ teaspoon garlic powder
¼ teaspoon ground ginger
¼ teaspoon white pepper

Wash beans and remove strings if necessary. Add to 2 quarts (2 L) boiling salted water. Boil for 3 minutes, drain, and quickly rinse beans under cold water so they stay crisp. Sauté chopped onion in oil for 1 minute, remove from heat, add white wine, and stir. Add beans, toss, and reserve. To prepare the fish, add parsley and 1 teaspoon salt to 1 cup (240 mL) water and bring to boil. Place fish filets in water, remove from heat, and set aside, covered, to cool. Pat fish dry and arrange on a plate with the beans. Combine all the dressing ingredients and mix well. Pour over fish just before serving.

Mussel Salad and Green Bean Salad with Flounder are elegant, small meals, delicious served with toast and a glass of Sauternes.

"Soup is to the meal what a beautiful foyer is to the house," according to the 18th-century gastronome and philosopher Balthasar Grimod de la Reynière. What he referred to was, of course, soup as an appetizer. It was the course that appeased his hunger but, because of its lightness, also prepared his palate for upcoming pleasures. Soups that make perfect appetizers include consommés with a garnish of vegetable julienne or dumplings, cream soups, and fantastic cold soups such as French vichyssoise or Spanish gazpacho.

In this chapter we offer an assortment of delicious soups that can as easily be served at the start of a good hot lunch as at dinner. Fortunately, these new mixtures have nothing in common with grandmother's flour-based soups. The ones presented here are very special not only because they are based almost entirely on flavorful stocks, but also because they include everything that typifies today's cuisine: they are thickened primarily with vegetable purées and finished with cream, egg yolk, or crème fraîche. It goes without saying that all ingredients must be of the finest quality.

The same is true of stews, those filling meals so popular in the colder seasons. They must be made with the freshest ingredients available to create a consistent, harmonious mixture. But as complicated as this sounds, each ingredient must also retain its individual character—only then will a combination succeed.

SOUPS AND STEWS

Garnishes for soups can be prepared ahead of time and frozen, and the same is true of broth or consommé. This way you can always have ingredients on hand for a quick appetizer or meal. Freeze soup in small containers; freeze garnishes in individual portions and use only the amount you need.

Try preparing quenelles from a delicate fish pâté mixture, or make a light meat dumpling using a meat pâté mixture and dumpling dough. Use semolina or wholewheat flour for fried dumplings, if you like. These meat or fish dumplings are classically shaped into ovals using two teaspoons, though you can also roll them into balls with your hands.

Cut vegetables into very fine (julienne) strips. Sauté firm vegetables, such as carrots or celery, in butter for 1 minute before adding them to stock. Add softer vegetables like leeks, bell peppers, and green onions raw to your stock, then let it come to the boil before serving.

Use chiffonade—leafy greens like sorrel, beet greens, or spinach that have been rolled up and cut into fine strips—and fresh herbs (we prefer basil, parsley, and chives) to flavor precious meat stocks.

1 **Milling your own flour.** You can grind whole wheat grain with a home flour mill. Follow the instructions for your machine, then mill the grain on high speed to a very fine powder similar to commercial flour.

2 **Making the dough.** Boil water and butter. Pour in fresh-ground flour all at once and stir with a wooden spoon until dough forms a ball.

Freshly cooked dumplings are served here in a double-strength stock garnished with parsley. Always warm bowls or plates before serving to prevent the contents from cooling down too quickly.

WHEAT DUMPLINGS

For 30 dumplings

¾ cup wholewheat berries or 1 cup wholewheat flour

½ cup (125 mL) water

2 tablespoons (25 g) butter

1 egg

¼ teaspoon salt

⅛ teaspoon each pepper and nutmeg

1 tablespoon chopped fresh parsley

Mill your own grain or buy flour. Make the basic dough, cool, and mix with remaining ingredients. Shape small balls and cook 15 minutes.

1 **Make crêpes.** Pour a small amount of the batter into a well-greased skillet, and quickly turn the pan to spread batter. When firm, cook on other side.

1 **Mix ingredients.** Scrape the bone marrow into a small bowl. Add eggs, breadcrumbs, parsley, salt, and nutmeg and mix well with a fork.

1 **Cook in a hot water bath.** Place a bowl of egg mixture in a pot of hot (almost boiling) water. Cover bowl and let stand for 15 to 20 minutes. Turn out onto a flat work surface.

2 **Cut and serve.** Spread crêpe with herbed cheese or liver pâté mixture if desired. Roll up, slice thinly, place in a cup and cover wth hot broth.

2 **Shape dumplings and cook.** Shape small dumplings using 2 teaspoons. Place into gently simmering water and cook for 10 minutes, being careful not to let water boil.

2 **Cut the mixture.** Using a sharp knife, dice the cooked egg mixture, or use small cookie cutters to make decorative shapes. Save any scraps for later use.

CRÊPES CÉLESTINES

2/3 cup (70 g) all-purpose or wholewheat flour
1 egg
1/2 cup (125 mL) milk
1/4 teaspoon salt
oil or butter for frying

Mix flour with egg, add milk and salt, and stir to make a smooth batter. Heat oil or butter in an 8-inch (20-cm) skillet over medium heat and fry 6 thin crêpes.

MARROW DUMPLINGS

For 25 dumplings
about 1/4 cup (60 g) marrow (from 4 large marrow bones)
2 eggs
1/2 cup (80 g) fresh breadcrumbs
2 tablespoons chopped fresh parsley
1/4 teaspoon salt
1/8 teaspoon freshly grated nutmeg

Over low heat, bring 1 quart (1 L) water to a boil with 1 tablespoon salt. Cook dumplings in gently simmering water, then remove with a spoon.

EGG CUTOUTS

2 eggs
1/4 cup (60 mL) milk
1/4 teaspoon salt
1/8 teaspoon freshly grated nutmeg

Gently mix, but do not beat, eggs, milk, and spices. Butter a flat-bottomed bowl, pour in egg mixture and let cook in a hot water bath as explained in captions.

CREAMED SOUPS

Made in the blender, these soups are always fresh, smooth, and ready in minutes. They don't need floury thickeners. Today's elegant creamed soups are thickened with puréed vegetables, which make them both delicate and healthy. Finish these creamed soups with cream and egg yolk, or leftover light sauces, soups, or puréed vegetables. Create your own soups with celery, carrots, and mushrooms, using the recipes on these pages as guidelines.

CREAMED PEA SOUP

1½ tablespoons (20 g) butter
1 medium onion
10 ounces (300 g) young peas, shelled
3 cups (700 mL) chicken stock
½ cup (125 mL) heavy cream
salt
white pepper
1 tablespoon chopped fresh mint or parsley

2 Sauté peas. Add shelled peas to onion and stir until they are hot and give off a good, fresh aroma.

3 Pour in stock. Add either hot or cold stock. Bring to a boil and cook peas for 5 to 10 minutes, depending on their age and freshness.

1 Sauté onion. Melt butter over medium-low heat until it foams. Chop onion finely, add to butter, and sauté until transparent.

4 Purée peas. Strain pea and onion mixture, reserving stock. Purée in blender on high speed, pouring them through the opening in lid.

5 Cream soup. Slowly add enough stock to liquefy puréed vegetables, then transfer mixture to a pot and add remaining stock. Bring to a boil, stirring constantly.

CREAMY SPINACH SOUP

1 small baking potato
1 tablespoon (15 g) butter
1 clove garlic
3 cups (700 mL) milk
⅛ teaspoon meat glaze
10 ounces (300 g) fresh spinach
1 teaspoon salt
¼ teaspoon white pepper
¼ teaspoon freshly grated nutmeg
1 hard-cooked egg (garnish)

Peel, rinse, and dice potato. Melt butter over medium heat, add potatoes and peeled garlic clove, and sauté for 2 minutes. Add milk and meat glaze and cook for 10 minutes. Meanwhile, wash and dry spinach leaves. Add to soup, stir, and when spinach leaves have wilted (after about 1 minute), strain soup, reserving liquid. Pour vegetables into blender and purée, adding as much reserved liquid as necessary. Transfer mixture to a pot, bring to boil, and add remaining liquid. Season with salt, pepper, and nutmeg. Serve soup garnished with chopped egg.

6 **Enrich with cream.** Whisk cream into the pea soup and season to taste with salt and pepper. Reheat and garnish with finely chopped mint or parsley.

CREAMY ASPARAGUS SOUP

1 generous pound (500 g) fresh asparagus
½ cup (125 mL) heavy cream
1 egg yolk
1 teaspoon salt
½ teaspoon freshly grated nutmeg
1 tablespoon (15 g) butter

Peel asparagus; cut off tips and reserve. Snap off tough ends and coarsely chop stalks. Boil for 10 minutes in 2 cups (450 mL) water. Purée in blender. Transfer purée to a pot, add asparagus tips, and cook for 5 minutes. Mix cream and egg yolk, whisk into soup, and reheat. Whisk in salt, nutmeg, and butter.

CREAMY TOMATO SOUP

1 small onion
3 slices bacon
1 cup (240 mL) beef stock
2¼ pounds (1 kg) fresh tomatoes
½ cup (125 mL) crème fraîche
salt and pepper
1 tablespoon chopped fresh basil

Cut onion into chunks. Dice bacon and fry over low heat until golden brown. Add stock and cook for 10 minutes.

Quarter and seed tomatoes. Purée in blender. Strain into stock, discarding bits of skin. Boil soup for 2 minutes, add crème fraîche, and mix well. Season to taste with salt and pepper. Serve garnished with chopped fresh basil.

COLD SOUPS

These recipes are classic examples of cold soups, which are particularly refreshing on hot days. They taste pure and smooth because chilling creamed soups helps release their flavors. We hope the recipes below will stimulate you to prepare other cold soups. What is most important is that all the vegetables and fruits be ripe and fresh. Try using raw or steamed fruits to make sweet soups.

AVOCADO CREAM SOUP

3 ripe avocados
1 cup (240 mL) chicken stock
1 cup (240 mL) heavy cream
2 teaspoons fresh lemon juice
salt and white pepper
2 tablespoons minced fresh dill

Avocados are ripe when they are slightly soft and will peel easily. Cut avocados in half; pit and peel. Put avocado through a strainer or purée it in a blender, slowly adding enough chicken stock to make a smooth, creamy liquid. Add remaining stock, cream, and lemon juice and mix well. Season with salt and pepper and serve garnished with dill.

CRÈME VICHYSSOISE

2 to 3 small baking potatoes
3 leeks, with green tops
1 small onion
2½ tablespoons (40 g) butter
1 quart (1 L) chicken stock
¼ cup (60 mL) heavy cream (or more, if desired)
salt and black pepper
2 tablespoons finely chopped fresh chives

Wash, peel, and dice potatoes. Clean leeks, cut into rounds, and rinse well. Dice onion and sauté in butter until transparent. Add potatoes, leeks, and chicken stock and cook for 30 minutes. Remove from heat and strain; or cook soup for only 10 minutes, cool, and purée in blender. Stir in cream and season to taste with salt and freshly ground pepper. Serve vichyssoise cold or hot, sprinkled with chives. Thin soup by adding more cream or milk after it has cooled completely.

For fresh, appealing soups: Try Gazpacho made in a blender and garnished with croutons, chopped egg, and vegetables; Avocado Cream Soup with dill and fruit wedges; and Vichyssoise garnished with chives.

GAZPACHO

2 large cucumbers, peeled and seeded

1 each red and green bell pepper

2 large fresh tomatoes, peeled and seeded

1 medium onion

1 clove garlic

3 cups (700 mL) cold water

1/4 cup (60 mL) olive oil

2 slices day-old white bread, crusts removed

1 tablespoon white wine vinegar

2 teaspoons salt

1 teaspoon paprika

1/4 teaspoon white pepper

1/8 teaspoon ground cumin

For the garnish:

1 slice white bread, diced

2 tablespoons olive oil

2 tablespoons diced red bell pepper

2 tablespoons diced green bell pepper

2 tablespoons diced cucumber

1 hard-cooked egg, chopped

2 tablespoons chopped green onion

2 **Finely chop vegetables.** Using a large knife or cleaver, finely chop vegetables, holding the tip of the knife on the board while chopping.

4 **Add bread and seasonings.** Add finely diced bread, vinegar, and seasonings and mix well. Chill and season to taste. The soup will have a distinctive flavor, and all the vegetables will retain their individuality.

3 **Add water.** Combine all vegetables in a medium bowl, mix, and add oil and water.

1 **Dice vegetables.** The best way to dice vegetables is to slice them, then hold them together and cut across. Dice onion and mince garlic.

5 **To use blender.** Combine half the soup (including tomatoes with their skins) in a blender and purée. Repeat with remaining soup. The result is a smooth soup with all the flavors blended harmoniously. Season, chill, and season again to taste just before serving.

SUMMER STEWS

During long, hot summer days, light, simple stews with lots of fresh vegetables and herbs are tempting fare. They taste good, and they're good for you—and not just during summer, since most vegetables are available year-round, either fresh or frozen. You can take advantage of an abundant harvest by freezing a large variety of fresh vegetables, either individually or mixed.

SUMMER GARDEN STEW

10 ounces (300 g) large shell beans, hulled
3 teaspoons salt
3 cups (700 mL) water
6 medium carrots
6 new potatoes
10 ounces (300 g) green beans
10 ounces (300 g) shelled peas
3 cups (700 mL) milk
2 tablespoons (25 g) butter
1 cup (30 g) finely chopped fresh parsley

Add beans and 2 teaspoons salt to boiling water and simmer, covered, for 10 minutes. Peel and slice carrots and potatoes. Wash and string green beans and cut into 1¼-inch (3½-cm) lengths. Add to beans and cook 10 minutes. Add peas and simmer for an additional 10 minutes. Drain vegetables and transfer to a warmed tureen. Bring milk, butter, remaining 1 teaspoon salt, and parsley to a boil. Pour over vegetables, stir gently, and serve immediately. Try Westphalian or other smoked ham as an accompaniment.

RATATOUILLE

1 generous pound (500 g) eggplant, peeled
1 generous pound small (500 g) zucchini
1¾ pound (800 g) fresh tomatoes
2 green bell peppers
1 bunch green onions, with tops
6 tablespoons (75 mL) olive oil
2 teaspoons salt
2 cloves garlic
½ teaspoon freshly ground black pepper
2 tablespoons chopped fresh basil
3 tablespoons finely chopped fresh parsley

Cut eggplant and zucchini into 1¼-inch (3½-cm) pieces. Peel and seed tomatoes; cut into quarters. Quarter bell peppers, remove seeds, rinse under cold water, and cut into 1¼-inch (3½-cm) pieces. Wash green onions and chop finely.

Heat oil in a deep skillet over high heat until it smokes. Add each vegetable separately and sauté until crisp-tender. Combine all vegetables in a baking dish, add raw green onions, and mix gently. Deglaze the frying pan with enough water to loosen any browned bits. Sprinkle salt on garlic and crush using a mortar and pestle or heavy knife. Add to deglazing liquid, stir, season with pepper, and pour evenly over vegetables. Place baking dish on the bottom rack of a preheated 400°F (200°C) oven and bake for 30 minutes, or until vegetables are tender. Just before removing from oven, sprinkle with fresh herbs.

Serve ratatouille at the temperature you prefer, anywhere from hot to chilled.

CABBAGE STEW WITH LAMB

1¾ pounds (800 g) boneless lamb shoulder
2 tablespoons oil
2 cloves garlic, minced
1 sprig lovage or several celery leaves
2 cups (450 mL) dry white wine
2 medium carrots
2 medium potatoes
1 medium head of green cabbage
1 generous pound (500 g) fresh tomatoes
salt and pepper
2 tablespoons minced fresh parsley

Cut lamb into large chunks. Heat oil in skillet until it begins to smoke, add lamb, and brown on all sides. Add garlic and lovage (or celery leaves) and slowly pour in wine along the edge of the pan. Reduce heat and simmer for 45 minutes. Meanwhile, peel carrots and potatoes. Slice carrots in rounds and dice potatoes. Cut out ribs from cabbage leaves; slice leaves. Blanch carrots, potatoes, and cabbage for 2 minutes, drain, and rinse under cold water. Peel, quarter, and seed tomatoes.

Remove lamb from cooking liquid, discard bones, and cut meat into small pieces. Add carrots and potatoes to cooking liquid and cook for 10 minutes. Strain, reserving vegetables and cooking liquid. Season liquid to taste with salt and pepper. Layer meat, vegetables, and potatoes in a baking dish, pour cooking liquid over all, and bake, covered, in a 300°F (150°C) oven for 30 minutes. Serve garnished with chopped parsley.

Cabbage Stew with Lamb is a perfect summer and fall dish. It is hearty yet light, and it can easily be prepared ahead of time.

CASSOULET

Cassoulet is the famous bean stew from Gascony in southwest France. As with most regional specialties, there are many versions of cassoulet. Our recipe serves 12, and it can be prepared ahead of time and kept warm, which makes it ideal for a dinner party.

The ingredients in cassoulet are always cooked first, then layered in a baking dish. The cooking liquid is poured over the vegetables up to, but not covering, the top layer of beans. Pour stock evenly over the bread-crumb topping so it doesn't sink into the beans. Bake until the topping is crisp and golden. After 2 hours of baking time, press the crumbs gently down into the cassoulet to keep them from burning.

You can make any amount of cassoulet. Combine all ingredients in a baking dish. Place in a 425°F (220°C) oven until the liquid begins to boil. Reduce heat to 300°F (150°C) and continue baking for 1 to 2 hours. The cassoulet is done when it is still moist and so tender that the meat, beans, and vegetables melt in your mouth.

For *Cassoulet Toulousain* you will need: 1¾ pounds (800 g) goose confit. To make confit, rub a cut-up goose with salt, place in a bowl, cover, and refrigerate for 2 to 3 days. Wipe off the goose with a paper towel to remove excess salt and cook for 2 hours in equal quantities of lard and goose fat. Remove from heat and let cool. Remove meat from bones and place in earthenware pots. Pour fat over meat until it is covered by 1½ inches (4 cm). The confit will keep for several months if stored in a cool place. (This method of preserving meat was used long before there was refrigeration.) For smaller meals, use goose drumsticks.

Cassoulet à la Carcassonne is similar. Reduce the quantity of preserved goose by half and add 10 ounces (300 g)

CASSOULET AU CANARD

1 duck (about 2¼ pounds/1 kg)
1½ teaspoons chopped fresh herbs (thyme, rosemary, parsley)
1 teaspoon salt
½ teaspoon pepper
1¼ pounds (600 g) dried white beans
1 medium celery root with greens
1 parsley root with greens
4 medium leeks
2 sprigs fresh thyme
1 bay leaf
1 clove garlic
2 teaspoons salt
1¼ pounds (600 g) pigs' feet
3 ounces (100 g) bacon
1½ quarts (1½ L) water
1 tablespoon lard
1 onion
1 large carrot
12 ounces (100 g) fresh tomatoes
1 garlic sausage (such as kielbasa), cooked

each of lamb and pork. Cut meats into large pieces, add tomatoes, and cook for 1 hour.

The day before serving the cassoulet, cut duck along the back and front, using a boning knife. Separate drumsticks and wings and cut the body in half between the ribs. Mix herbs, salt, and pepper; rub into duck, cover, and refrigerate overnight. In a bowl, cover beans with twice their volume of cold water and soak for 6 to 8 hours. Or, bring to a boil over high heat, remove from the flame, and set aside for 1 hour to soak.

The next day, drain excess water from soaked beans and place them in a large pot. Peel celery root and parsley root and rinse other vegetables. Tie vegetables together with thyme and bay leaf to make a bouquet garni. Peel

and slice garlic, sprinkle with salt, and crush with a knife blade. Add garlic, bouquet garni, pig's feet, and bacon to beans. Add 1½ quarts (1½ L) cold water and proceed as shown in the photographs.

Brown duck as shown in photograph 2. (You may also brown duck in the oven.) Cut onion into large dice. Peel and slice carrot. Peel, seed, and quarter tomatoes. Peel and slice sausage. Continue as shown in photograph.

When beans are cooked, remove bouquet garni, squeezing out any liquid, and discard. Remove pigs' feet and reserve for another meal, remove soft skin and meat from pigs' feet, cut into ¾-inch (2-cm) pieces, and add to cassoulet. Layer cassoulet: First, place ⅓ of beans in a large pot, baking dish, or roasting pan. Add meat, bacon, and sausage. Fill any gaps in pan with vegetables and cover well with remaining beans. Combine duck cooking juices and bean cooking liquid and bring to boil. Pour over stew just to the top bean layer. Place cassoulet, uncovered, on the bottom rack in oven and bake for 2 hours; do not stir during baking.

1 **Cover with water.** Place beans and pigs' feet in a pot. Add bacon, bouquet garni, and garlic. Cover with water and bake, covered, in a 350°F (180°C) oven for 2 hours.

2 **Sear duck.** Melt lard in a skillet over medium-high heat. Brown duck pieces, reduce heat to low, cover, and cook for 45 minutes.

3 **Sauté carrots and onions.** Heat some fat from the duck in a saucepan. Add onion and carrot and sauté for 10 minutes, then add tomatoes.

4 **Layer cassoulet.** Place ⅓ of the beans on bottom of roasting pan or Dutch oven. Add meat, sausage, and vegetables. Top with beans and cover with drippings from duck and stock.

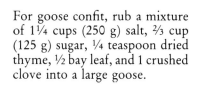

For goose confit, rub a mixture of 1¼ cups (250 g) salt, ⅔ cup (125 g) sugar, ¼ teaspoon dried thyme, ½ bay leaf, and 1 crushed clove into a large goose.

Cassoulet with duck is a juicy, hearty dish. Serve it with cold beer or a robust red wine.

WINTER STEWS

Hearty stews can still be light and easy on your stomach. They must be cooked only as long as necessary, using a small amount of fat to bring out all the flavors and retain as many vitamins as possible.

BORSCHT

1 quart (1 L) beef stock
1 generous pound (500 g) beef brisket or short ribs
1 onion
14 ounces (400 g) beets
8 ounces (200 g) fresh tomatoes
1½ tablespoons (20 g) butter
2 tablespoons red wine vinegar
1 teaspoon sugar
1 teaspoon salt
1 cup sliced green cabbage
2 ounces (60 g) boiled ham
2 frankfurters
4 sprigs, fresh parsley
1 small bay leaf
black pepper
½ cup (125 mL) sour cream

Heat beef stock, add beef brisket, and cook for 1 hour. Separate meat from bones; discard bones and any fat or gristle. Return meat to stock, cover, and refrigerate until cold. Cut meat into ½-inch (1½-cm) pieces. Dice onion; peel beets and slice them ⅛ inch (½ cm) thick. Peel, seed, and coarsely chop tomatoes.

Melt butter in a large pot until it foams. Sauté onions in butter until soft. Add beets, tomatoes, vinegar, sugar, ½ teaspoon salt, and ½ cup (125 mL) beef stock, cover, and simmer for 30 minutes over low heat. Reserve.

Meanwhile, core the cabbage and thickly slice the leaves. Cut ham into ½-inch (1½-cm) pieces and slice franks into ½-inch (1½-cm) rounds. Bring remaining beef stock to a boil; add cabbage, ½ teaspoon salt, ham, sausage, beef, parsley, and bay leaf. Partially cover and simmer for 20 minutes. Add soup to beet mixture. Season to taste with pepper and sugar, if necessary. Serve in soup bowls, passing sour cream separately. Garnish with chopped parsley and dill if desired.

PICHELSTEINER STEW

10 ounces (300 g) boneless shoulder
10 ounces (300 g) leg of lamb or pork neck
3 medium onions
1 tablespoon lard
1 teaspoon salt
½ teaspoon pepper
pinch of marjoram
2 cups (450 mL) beef stock
5 medium carrots
1 large celery root
2 medium baking potatoes
3 leeks, without tops
¼ cup finely chopped fresh parsley

Cut meat into ¾-inch (2-cm) pieces. Dice onions. Melt lard in a heavy skillet or Dutch oven over medium–high heat, add meat, and brown quickly, stirring occasionally. Add onions and cook until golden. Add salt, pepper, marjoram, and hot beef stock; cover and simmer for one hour over low heat. Meanwhile, peel and dice carrots, celery root, and potatoes. Clean leeks, then quarter them lengthwise and crosswise. Add vegetables to soup, stir, and simmer for an additional 30 minutes, shaking pot occasionally to prevent sticking. Season to taste. Serve sprinkled with chopped parsley, and have plenty of cold beer on hand.

Pichelsteiner is perfect for a dinner party. To make a large quantity, preheat oven to 350°F (175°C). Tightly layer ingredients in a large roasting pan to ¾ inch (2 cm) below the rim, starting with browned, seasoned meat and ending with vegetable mixture. Season with salt and pepper and dot with butter if desired. Or, arrange overlapping slices of marrow on vegetable mixture. Pour stock over all to a depth of 1¼ inches (3½ cm), cover pan tightly with foil, and place in oven. Cooking time will depend on the amount in the pan; once stock has come to a boil, cook for an additional hour.

Specialties rich in tradition include bright red Russian Borscht served in a white cup and, in the copper pot, a hearty Pichelsteiner Stew that may be varied by adding cabbage as well. Today's cooking methods call for reduced cooking time, which gives these dishes extra texture from still-crisp vegetables.

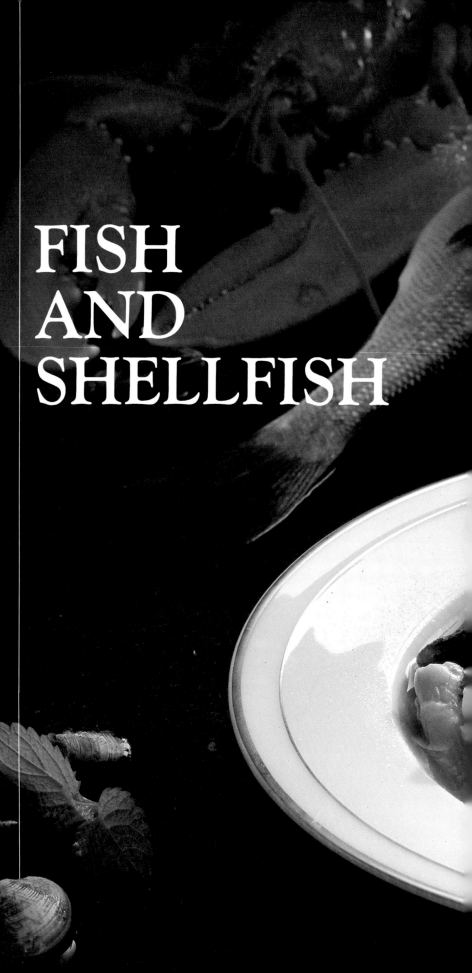

The new cuisine has discovered fish for the wonder that it is—bravo! Until recently, fish was prepared without imagination and usually overcooked, which presented us with sad excuses for the many varieties of salt- and fresh-water fish available.

As it is served in fine meals today, fish is a revelation to the gourmet. The tender trout balls with spinach and saffron velouté in this chapter are a good example, as is the stuffed flounder cooked in its own juices and served with creamy sauce and tomato wedges.

Shellfish wasn't much better off in yesterday's cooking. Think of lobster, buried under too much dressing or so much mayonnaise that its unique taste (which had probably been cooked out of it anyway) was lost. No, today we cook shellfish *à la minute*—fresh to order—then add light sauces to enhance its delicate flavor and vegetables to complement it.

Serving fish and shellfish at least once a week is a good idea, not only because it can be turned into a real delicacy. Fine seafood is a joy to the palate, confirming the words of Oscar Wilde: "After a good meal you can forgive anyone, even your relatives." Fish filets should be wrapped to stay moist and juicy during cooking, while a whole fish is protected by its own skin. Follow the directions for frying flounder when preparing sole or other white fish filets.

FISH AND SHELLFISH

FRIED FISH

When frying fish, use a heavy stainless steel, cast-iron, or enamel pan. Use plenty of fat to fry fish evenly and shake the pan occasionally so it doesn't stick. If you enjoy the flavor of melted butter, pour some over the fish after you've turned it once, but first pour out the excess cooking fat. Temperature is extremely important when frying fish. Heat the fat over a medium flame until it is hot enough to sizzle when the fish is added. If the fat isn't hot enough, the fish will absorb it and lose its own juices. On the other hand, if the fat is too hot, the fish will burn before it is done. Seasoning the fish with fresh lemon juice or vinegar before frying will make it more firm.

FISH PATTIES

12 ounces (350 g) white fish filets
3 slices bacon
1 large onion
1 bunch fresh parsley
1 dinner roll, soaked in milk and squeezed dry
1 egg
1/2 teaspoon salt
pepper and freshly grated nutmeg
butter or oil for frying

Put filets, bacon, onion, parsley, and dinner roll through a meat grinder. To ensure that all of the ingredients go through the grinder, press a piece of wax paper through it as the last step. Combine the fish mixture with egg, salt, pepper, and nutmeg. Mix well and correct seasoning. Shape into 4 round patties and fry in butter or oil over medium heat for 10 minutes, turning occasionally.

FRIED FLOUNDER FILETS

4 large flounder filets
flour
oil for frying
1/2 teaspoon salt
1/4 teaspoon pepper
1 1/2 tablespoons (20 g) butter

Prepare flounder as shown earlier and pat dry. Just before frying, dust with flour to prevent sticking. Pour oil into a skillet to a depth of about 1/8 inch (1/2 cm) and heat over medium heat. Place flounder into pan white side down, shaking pan occasionally to keep the fish from sticking. Fry fish for 4 to 8 minutes, turn with two wooden spatulas, season with salt and pepper, and fry for an additional 4 to 5 minutes. Place on a warm platter and keep warm in a low oven. Discard oil used in frying, add butter to skillet, and heat until browned. Pour over fish.

BREADED FISH FILETS

1 1/4 pounds (600 g) fish filets
flour
1 egg
1/2 teaspoon salt
1/4 teaspoon white pepper
fine breadcrumbs
oil for frying

Cut fish into serving-size portions, which are easier to work with than large filets. Dust with flour and shake off excess. Beat egg with salt and pepper. Dip fish pieces into egg mixture and coat with breadcrumbs on both sides, pressing lightly to make them adhere. Refrigerate for at least 20 minutes to harden the coating, which will prevent the crumbs from burning. Fry in hot oil, turning once (see above recipe for flounder). Always fry breaded fish just before serving so the coating stays crisp.

BATTER-FRIED FISH FILETS

1 1/4 pounds (600 g) fish filets
juice of 1/2 lemon
3/4 cup (125 g) flour
1 to 2 eggs
1/2 cup (125 mL) beer or milk
1 tablespoon oil plus additional oil for frying
1/2 teaspoon salt
1/4 teaspoon pepper

Rub fish with lemon juice. Mix flour and egg in a bowl, add beer or milk to make a batter, and mix well. Add oil, salt, and pepper; stir and set aside for 30 minutes to allow the starch in the flour to swell. Pour oil into skillet to a depth of 3/4 inch (2 cm). Test temperature of oil with a small piece of bread; if it sizzles immediately, the oil is ready for frying. Dip fish into batter, and fry until golden on both sides.

59

FISH COOKED IN FOIL

Fish cooked in aluminum foil retains its vitamins, minerals, and delicate tenderness because it cooks in its own juices. We even recommend placing tightly sealed portions of fish in simmering water. This method saves energy, because the fish cooks faster than it would in the dry heat of the oven.

Cooking in aluminum foil works well for frozen fish, too. Double the cooking time to allow for thawing. If you use frozen fish, add raw vegetables before cooking. The foil keeps fish from drying out and getting tough. Fish is done *before* it flakes—at this point it is still juicy and delicious. Cooked in foil, it is also low in calories since it is prepared with little or no fat.

HERRING WITH THYME

8 small herrings, 7 ounces (200 g) each
juice of 2 lemons
1 teaspoon salt
1/2 teaspoon pepper
24 sprigs fresh parsley
24 sprigs fresh thyme
1 1/2 tablespoons (20 g) butter

Clean herrings, cut off heads and tails, rinse, and pat dry. Place in a dish just large enough to hold them side by side. Pour lemon juice over fish, cover, and refrigerate for 1 hour; this will allow the lemon flavor to penetrate and will firm the fish.

Pat fish dry, sprinkle with salt and pepper, and stuff with herbs. Wrap individually in buttered aluminum foil and simmer until done.

HALIBUT WITH HERBS

4 halibut steaks, 8 ounces (250 g) each
1 1/2 tablespoons (20 g) butter, softened
2 tablespons minced onion
1 teaspoon each chopped fresh basil, savory, fennel, and lovage or celery leaves
1 tablespoon each chopped fresh dill, chervil, and parsley
1 tablespoon fresh lemon juice
1 teaspoon salt
dash of Worcestershire sauce

Place halibut pieces on aluminum foil and brush with butter. Combine onion, herbs, lemon juice, salt, and Worcestershire and mix well. Spread evenly over halibut, seal aluminum to form a pouch, and steam until done. If you wish you may substitute other herbs or just use parsley. Serve with boiled potatoes and a green salad with yogurt dressing.

HOW TO COOK FISH IN ALUMINUM FOIL

Cut heavy-duty aluminum foil into long 16-inch (40-cm) pieces. Place fish and other ingredients in the center of each piece. Bring long sides together and fold over several times to seal. Press ends together and fold over to seal. Bring 2 inches (5 cm) of water to boil in a large, heavy-bottomed pot and place foil packages next to each other in water. Cover pot and reduce heat to low. If using an electric stove, turn heat off after 5 minutes. After 12 minutes, pieces that are approximately 3/4 inch (2 cm) thick, weighing 8 ounces (200 g) each will be fully cooked. For larger pieces or for a whole fish, allow 5 minutes extra cooking time per 1/2 inch (1 1/2 cm) thickness.

FILETS WITH VEGETABLES

1 3/4 pounds (800 g) filet of salmon, ocean perch, or haddock
1 teaspoon fresh lemon juice
1 teaspoon salt
1 large carrot
2 1/2 tablespoons (40 g) butter
1 medium tomato
1 leek
1 tablespoon chopped fresh herbs (basil, lemon balm, parsley)
1/2 cup (125 mL) dry white wine
2 tablespoons heavy cream
1/8 teaspoon ground ginger
dash of hot pepper sauce

Cut fish into 4 pieces; rub with lemon juice and salt. Peel carrot and cut into thin sticks. Sauté in butter for 2 minutes. Blanch tomatoes in boiling water, then peel, quarter, seed, and chop coarsely. Wash leeks and cut into thin sticks. Combine vegetables and mound evenly over fish. Sprinkle with chopped herbs, seal in foil, and steam over simmering water. Meanwhile, in a saucepan, combine white wine, cream, ginger, and hot pepper sauce and bring to boil. Arrange fish and vegetables on warm plates. Season cooking juices to taste and spoon over fish. Serve with boiled potatoes.

A tender fish filet, cooked in its own juices, is a true delicacy. Serve it with boiled potatoes tossed in butter; accompany with a glass of chilled white wine.

OTHER WAYS OF COOKING FISH

Poaching fish is a highly respected, thoroughly traditional cooking method. It takes little time and it enhances the subtle, delicate flavors of fish. When poached in its skin, fish often looks blue—an effect created by exposure to heat. It will turn a more intense blue if rinsed in vinegar before cooking, though this tends to cause a certain loss of flavor.

When cooking fish in water the most important element is the salt. Ocean fish needs about 1½ teaspoons salt per quart of water, or it will be watery when cooked. About half that amount is needed for fresh-water fish, because they will dry out if cooked with too much salt.

To make a full-flavored court bouillon or poaching liquid, add vegetables, spices, and 1 tablespoon vinegar or fresh lemon juice per 5 quarts (5 L) water. For cooking trout or other tender fresh-water fish, add onion, carrot, parsley, and peppercorns to the cooking liquid. For carp or pike add leeks, celery leaves, and a bay leaf as well, and add dry white wine to the court bouillon for cooking ocean fish. Allow at least 2 quarts (2 L) water per pound of fish.

Make the stock with finely chopped vegetables and spices and boil over high heat for 15 minutes. Add salt, wine, and vinegar or lemon juice and place fish in the stock. Cover loosely so you can see when bubbles begin to rise to the surface of the water. At this point add 1 cup cold water, which will make the fish tender and flaky. Cover pot tightly and remove from heat. Small fish such as trout will be done after 8 minutes. Larger fish such as carp will need up to 20 minutes. To calculate the correct cooking time, measure the fish at its thickest part and allow 10 minutes cooking time for every inch. To test for doneness insert

Clean the fish (or have your fishmonger clean it for you). If you plan to cook a whole fish, scale it first. To scale fish, begin at the tail and scrape with a knife toward the head.

Hold the fins out with one hand and cut off with scissors. Butterfly the fish by cutting along the backbone on each side, then gently push back the filets and remove the entrails. If there is any roe in the fish, it is delicious when fried in butter or poached in milk. Cut the backbone at the tail and slowly pull it up towards the head to remove as many small bones as possible at the same time. Use your fingers or tweezers to remove any bones that remain in the fish.

a needle into the thickest part of the fish, right behind the head. The fish is done when there is only slight resistance.

Steaming fish is another cooking method that has been revived lately as a way of retaining more flavor and nutrition. Generally, you should filet the fish first, then make a court bouillon from the scraps. Reduce it to make a delicate sauce similar to velouté.

We have chosen sole to demonstrate how to filet flat fish. Prepare rounded fish like perch as shown in the box on this page, though you need only scale them if you want to use the skin for fish stock or if the scales are extremely large. If you plan to stuff the filets, remove the head and cut open the front of the filet. Place filets on a cutting board skin side down. Using a pointed knife, loosen enough skin from the filet so you can hold on to it firmLy. Then, holding the knife flat with the sharp edge forward, work it toward the end of the filet, pulling on the skin, until skin and filet are separated. Trim any ragged edges from filet.

Vegetables such as onion, shallots, celery, carrots, and leeks are best suited to steaming fish. Clean them and cut into matchstick-size pieces. Sauté them in butter before steaming them with the fish; they will then cook in the same amount of time as the fish.

Deep saucepans, Dutch ovens, or steamers work well for steaming fish, as long as they have tight lids. Stovetop steaming is more efficient than oven steaming. Melt butter over low heat; sauté onions and firm vegetables, then add soft vegetables. Arrange filets skin side down on top of vegetables, season, cover, and reduce heat as low as possible. Steam fish for 4 to 8 minutes, depending on its thickness. When the vegetables are done, add wine and reheat; the acid in the wine will help keep the vegetables crisp.

PERCH IN PARCHMENT PAPER

1 1½-pound (675-g) whole perch or trout

2 tablespoons (30 g) butter, softened

1 teaspoon salt

6 tablespoons chopped fresh herbs (dill, parsley, and basil with a bit of tarragon, thyme, and sage)

1 onion

Follow directions on this page for preparing fish. Scale, wash thoroughly, and rinse. Pat dry with a paper towel. Cut off fins and make small slits on both sides of fish.

Place parchment paper on a baking sheet and brush with butter. Preheat oven to 425°F (225°C). Insert remaining butter into slits and coat fish with salt and herb mixture. Place perch in center of parchment paper and arrange onion around fish. Fold paper over fish and crimp the edges tightly. Place baking sheet on the center oven rack and bake fish for 20 minutes, opening the paper for the last 5 minutes of cooking time.

Make slits across the fish right down to the bones, as shown in the photograph. The fish will cook evenly and absorb the flavors of the herbs, spices, and butter. Cook fish in parchment paper or on the grill.

Perch steamed in parchment paper is fragrant with tender herbs fresh from the garden. Serve it with mashed potatoes and a mild cucumber salad with cream dressing. If desired, you may bone the fish before it is cooked and stuff it; allow 10 additional minutes cooking time.

PIKE QUENELLES ON SPINACH LEAVES

7 ounces (200 g) pike fish filets
1 egg
½ teaspoon salt
⅛ teaspoon pepper
2 tablespoons (25 g) butter, softened
½ cup (125 mL) chilled heavy cream
1 pound (450 g) fresh spinach
2 tablespoons (25 g) butter
Velouté sauce (see Index), flavored with fresh sage

Cut the filets into small pieces. In a bowl mix fish, egg, salt, and pepper. Cover and refrigerate. When chilled, purée in a blender, adding soft butter and chilled cream. Bring a large pot of salted water to boil. Shape fish mixture into small dumplings and place gently in water (see photographs at right). Cover loosely and simmer gently for 10 minutes or until done, being careful not to let water boil. Remove dumplings from water with a slotted spoon, drain, and keep warm.

Meanwhile, carefully wash spinach and discard stems. Blanch leaves, drain, and rinse under cold water. (Blanching spinach removes its astringent qualities.) Carefully press out excess water and separate leaves. Melt 2 tablespoons butter in a skillet over low heat until it foams. Add spinach, season with salt and pepper, and heat through, stirring occasionally. Divide spinach between 2 plates for a main course or arrange on 4 plates for an appetizer. Arrange quenelles on spinach and nap with velouté sauce seasoned with sage.

1 **For pike quenelles add cream** after fish, egg, seasonings, and soft butter are combined in blender. Purée quickly so mixture remains chilled.

1 **Prepare flounder.** Remove head using a sharp knife; cut off fins with scissors. Scrape any darkened areas from inside fish and rinse fish well.

2 **Shape quenelles.** Place the chilled mixture in the palm of your hand and, using a teaspoon, shape into smooth oval dumplings. Arrange on a buttered plate.

2 **Cut pockets for stuffing** using a sharp, pointed knife. First cut along the center, then loosen both filets from the bones, holding the knife blade flat and being careful not to cut through the filets.

3 **Poach quenelles.** Bring salted water to gentle simmer in a saucepan. Using 2 tablespoons, drop quenelles into water and poach for 10 minutes or until firm.

3 **To stuff flounder,** place stuffing mixture into the pocket and smooth it with a spatula. Pull the filets from both sides over the stuffing to cover it, pressing firmly to keep them in place.

STUFFED FLOUNDER

4 whole flounders

stuffing mixture, made from 7 ounces (200 g) flounder filets according to recipe for Pike Quenelles above

2 tablespoons finely chopped fresh dill

1 tablespoon finely chopped fresh basil

1½ cups (350 mL) dry white wine

1 cup (240 mL) water or fish stock

1½ tablespoons (20 g) butter

½ onion, diced

1 cup (240 mL) heavy cream

½ cup (125 mL) fish stock

salt and white pepper

2 tomatoes, diced

Prepare and clean flounders. Prepare stuffing mixture according to directions for Pike Quenelles, substituting flounder for pike and adding dill and basil. Pour 1 cup (125 mL) each white wine and water (or fish stock) into a deep baking dish that is large enough to hold fish next to each other without overlapping. Heat liquid in 400°F (200°C) oven until bubbles rise to the surface. Add fish and cover with

oiled parchment paper. After 5 minutes turn off oven; after another 5 minutes remove fish from cooking liquid and arrange on warm plates.

Meanwhile, prepare sauce. In a medium saucepan, melt butter, add onion, and sauté until translucent. Stir in cream with ½ cup (125 mL) each white wine and fish stock. Let simmer for 15 minutes, or until sauce has reduced by half. Strain sauce, pressing onion through strainer. Quickly reheat sauce, season to taste, and pour around flounder. Garnish with diced fresh tomato.

chilled dry Riesling is superb with delicate fish dishes such as Stuffed Flounder and Pike Quenelles.

65

Sole is one of the tastiest of ocean fish. The filets are as delicious steamed as they are when stuffed, rolled, and sautéed in butter.

Steamed fish has a wonderful aroma, like the salty sea from which it came. Fish can be steamed simply, without salt or other seasonings, or spices and fresh herbs can be added to create a pleasing treat for the palate. Fruity wines, a whiff of garlic, and softened sweet butter are also natural flavorings for steamed fish. Any filet is suitable for steaming, but a fresh-water fish will require more seasoning since it doesn't have as much natural salt as ocean fish.

The Chinese steam fish by placing it on a plate and letting it cook in its own juices. The European method is usually to place the fish in a steamer set over simmering water, though much of its flavor is lost when the juices drain off. Every kitchen has utensils suited for steaming. All you need is a round or oval pan and a plate small enough to leave space between its edge and the rim of the pan, allowing the steam to circulate freely. You will also need either a steamer rack or two heatproof cups to raise the plate from the bottom of the pan.

SOLE BRAISED IN DRY SHERRY

2 large whole sole
1 tablespoon fresh lemon juice
¼ teaspoon white pepper
2 onions
2 tablespoons finely chopped fresh chives
2 tablespoons finely chopped fresh parsley
½ teaspoon salt
½ cup (125 mL) each dry sherry and water
3½ tablespoons (50 g) butter (optional)

Remove heads from sole and filet the fish. To remove the skin, cut sideways into the skin above the tail and peel it back far enough to get a good grip on it. Hold the tail down with one hand and pull the skin towards the head with the other. Cut filets, rinse, and pat dry. Rub with lemon juice and pepper. Cover and refrigerate for 1 hour. Slice onions as thinly as possible and arrange on a large plate or platter. Pat filets dry and arrange on top of onion slices, skin side down. Sprinkle with herbs and salt and steam over mixture of sherry and water. If desired, reduce sherry mixture to several tablespoons, add fish juices and butter, and whisk until light and creamy. Spoon over fish. Serve with a chilled white wine. (Note: Dry white wine can be substituted for the sherry.)

1 **Loosen skin.** Beginning at the head, loosen the dark skin at the fins with your thumb to make skinning easier. At the tail, use a sharp pointed knife.

2 **Remove skin.** Hold onto the tail tightly; forcefully pull the skin up and towards the head, as shown in the photograph. Scale the white skin or remove it entirely.

3 **Cut off fins and use scissors** to trim the filets. Dust with flour if you are frying them, or prepare any way you like.

6 **Sprinkle with herbs.** Place a bed of onion rings on a platter. Arrange filets on top, skin side down, and sprinkle with chives and parsley.

7 **Pour water and wine** into a deep pot, place a heatproof bowl upside down in the center, cover and bring to simmer over medium heat.

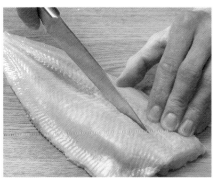

4 **To filet,** cut along the center line of the fish right down to the bone.

5 **Loosen filets.** Press a flexible knife flat against the bones and, starting at the head of the fish, cut towards the tail, continually cutting deeper until the filets are separated.

8 **Sprinkle fish with salt** just before cooking. Set platter in the pot as shown in the photograph. Cover tightly and steam fish until done; the cooking time depends on the thickness of the fish. Thin sole filets are cooked in 5 to 6 minutes. Serve immediately.

FISH AND VEGETABLE STEW

1 generous pound (500 g) cod or perch filets
1/4 cup (60 mL) dry white wine
2 onions
3 large carrots
1/2 medium celery root
2 1/2 tablespoons (40 g) butter
1 tablespoon paprika
1/2 teaspoon hot paprika or ground red pepper
1 teaspoon salt
1 bay leaf
1 quart (1 L) water
3 large tomatoes
2 tablespoons finely chopped fresh parsley
crème fraîche (optional)

Garlic Mayonnaise (rouille—see page 33)

Cut the fish into bite-size pieces and remove as many bones as possible. Place fish in a bowl, add wine, mix well, and set aside. Peel onions, carrots, and celery root and cut into 3/8-inch (1-cm) pieces. Melt the butter in a Dutch oven or heavy skillet over low heat until it foams. Add vegetables and stir until onions are translucent. Stir in seasonings, add water, and bring to a boil. Cover, reduce heat to low, and cook until vegetables are tender.

Meanwhile, peel, quarter, and seed tomatoes. Add to stew along with fish and simmer for 10 minutes, being careful not to let mixture boil. Add parsley and season broth to taste. If desired, stir in crème fraîche. Serve with boiled potatoes or rice seasoned with sage. Serve with *rouille*.

FISH SOUP WITH MUSSELS

14 ounces (400 g) fish filets
2 tablespoons olive oil
salt and pepper
1/8 teaspoon powdered thyme
1 clove garlic, minced
1 3/4 pounds (800 g) mussels
1/2 cup (125 mL) dry white wine
1 quart (1 L) fish stock
1 cup (100 g) chopped cooked shrimp
1 small onion
2 tablespoons (25 g) butter
4 fresh tomatoes
2 leeks

Cut fish into 3/4-inch (2-cm) pieces. Combine olive oil, 1/2 teaspoon salt, 1/4 teaspoon pepper, thyme and garlic and mix well. Coat fish pieces with mixture and refrigerate for 1 hour. Steam mussels in white wine until shells open. Strain cooking liquid. Bring 1 cup (175 mL) fish stock to boil, season with salt and pepper, and pour over shrimp. Cover and set aside.

Dice onion. Melt butter over low heat, add onion, and sauté until translucent. Add 3 cups (700 mL) fish stock and mussel liquid and cook for 15 minutes. Peel, seed, and dice tomatoes. Cut leeks into small rounds and rinse well. Add vegetables to soup and bring to boil. Reduce heat, add fish, mussels, and shrimp, and simmer for 5 minutes. Serve with bread and herb butter.

Herb Butter

Crush 2 cloves garlic, 2 teaspoons green peppercorns, 10 fresh basil leaves, and 1 teaspoon salt with mortar and pestle. Stir in 10 tablespoons (150 g) softened butter and mix well. Season with fresh lemon juice and crushed black pepper.

FRENCH-STYLE FISH SOUP

For 8 servings
2¼ pounds (1 kg) assorted fish
5 shallots, finely chopped
⅛ teaspoon powdered sage
1 generous pound (500 g) mussels
2 quarts (1 L) water
2 tablespoons salt
1 small lobster
8 ounces (200 g) fresh eel
8 jumbo shrimp in shells
2 onions
4 cloves garlic
white part of 6 leeks
1 large fennel bulb
4 fresh tomatoes
1 bunch fresh parsley
6 tablespoons (80 mL) olive oil
1 bouquet garni
1 piece each orange and lemon peel
white pepper
2 tablespoons Pernod or other anise aperitif

Use as many different kinds of fish as possible; cod, halibut, flounder, salmon, sole, turbot, and perch are all good choices. Remove as many bones as possible, cut fish into bite-size pieces, add shallots and sage, and toss to mix. Reserve all fish scraps.

Prepare mussels as shown on page 40 and steam in 2 quarts boiling water with 2 tablespoons salt until the shells open. Remove and reserve. To kill lobster, drop into same water, then remove and reserve. Add fish scraps to water and simmer for 20 minutes to make a stock. Strain stock through cheesecloth. Meanwhile, remove mussels from their shells. Break off lobster tail and cut lengthwise into 4 pieces using a heavy knife. Cut claws length-

wise and halve body lengthwise. Cut eel into 8 pieces. Rinse shrimp. Dice onions and garlic. Cut leeks and fennel into very thin slices. Peel, seed, and dice tomatoes. Finely chop parsley and have all remaining ingredients ready to add to soup.

Heat olive oil in a large pot, add onion, garlic, half the vegetables, bouquet garni, ¼ teaspoon pepper, and orange and lemon peel and sauté for 10 minutes. Add lobster meat and shrimp and sauté quickly. Add mussel stock, bring to a boil, and simmer for 15 minutes. Add eel and cook 5 minutes, then remove from heat. Remove lobster and shrimp shells and cut large pieces of lobster into bite-size pieces.

Strain cooking liquid. Shortly before serving, reheat cooking liquid, add remaining vegetables and tomatoes, and cook for 1 minute. Add Pernod and parsley. Season to taste with salt and pepper. Add all seafood and simmer gently for 10 minutes, being careful not to boil. Using a slotted spoon, remove fish and vegetables from broth and arrange on a preheated platter. Pour broth into a tureen. Garnish fish and vegetables with thin rounds of French bread spread with garlic butter and toasted. To serve, place fish and rounds of bread in soup plates and ladle hot broth over them.

SHELLFISH

Most shellfish are either bivalves or crustaceans. Bivalves include clams, mussels, and oysters, while crustaceans are shrimp, crawfish, lobster, and crab. Their names may be confusing, but cooking with them is simple. They are best when fresh and barely cooked. One method of cooking crustaceans is to place them in hot fish stock, remove it from the heat, let cool, and serve chilled. Or, remove the juicy meat from its shell and heat it gently in soups or sauces. Prepared this way the meat will retain its delicate flavor. Never boil the meat; it will become bitter, tough, and dry. High-quality seafood is available either fresh or frozen. Whenever possible, select seafood in the shell, because it is much fresher that way.

CRAWFISH IN WINE SAUCE

| 1 onion |
| 1 carrot |
| 1 medium celery root |
| 2 bunches fresh parsley |
| 2 bunches fresh dill |
| 1½ tablespoons (20 g) butter |
| 1 quart (1 L) dry white wine |
| 1 quart (1 L) water |
| 2 tablespoons salt |
| 30 live crawfish |

Peel and slice onion, carrot, and celery root. Tie parsley and dill together into a bouquet garni. Melt butter in a large pot over low heat and sauté onion, carrot, and celery root until onion is translucent. Pour in wine and water; add salt and bouquet garni. Bring to boil over high heat. Drop in crawfish head first and boil until all crawfish have turned bright red. Cov-

er, reduce heat, and simmer until crawfish are cooked, about 7 minutes, stirring occasionally. Remove from heat and let mixture cool to lukewarm. Remove crawfish and serve garnished with parsley tied in small bunches. Accompany with freshly toasted French bread and whipped butter. Reduce cooking liquid, cool, and freeze for later use as fish stock.

LOBSTER IN DILL CREAM

| 4 small lobsters, approximately 1 pound (450 g) each |
| 3 tablespoons sea salt |
| 2 tablespoons caraway seed |
| 2 bunches dill, stems cut off and reserved |
| 1 cup (240 mL) heavy cream |
| 1 tablespoon mayonnaise |
| 1 teaspoon hot prepared mustard |

Thoroughly wash lobsters. Pour 3 quarts (3 L) water into a pot large enough to hold all the lobsters and bring to boil. Add sea salt, caraway, and dill stems and boil for 5 minutes. Add lobsters head first, cover, and boil for 25 minutes. (Allow 1 minute cooking time for each additional 4 ounces [100 g]).

Meanwhile, finely chop dill leaves. Whip the cream until stiff. Fold in mayonnaise, mustard, and chopped dill. Remove lobsters from pot, drain, and serve in a white cloth napkin. Accompany with new potatoes and French bread, and have finger-bowls with lemon wedges ready—you'll need to use your fingers. To eat lobster, remove claws from body, crack with a nutcracker, and remove meat with a long narrow fork. Then break open the body and tail and remove the meat. Crack the smaller claws and carefully extract meat, using a nut pick if necessary.

SHRIMP WITH TARTAR SAUCE

| 2¼ pounds (1 kg) cooked jumbo shrimp |
| 2 celery stalks |
| 4 green onions, with tops |
| 2 tablespoons olive oil |
| 1 cup (240 mL) dry white wine |
| 1 teaspoon hot prepared mustard |
| ¼ teaspoon salt |
| ⅛ teaspoon ground red pepper |
| Tartar Sauce (see Index) |

Shell the shrimp; reserve shells. Wash and slice celery stalks and green onions. Heat olive oil in a deep skillet until it smokes. Add shrimp shells and vegetables, cover, and cook, stirring occasionally, for 5 minutes. Add white wine, cover, and cook an additional 10 minutes. Remove from heat, strain broth through a fine sieve or cheesecloth, and reduce by half over medium heat. Season with mustard, salt, and red pepper. Add shrimp to broth and heat through, being careful not to boil. Serve with rice or new potatoes, tartar sauce, and a watercress salad with lemon cream dressing (see Index).

Crawfish are an appetizing red after cooking. Use a broth made with the same type of wine as will be served with the meal.

New cuisine or not, many of us still clamor for our Sunday roast. But most of us are beginning to experiment with recipes for light meat dishes as well. These new recipes add variety and lead us away from fatty meats with thick gravies. But only high-quality meat guarantees a good meal. As Winston Churchill said, "Offer something to your body so the soul enjoys living in it."

For roasting and grilling, always use fine, tender meat like leg, rib, round steak and high-quality sirloin and tenderloin steaks. For these steaks to be as juicy and tender as possible they must be aged, then cut against the grain at least ¾ inch (2 cm) thick. A few fatty streaks—or marbling—in the meat guarantee a tasty cut. After you buy a steak, rub it with cooking oil, wrap it tightly, refrigerate, and use within three days.

MEATS

STEAKS AND CHOPS

Frying Steaks

The meat should be at room temperature, and it should be completely dry. Remove from the refrigerator ahead of time and pat it dry with a paper towel. Slash the edges of the steak to prevent it from curling, but don't remove the fat because it adds flavor and moisture to the meat.

You'll need a heavy cast iron, steel, or enamel skillet strong enough to withstand and conduct heat well. Heat pan over a high flame and, to test the temperature, add a drop of water; if it pops and crackles immediately, the pan is hot enough. Add steaks and fry for 1 minute on each side, or until small drops of red juice rise to the surface. Turn steaks again and fry until the drops are clear. Reduce heat to medium and carefully turn steaks again. Do not prick them or you will lose precious juices; for the same reason don't salt them until they are cooked. Dot steaks with butter if desired. Steaks fried this way will be juicy and pink.

Follow the same procedure for other thick cuts of meat; the frying time depends on the meat's thickness. For example, a piece of meat that is 2½ inches (6 cm) thick will take approximately 30 minutes to cook. Let steaks sit for a few minutes before slicing so they will retain their juices.

Broiling Steaks

Broiling works well if you plan to serve more than 4 steaks at a time. Brush a broiler pan with oil and place on top broiler rack. Brown steaks on both sides under broiler, then lower the rack and cook steaks according to their thickness. Watch them closely and adjust heat and/or rack if necessary.

Testing for Doneness

The longer meat is cooked the more it loses its elasticity; it becomes firm and eventually dry and tough. To test meat for doneness, press it with your finger. It should be springy, indicating that the juices are still within the meat.

1 **Medium-rare steak** looks dark pink and barely cooked in the center. It is warm through, very juicy and just the way most steak lovers prefer it.

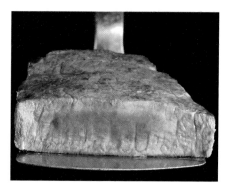

2 **Medium steak** is pink throughout, with a juicy, red center. It is hot through and perfectly cooked.

3 **Well done** steaks should still be juicy; the center is light pink and the meat has toughened just slightly. If fried any longer, the steak will be dry.

SIRLOIN STEAK WITH MORELS

4 small slices beef sirloin,
approximately 4 ounces (125 g) each

1 tablespoon oil

12 dried morels

1 cup (240 mL) beef stock

½ cup (125 mL) heavy cream

1½ teaspoons crushed green
peppercorns

4 green onions, with tops

1½ tablespoons (20 g) butter

salt

Rub meat with oil and set aside for 30 minutes, covered. Heat morels in stock until hot, cover, and let soak for 30 minutes. If the morels are still sandy, strain the stock, rinse morels thoroughly, and return both to clean saucepan. Add cream and reduce by half. Add green peppercorns. Clean green onions and cut into 1½-inch (4-cm) strips. Heat a skillet over high heat and brown steaks for 1 minute on each side. Reduce heat, melt butter on top of steaks, and fry to desired doneness. Sprinkle with salt and arrange on preheated plates. Quickly sauté green onions in the same skillet. Stir in morel sauce and bring to a boil. Season to taste and pour over steaks. Serve with fried matchstick potatoes.

Chops and cutlets from lamb, pork, and veal are ideal for frying as well. Pork and veal cutlets are juicier if they are breaded first, then fried or deep-fried. When frying breaded meats, always brown both sides in sufficient oil over medium-high heat first, then reduce heat and finish cooking, turning meat several times so breading stays crisp and browns evenly but doesn't burn. Boneless cuts require about 12 minutes frying time; cuts with bones require an additional 5 minutes.

The following three recipes will show you how to handle the best cuts of meat, how to fry them to perfection, and how to serve them so they are as pleasing to the eye as they are to the palate, and so they make you look like a pro. The side dishes are simple to prepare as well, and they help create a perfect meal.

LAMB CHOPS WITH HERB BUTTER

8 loin lamb chops, about 1¼ inches (3 cm) thick
2 tablespoons oil
1 clove garlic
2 pimentos, diced
½ teaspoon chopped fresh rosemary
½ teaspoon chopped fresh sage
8 white peppercorns
salt
For the herb butter:
7 tablespoons (100 g) butter, softened
1 tablespoon minced fresh dill
¼ teaspoon celery salt
⅛ teaspoon white pepper

Slash fat on chops in several places. Combine oil and seasonings in a mortar and pestle, crush to a paste, and rub lamb chops. Wrap tightly in foil and set aside for 4 to 5 hours. For herb butter, cream butter with a whisk, add seasonings, and mix well. Shape into a roll, wrap in parchment or wax paper, and refrigerate.

Over high heat, fry lamb chops in a ribbed-bottom cast iron skillet for 1 minute on each side. Reduce heat to medium and fry for an additional 5 minutes. (Or broil them if you prefer.) Remove fat if desired. Slice herb butter into rounds and place a round on each steak. Serve with boiled potatoes and puréed green beans (see Index).

VEAL TENDERLOIN WITH CARROT FLAN

1 veal tenderloin, about 1¼ pounds (600 g)
flour
½ teaspoon salt
¼ teaspoon pepper
½ teaspoon paprika
⅛ teaspoon ground ginger
½ cup (125 mL) heavy cream
3 tablespoons (40 g) butter
½ cup (125 mL) dry white wine
½ cup (125 mL) veal stock
1 tablespoon chopped fresh parsley
Carrot Flan (see Index)

To remove skin from veal, use a small, sharp, pointed knife. Cut into the meat just underneath the white skin, take hold of the skin and, holding knife flat, move it between the skin and the meat, being careful to cut off as little meat with the skin as possible. Dust meat with flour and shake off any excess. Combine seasonings. Whip cream just until thickened; reserve. Melt butter in a skillet over medium heat until it foams. Add veal and fry for 5 minutes, turning frequently. Pour white wine and veal stock slowly into the skillet at the edge, so it is already boiling when it reaches the meat. Sprinkle seasoning mixture over meat, cover, reduce heat to low, and cook 5 to 7 minutes, or until cooked to desired doneness. Strain the sauce, add parsley and cream, mix well, and season to taste. Slice the veal ½ inch (1½ cm) thick and serve with sauce, spaetzle (see Index), and carrot flan; replace 1 carrot in the flan with ¼ cup minced fresh parsley for heartier flavor. Or serve veal with steamed watercress: Trim stems from watercress and steam just until tender, then toss with melted butter.

CABBAGE-WRAPPED PORK FILET

1 pork tenderloin (filet), about 10 ounces (300 g)
salt
1 teaspoon crushed green peppercorns
3 tablespoons brandy
6 large Savoy cabbage leaves
4 ounces (125 g) ground beef
1 teaspoon paprika
½ teaspoon fresh thyme
1 egg yolk
½ cup (125 mL) heavy cream
2 tablespoons oil for frying
¾ cup (175 mL) chicken stock

Using a sharp, pointed knife, remove any membrane from pork and rub meat with ½ teaspoon each salt and green peppercorns. Place on aluminum foil, pour brandy over meat, wrap tightly, and marinate for 4 to 5 hours. Blanch cabbage leaves, rinse under cold water, and spread on paper towels to drain. Cut the ribs from the leaves and reserve. Blend ground beef, paprika, thyme, egg yolk, and 2 tablespoons cream. Add pork marinade and salt to taste. Spread mixture on pork, completely covering it. Wrap with cabbage leaves and tie with kitchen string. In a skillet just large enough to hold the cabbage "package," heat oil over medium heat. Quickly brown cabbage package on all sides. Slowly add stock and remaining cream. Reduce heat to low, cover, and cook for 15 minutes. To serve, discard string, slice the filet, arrange on plates, and nap with sauce. Accompany with au gratin potatoes (see below).

Au gratin potatoes

Peel 1 generous pound (500 g) baking potatoes and slice thinly. Brush a soufflé dish with butter. Layer potatoes and 1 cup (100 g) grated Emmenthal cheese in the dish. Blend 1 cup (240 mL) heavy cream with 1 teaspoon salt and ⅛ teaspoon freshly grated nutmeg and pour over potatoes (cream should reach to about ¾ inch [2 cm] below the rim). Bake in a preheated 400°F (200°C) oven for 40 minutes, or until golden.

Arrange delicate dishes like Veal Tenderloin with Carrot Flan and Cabbage-Wrapped Pork Filet on preheated plates and serve immediately so you can enjoy them fresh and hot from the fire.

SKILLET MEATS

Stir-fried meats are cooked quickly, and preparing them for cooking takes very little time as well. Fine cuts like loin, leg, and chops work well for stir-frying, as do less expensive cuts from beef, pork, or lamb. Any skin or tendons should be removed. For easiest slicing, we recommend putting meat in the freezer for 30 minutes before cutting it. In general, cut slices against the grain—but when a recipe calls for "strips" they should be cut *with* the grain. When cutting meat, use a sharp knife with a thin blade to retain as much juice in the meat as possible.

SHREDDED VEAL

10 ounces (300 g) boneless veal loin or round
1 medium onion
6 ounces (150 g) fresh mushrooms
1 tablespoon oil
salt and pepper
1½ tablespoons (20 g) butter
2½ tablespoons flour
½ cup (125 mL) white wine
⅔ cup (150 mL) crème fraîche
fresh lemon juice
2 tablespoons finely chopped fresh parsley

Remove any skin and tendons from meat and cut into ¼-inch (¾-cm)-thick strips. Dice onion. Clean and slice mushrooms, trimming bottoms of stems.

In a deep skillet heat oil until it smokes. Add meat and stir-fry for 2 minutes, or until lightly browned. Use a slotted spoon to transfer meat to a plate; season with salt and pepper and reserve. Add butter to skillet and heat until it foams. Stir-fry mushrooms for 2 minutes; transfer to plate with meat using a slotted spoon. Sauté diced onion until translucent. Sprinkle with flour, pour in white wine, and stir to make a roux. Reduce heat to low and simmer for 10 minutes. Stir in crème fraîche, increase heat, and bring to boil. Add meat and mushrooms with all their juices and heat through, being careful not to boil. Season to taste with salt, pepper, and lemon juice and serve garnished with chopped parsley.

STIR-FRIED PORK

10 ounces (300 g) boneless pork shoulder
1 tablespoon cornstarch
3 tablespoons soy sauce
2 large leeks
7 ounces (250 g) bean sprouts, fresh or canned
½ cup (125 mL) beef stock
½ teaspoon salt
1 tablespoon dry sherry
1 clove garlic
2 to 3 tablespoons grated fresh ginger
3 tablespoons oil

Cut meat into 1¼-inch (3-cm)-thick strips, then into paper-thin slices. In a bowl, mix cornstarch with 1 tablespoon soy sauce. Add pork and stir until all the pieces are coated. Let marinate for 15 minutes, stirring occasionally. Slice leeks lengthwise, wash and cut into ¼-inch (¾-cm) rings. Rinse bean sprouts under cold water and drain. Combine meat stock with ¼ teaspoon salt, 2 tablespoons soy sauce, and sherry; mix well. Peel and mince garlic and ginger.

Heat a large, deep skillet over a high heat, add 1 tablespoon oil and ¼ teaspoon salt, and stir. Quickly brown garlic. Add pork and stir-fry for 3 minutes, or until it begins to brown. Remove meat, add remaining oil and stir in ginger and vegetables. Stir-fry for 1 minute, or until vegetables are coated with oil. Add sherry mixture and cook for 1 minute, stirring constantly. Add meat and stir until all ingredients are heated through. Serve immediately with steamed rice.

LAMB CURRY

1 pound (450 g) boneless lamb neck or shoulder
1 tablespoon flour
1 apple
1 onion
2 tablespoons oil
4 teaspoons curry powder
1 cup (240 mL) beef stock
3 tablespoons fresh lemon juice
½ teaspoon salt
¼ teaspoon white pepper

Cut lamb into ¼-inch (¾-cm)-thick strips and dust with flour. Peel, quarter, core, and slice apple. Dice onion. Heat oil in a large skillet over high heat. Add lamb and stir-fry for 2 minutes, or until golden brown. Remove meat and reserve. Stir-fry apple and onion until soft and transparent. Remove from heat. Add curry powder and pour in meat stock. Season with lemon juice, salt, and pepper and cook sauce for 10 minutes, or until slightly thickened. Add lamb and heat but do not boil. Serve with rice, fried bananas, peanuts, or a mixture of hard-cooked eggs and chopped fresh chives.

Shredded veal, a famous Swiss specialty known in its homeland as *Kalbsgeschnetzeltes* tastes particularly good with pan-fried potatoes and a tossed green salad.

ROASTS

Large roasts from top-quality meat are the stars of many cuisines, particularly when they are cooked so they are still juicy inside. Always use a meat thermometer to guarantee a perfect roast. Using a frying pan for roasts weighing less than 2 pounds (1 kg)—it saves energy. Tough cuts of meat should not be oven-roasted; they are best when braised on top of the stove.

LEG OF LAMB WITH HERB CRUST

4 cloves garlic
1 onion
1/4 cup chopped fresh herbs (oregano, sage, basil, parsley)
1/4 cup (60 mL) oil
1 1/2 teaspoons salt
1/2 teaspoon pepper
1 teaspoon hot prepared mustard
1 4 1/2-pound (2-kg) leg of lamb, bone in
1 cup (240 mL) dry red wine
1 cup (240 mL) beef stock

Cut garlic cloves into slivers. Pierce meat all over with paring knife and insert garlic. Chop onion and combine with herbs, oil, salt, pepper, and mustard. Blend to make a paste and rub all over leg of lamb. Preheat oven to 500°F (250°C), place lamb in roasting pan on lower rack and brown for 10 minutes. Reduce heat to 350°F (175°C) and add wine. Continue roasting, basting with wine and stock every 15 minutes; there should always be enough liquid in the roasting pan to prevent juice and meat from burning or sticking. If you want the lamb to be juicy and pink in the center, roast it for 45 minutes; for well-done lamb, double this roasting time. Insert a meat thermometer into the thickest part of the leg, not touching the bone. At 140°F (60°C) the lamb will be pink; at 180°F (80°C) it will be well done. When lamb is cooked, turn off oven. Transfer lamb to a platter and let it rest in the still-warm oven for 15 minutes. Pour cooking juices into a saucepan, reduce, season to taste, and strain into sauceboat.

RACK OF LAMB WITH HERBS

For 6 servings
1 2 3/4-pound (1 1/4-kg) rack of lamb
5 cloves garlic, cut into slivers
3 tablespoons oil
2 tablespoons chopped fresh herbs (thyme, basil, rosemary, parsley)
1 teaspoon paprika
1 teaspoon salt
1/2 teaspoon pepper

With a sharp paring knife make evenly spaced incisions in the lamb fat and insert garlic. Combine remaining ingredients, mix to a paste, and rub all over lamb. Place lamb in roasting pan, pour in 1 cup (240 mL) water, and brown in 450°F (225°C) oven for 10 minutes. Reduce heat and roast lamb for an additional 30 minutes, or until still pink in the center. For well-done lamb, increase roasting time (see above recipe).

Let lamb rest for 10 minutes before slicing. Meanwhile, reduce cooking juices to desired sauce consistency.

Let roasts such as rack of lamb rest before slicing so they retain their juices. Serve with green beans, broccoli, or cauliflower that have been steamed until crisp-tender then tossed in butter.

HERBED ROAST BEEF

For 12 servings

1 3½-pound (1½-kg) beef roast, with fat
2 bunches fresh parsley, chopped
1 small bunch celery leaves, chopped
6 fresh basil leaves, chopped
1 teaspoon fresh marjoram
1 teaspoon fresh thyme
3 cloves garlic, chopped
1 teaspoon finely ground black pepper
¾ cup (175 mL) vegetable oil
1 cup (240 mL) water or dry red wine
2 teaspoons salt

Prepare meat as shown in the photograph. Cover with herbs, garlic, and pepper, then pour oil over to prevent herbs from burning. Place meat in a roasting pan and place on the bottom rack of a preheated 400°F (220°C) oven. Pour in 1 cup (240 mL) water or red wine and roast for 40 minutes; during the last 15 minutes, cover meat with oiled parchment paper to keep herbs from burning. Test for doneness and season to taste with salt. Wrap meat once with aluminum foil and again with a cotton towel, if desired, so the temperature will be even throughout the roast and it won't cool before serving.

Reduce drippings to desired sauce consistency, adding more meat stock if you are serving the roast as the main course of a full meal.

Cooking a large roast is worthwhile even if you only serve 4, because you can slice the next day and serve it cold with tartar or herb sauce and pan-fried potatoes.

1 Trim roast. Using a sharp paring knife, trim fat and tendons from one side of the roast. Use any scraps to make stock or sauces. Leave the fat on the other side of the roast.

2 Cover with herbs. Finely chop fresh herbs, blend with garlic and pepper, and sprinkle evenly over meat, pressing firmly to make them adhere.

3 Add oil. Pour oil over roast in roasting pan (or the convenient spatterproof dripping pan available in some new ovens) to soak all the herbs evenly.

4 Test for doneness. When you press the meat firmly with your thumb and it springs back, the temperature in the center is about 115°F (45°C). Use a meat thermometer for an exact reading.

5 Let meat rest, wrapped in aluminum foil. Wrap meat well in several layers of foil so the temperature will be even throughout and the juices will stay in the meat.

6 Slice. After roast has rested for 30 minutes, slice it with a very sharp knife.

WRAPPED ROASTS

Small roasts wrapped in dough are a juicy delight. They are easy and fun to prepare, and wrapping the meat in dough protects it. Once you are familiar with the technique, you can use filo sheets or any bread dough of your choice. Corned beef, cooked ham, even rack of lamb or veal can be wrapped in dough. Fresh meats must always be seared first, preferably the day before. After searing, wrap meat tightly and store it in the refrigerator overnight to enhance its flavor.

STUFFED BEEF TENDERLOIN

1¼ pounds (600 g) boneless beef tenderloin
2 tablespoons oil
1 teaspoon salt
¼ teaspoon pepper
½ cup (125 mL) dry red wine

Stuffing:
8 ounces (200 g) lean ground veal
1 egg
¼ cup (30 g) grated onion
3 tablespoons finely chopped fresh parsley
2 tablespoons heavy cream
1 tablespoon breadcrumbs
1 teaspoon green peppercorns
½ teaspoon each prepared mustard and salt

Dough:
1¾ cups (200 g) flour
½ teaspoon salt
6 tablespoons (100 g) butter, cut into small pieces
2 tablespoons water

For glaze:
1 egg yolk
2 tablespoons heavy cream

Rub beef with oil and set aside for 30 minutes. Heat skillet over high heat and sear meat for 10 minutes, turning often. Place meat on aluminum foil and sprinkle with salt and pepper.

Deglaze pan with red wine, scraping up any browned bits, and reduce to 2 to 3 tablespoons liquid. Brush beef with wine mixture, wrap tightly in foil, and refrigerate until cold.

Combine the stuffing ingredients, mix well, and season to taste. (If desired, grind your own veal using a meat grinder.)

To make the dough, sift the flour and salt into a bowl and cut in butter until mixture is the consistency of fine meal. Sprinkle water over and gather quickly into a ball. Wrap tightly and refrigerate for 30 minutes. Roll dough out to ⅛ inch (½ cm) thickness. Spoon ¼ of the stuffing in the center of dough, place tenderloin on top, and cover with remaining stuffing. Wrap dough around the meat, press to seal edges, and place on a baking sheet seam side down. Seal any openings with dough trimmings. Cut remaining dough trimmings into strips and use them to decorate the top. Brush with egg glaze, cover, and refrigerate until 1 hour before serving.

Preheat oven to 400°F (200°C) and place baking sheet on center rack. Bake for 50 minutes, or until golden brown. Let rest for 10 minutes before slicing. Serve with vegetables—for example, green beans, peas and carrots, asparagus, or cauliflower—tossed in butter. Or, for a perfect vegetable accompaniment, combine ¼ cup (30 g) breadcrumbs, 2 tablespoons olive oil, 1 minced garlic clove, 2 tablespoons minced fresh parsley, 1 teaspoon finely chopped fresh basil, ½ teaspoon salt, and ½ teaspoon pepper. Spoon this mixture over 8 small tomatoes and broil.

SMOKED PORK IN A SALT CRUST

1¼ pounds (600 g) boneless smoked pork
2 tablespoons chopped fresh parsley
1 tablespoon minced fresh mint
1 tablespoon chopped fresh thyme
1½ teaspoons chopped fresh rosemary
1 teaspoon minced fresh sage
1 teaspoon freshly ground black pepper
2 tablespoons oil
4½ pounds (2 kg) coarse salt
½ cup (125 mL) water
2 egg whites

With a sharp paring knife remove skin from pork. Combine herbs with pepper and oil and spread evenly on pork. Mix salt with water and egg whites and fill a roasting pan with mixture to a depth of ¾ inch (2 cm). Place pork in the center and cover with remaining salt mixture to form a crust; reserve some of the mixture to patch the crust if it breaks during baking. Preheat oven to 400°F (210°C), place pan on center rack, and bake for 45 minutes, spraying salt crust with water every 10 minutes to prevent cracking. Remove from oven and let rest for 5 minutes. Break salt crust and remove pork. Cut into ⅜-inch (1-cm) slices and serve with au gratin potatoes and a tomato salad.

TIP

Foil is an alternative to dough for covering lean meats to protect them from drying out. All of the flavors are concentrated and held in a moist environment. Heat the juices and serve them as is, or use them as the basis for a luscious sauce.

A salt crust encourages all ingredients to retain their flavors. The salt is not absorbed by the meat. We've provided a recipe for smoked pork, but fish or chicken are also delicious cooked in a salt crust. No matter what you put in it, always remember to reserve a small amount of the crust mixture to use for patching if the crust breaks during baking.

BRAISED MEATS

Goulash is a braised meat dish that is cooked slowly until it is so tender that it melts in the mouth. For this recipe we don't sear the meat; we'll prepare it Hungarian style, which is particularly moist and juicy. Be sure the pot is tightly covered. If necessary, replenish evaporated cooking liquid with stock or wine. Goulash can be prepared with lamb, beef, or pork. The meat should be marbled with fat and somewhat stringy, which will help thicken the sauce and make it good and hearty. Our first recipe comes from the dish's country of origin, Hungary. It is named for the University town of Szeged, on the river Tisza.

SZEGED-STYLE GOULASH

1¼ pounds (600 g) boneless pork shoulder
2 large onions
2 tablespoons lard
1 tablespoon Hungarian paprika
12 ounces (375 g) sauerkraut
1 teaspoon caraway seed
⅔ cup (150 mL) sour cream
2 tablespoons tomato paste
salt, pepper, and additional paprika

Cut pork into ¾-inch (2-cm) pieces. Chop onions. Melt lard in a skillet or Dutch oven over medium heat. Add onions and sauté until golden. Remove from heat and stir in paprika and pork. Cover and braise for 30 minutes. Add sauerkraut and caraway seed and braise for an additional 30 minutes. Stir in sour cream and tomato paste and season with salt, pepper, and paprika. Let stand, covered, for 10 minutes. Serve with noodles or boiled potatoes and, for a beverage, cold beer.

Around Hortobágy, where the herdsmen known as the *Csikós* live, Hungarian goulash is stewed in enormous cauldrons over open fires and poured into soup plates with huge ladles. It tastes wonderful, and it's named, quite appropriately, after its cooking vessel.

CAULDRON GOULASH

1¼ pounds (600 g) boneless beef chuck
2 small onions
2 cloves garlic
6 tablespoons (60 g) lard
2 tablespoons Hungarian paprika
⅛ teaspoon ground caraway seed
⅛ teaspoon crushed dried marjoram
2 cups (450 mL) beef stock
1 medium-large fresh tomato
2 large green bell peppers
1¼ pounds (600 g) baking potatoes
salt
1 egg
6½ tablespoons (60 g) flour

Cut beef into ¾-inch (2-cm) pieces. Dice onions and garlic. Melt lard in a Dutch oven or skillet over medium heat and sauté onions and garlic until golden. Remove from heat and add beef, paprika, caraway, and marjoram. Pour in hot stock, stir well, cover, and braise over low heat for 1 hour. Chop tomato and bell pepper; peel and dice potatoes. Add to goulash and braise for an additional 20 minutes. Season to taste with salt. (The goulash will be somewhat soupy.) Mix egg and flour to make a smooth dough. Pull off small pieces, add to goulash, and let stand for 10 minutes, season to taste and serve with fresh bread. For a real treat, serve Cauldron Goulash with a full-flavored Hungarian red wine such as Egri Bikáver.

LAMB GOULASH

1¼ pounds (600 g) boneless lamb shoulder
1 pound (450 g) shallots
2 cloves garlic
2 large carrots
1 small celery root
3 tablespoons (40 g) butter
1 teaspoon crushed dried rosemary
1 bay leaf
½ cup (125 mL) beef stock
½ cup (125 mL) dry red wine
2 tablespoons tomato paste
salt
black pepper
¼ cup chopped fresh Italian parsley

Cut meat into ¾-inch (2-cm) to 1¼-inch (3-cm) pieces. Mince shallots and garlic. Peel and dice carrots and celery root. Melt butter in a Dutch oven or skillet over medium heat until it foams. Sauté shallot and garlic until golden. Add carrots and celery root and sauté until golden. Add lamb, rosemary, and bay leaf and stir until lamb turns gray. Slowly pour in meat stock and red wine at the edge of the pot so the liquid is warm when it reaches the meat and vegetables.

Reduce heat, cover, and simmer until meat is cooked and tender, about 1 hour. Stir in tomato paste, season to taste with salt and pepper, and let stand briefly for flavors to meld. Remove bay leaf and sprinkle with chopped Italian parsley, which is more flavorful than ordinary curly-leafed parsley.

Lamb Goulash at its best: juicy lamb in a concentrated sauce that is delicately thickened with vegetables. Accompany with crisp sautéed green beans and fresh tomatoes tossed in butter.

BOILED MEATS

Boiled meat isn't really boiled, which would make it tough and dry, but rather cooked in water that is just under the boiling point so it emerges tender and juicy. The best meats for boiling are lean cuts with gelatinous connective tissues that soften slowly, tenderizing the meat and holding it together. Rump, rib, and brisket are good, flavorful cuts that are best when cooked slowly. It doesn't matter if you put the meat in cold or hot water first; experiments have shown that the meat turns out the same either way. It is important to regulate the heat so that the liquid reaches the simmer after 30 minutes cooking time, then simmers gently until the meat is done. Skim off foam to get a good, clear broth, and season with herbs and spices after skimming. Do not add vegetables until the meat is almost cooked, so they will still be colorful and crisp. The cooking time will depend on the kind of vegetables you use and their size. Thinly sliced leeks take only a few moments, whole carrots require up to 30 minutes. Blanch cabbage before adding it to avoid a bitter taste in the broth.

The meat is cooked when it is soft and tender. To test for doneness, use the tip of a sharp knife; it should pierce the meat with little or no resistance.

To prepare the day before, cook meat about 30 minutes less, cover, remove from heat, and let cool for 1 hour, then refrigerate in its cooking liquid. The meat will be particularly juicy and still slightly pink when prepared this way. To serve cold, cut meat into attractive thin slices. Before cooking, tie any uneven pieces of meat into compact bundles for easier slicing and serving. To serve hot, reheat meat in its cooking liquid, but don't let it boil. Let it rest for 10 minutes before slicing so it will retain its juices. Season to taste before serving. Use the cook-ing liquid to make bouillon or sauces, or for cooking potatoes. To serve it as a first-course broth, strain it and garnish it decoratively.

Serve meat with vegetables and potatoes, accompanied by horse-radish, onion sauce, or a green sauce (see Index). Let the possible combinations stimulate your own creativity.

BOLLITO MISTO

For 12 servings
1¾ pounds (800 g) beef neck
1¾ pounds (800 g) veal shank
1 generous pound (500 g) pickled beef or veal tongue
1 roasting chicken
4 marrow bones
2 onions
1 carrot
¼ celery root
2 leeks
2 tablespoons peppercorns
salt
chopped fresh parsley (optional)

In a large pot, heat 3 quarts (3 L) water over medium heat. Add the meats in the order listed so they will all be done at the same time. The beef will take 3 hours to cook, the veal 2 hours, the chicken and the marrow bones 40 minutes. Add vegetables and season-ings when you add the marrow bones. When the meats are cooked, transfer them to a large cutting board that has a groove to collect the juices. Skin from the tongue and arrange meats on a platter. Add the marrow bones and sprinkle with salt and parsley if de-sired. Strain the broth, season to taste, and serve by itself or with noodles as a first course, keeping the meat warm in a low oven. Do not cut the meat until just before serving. Serve with Italian Green Sauce (see right), boiled pota-toes, and pickle relish. According to the original Italian version of Bollito Misto, zampone (stuffed pigs' feet) and cotechino or luganighe (Italian saus-ages) should be cooked separately, then served with the other meats; add them if available. Serve the vegetables with the meat, or chop them and add to soup made with the leftover broth.

GREEN SAUCE

2 tablespoons each chopped fresh borage, watercress, parsley, salad burnet, chives, sorrel, and young spinach
1 teaspoon each chopped fresh dill, tarragon, lovage or celery leaves, and lemon balm
⅔ cup (150 mL) plain yogurt
6 tablespoons (100 g) mayonnaise
1 hard-cooked egg
2 tablespoons fresh lemon juice
1 shallot
1 teaspoon medium-hot prepared mustard
½ teaspoon sugar
½ teaspoon salt
¼ teaspoon black pepper

Turn on blender and add herbs gradually. Add all the remaining ingre-dients and purée until well blended and smooth. Taste for seasoning. (If you don't have a blender, finely chop the herbs on a cutting board, then stir in the remaining ingredients. When made by hand the sauce is not as smooth or as brilliant green as when made in a blender, but it will taste the same.) Refrigerate sauce, covered tightly, for several hours before serv-ing.

FRIESIAN CORNED BEEF

1¾ pounds (800 g) corned beef brisket, rinsed
1 bay leaf

4 whole cloves

2 onions

1 bunch parsley stems

¼ celery root

4 carrots

Place the corned beef in a large pot, cover with water, and bring to a boil. Add seasonings and simmer for 2 hours. Rinse and peel vegetables and add during the last 30 minutes of cooking. To serve, slice meat and serve with boiled potatoes and creamed horscradish, or with fresh applesauce, cranberry sauce, sweet and sour or mustard pickles, and beets. Save the cooking liquid to add to a hearty stew.

ITALIAN GREEN SAUCE
(Salsa Verde)

1 onion

1 clove garlic

2 cornichons (small sour pickles)

10 capers

¼ cup chopped fresh parsley

1 tablespoon finely chopped fresh basil

½ teaspoon minced fresh thyme

½ cup (125 mL) olive oil

¼ cup (60 mL) white wine vinegar

salt and black pepper

Dice onion and garlic. Chop pickles. Add capers and herbs and mince or purée in blender. Add oil and vinegar, mix well, and season to taste with salt and pepper.

POT AU FEU

For 8 servings

1¾ pounds (800 g) beef brisket

1 bay leaf

1 teaspoon salt

10 white peppercorns

1 onion

10 sprigs parsley

1 3½-pound (1½-kg) chicken

2 large turnips

6 medium carrots

1 large celery root

4 medium leeks

Place meat in a large pot, add 2 quarts (2 L) water, and bring to boil over medium heat. Skim off foam, add seasonings, onion, and parsley, reduce heat to low, and simmer for 3 hours. Meanwhile, cut chicken into 6 or 8 pieces and rinse well. Peel turnips, carrots, and celery root and cut into ¾-inch (2-cm) slices. Slice leeks lengthwise, then cut into 1¼-inch

(3-cm)-long pieces. After 2½ hours, add chicken to pot. Add root vegetables 10 minutes later; add leeks during the last 10 minutes of cooking. Serve beef with chicken and vegetables. Heat broth, season to taste, and pour over beef and chicken. If desired, serve Pot au Feu with peeled potatoes that have been cooked in the broth, or serve with a French baguette. You may serve the broth separately as a first course, garnished with chopped fresh chives.

French *pot au feu* is a dish which, like many other regional specialties, can be prepared in many ways. It has a pleasingly simple flavor when prepared with one kind of meat, but it is much more flavorful when many varieties are combined: Try chicken, veal, and lamb shanks. Serve the different meats all together as a main course or in individual courses: You might have chicken and marrow bones in broth, the lamb with tomato sauce and rice, the veal with mustard sauce and beans, and the beef with horseradish sauce and vegetables.

VARIETY MEATS

Beef tongue adds variety to many stews, including the Italian *bollito misto* and the French *pot au feu*. It is delicious by itself as well, served with vegetables, rice, or boiled or mashed potatoes. We prefer tongue that has been pickled or smoked.

Place tongue in cold water for several hours to remove excess salt and impurities. Drain, cover tongue with cold water, bring to a boil, and drain again. Rinse pot and tongue, cover with fresh water, and simmer over low heat for 2 hours. Let tongue cool in its cooking liquid; then, using a sharp paring knife, loosen the skin on the underside and pull it off. Cut away all fat and gristle and remove small bones from the base.

Strain the broth, return the tongue to it and season to taste. Add vegetables, onion or garlic, bouquet garni, and seasonings such as bay leaf, peppercorns, and whole cloves. Simmer the tongue until the tip feels soft, about 1 hour. By the time the tongue is cooked, all of the flavors will have blended and the vegetables will be fully cooked.

Preparing tongue takes time, but it's not much work. Use a timer to remind you when specific steps are completed. Everything may be prepared a day ahead; leave the meat in its cooking liquid to absorb all the flavors and stay moist and juicy. To serve, slice it diagonally, beginning at the tip, to get even slices. Reheat in broth or sauce, being careful not to let it boil.

Serve pickled beef tongue with horseradish or a light sweet and sour sauce made with Madeira, red wine, or cider. It is also good served with glazed shallots, plumped raisins or currants, blanched, sliced almonds or pine nuts. Serve fresh tongue with light, mild sauces like a velouté sauce (see Index) seasoned with fresh herbs like chives, basil or tarragon.

Onion Sauce

Boil 1 large onion (about 8 ounces/200 g) in the tongue cooking liquid for 1 hour. Peel and force through a strainer or purée in blender. Melt 3 tablespoons (45 g) butter in a saucepan until it foams and turns golden. Add onion, ½ cup (125 mL) heavy cream, and 1 teaspoon hot prepared mustard or 1 small grated apple. Season to taste with salt and pepper.

Devil's Sauce

Combine 2 finely chopped shallots with 1 cup (240 mL) dry white wine and ¼ cup (60 mL) wine vinegar and reduce by ⅓ over medium heat. Add 1 cup (240 mL) tongue cooking liquid, making sure it isn't too salty, and 1 tablespoon breadcrumbs; stir and simmer for 10 minutes. Strain sauce and season with ground red pepper and finely chopped fresh parsley.

Red Wine Sauce

Reduce 1 cup (240 mL) cooking liquid from tongue and 1 cup (240 mL) red wine by half over medium heat. Add 1 cup (240 mL) beef stock and cook until slightly thickened. Season to taste with salt, pepper, and fresh lemon juice. Remove from heat and whisk in small pieces of cold butter until sauce emulsifies and becomes smooth and creamy.

Green Sauce

Rinse and dry 4 cups (300 g) fresh sorrel, steam for 15 minutes, toss with 3 tablespoons (45 g) butter, and purée in a blender. Reheat with ½ cup (125 mL) heavy cream and season to taste with salt, pepper, and a pinch of sugar. Serve immediately. Always serve sauce in an acid-resistant porcelain or enamel dish.

Celery Root Sauce

Cook ½ large peeled celery root with tongue until soft; purée in blender. Prepare 1 cup (240 mL) velouté sauce (see Index) using the cooking liquid from the tongue; add to celery root purée. Season to taste with salt, pepper, and a pinch of freshly grated nutmeg.

Pickled beef tongue is delicious served with a hearty red wine sauce, boiled potatoes, and vegetables. Zucchini, shallots, celery stalks, and tomatoes have been sautéed separately, then mixed together before serving.

Veal sweetbreads are glands that help calves to digest milk. The younger the animal, the larger the gland, which shrinks as the animal gets older. Sweetbreads are one of the most sought-after ingredients in sophisticated cuisine. They are always prepared the same way. Soak sweetbreads in cold water for several hours, changing the water occasionally so all impurities are rinsed away. Rinse, cover again with cold water, and bring to a boil. Pour off the hot water and place sweetbreads in cold water to cool. Separate the round part of the sweetbreads from the long part, peel both, and remove tubules. To firm sweetbreads, press them between a board and a plate weighted with 2-pound (1-kg) weight for at least 1 hour before slicing (this will make them easier to slice). Or separate the sweetbreads into their natural sections and add to a delicate, light ragout made with veal, chicken, or seafood.

To fry sweetbreads, melt butter in a skillet over high heat until it foams, add sliced sweetbreads, and brown for 1 minute on each side. Season with salt, pepper, and fresh lemon juice. Serve with mashed potatoes and young peas, spinach, asparagus, or puréed beans. If desired, dip sweetbreads into a seasoned egg mixture before frying, then toss them in finely chopped fresh parsley. Serve with a green salad tossed with herb dressing.

Even without the truffles, Veal Sweetbreads à la Vigneron are a culinary adventure that will delight the most discriminating gourmet.

VEAL SWEETBREADS À LA VIGNERON

1½ pounds (675 g) sweetbreads
3 medium leeks
2 large carrots
1 onion
1 clove garlic
1 stalk celery
4 tablespoons (60 g) butter
½ cup (125 mL) veal stock
½ cup (125 mL) dry white wine
½ cup (125 mL) heavy cream
1 teaspoon salt
¼ teaspoon white pepper
⅛ teaspoon freshly grated nutmeg
1 tablespoon fresh lemon juice
4 truffle slices

Prepare sweetbreads as shown. Trim leeks, cut into strips, rinse, and pat dry. Peel carrots and cut into matchsticks. Finely chop onion, garlic, and celery. Melt butter in a Dutch oven or deep skillet over medium heat until it foams. Add carrots and sauté until they start to soften. Add leeks and sauté for 30 seconds. Drain vegetables in strainer, reserving butter. Pour butter back into skillet. Add onion, garlic, and celery and cook until soft. Pour in veal stock, wine, and cream, bring to boil, and season with salt and pepper. Reduce heat to low, add sweetbreads, cover, and cook for 20 minutes, turning occasionally. Strain sauce, reserving vegetables and sweetbreads, and pour into another pot. Quickly boil down sauce until creamy, season with nutmeg and lemon juice, add vegetables, and heat through. Slice sweetbreads. Arrange on a platter, nap with sauce, and garnish with truffle slices. Serve with white or green fettuccine.

Lamb kidneys can be a delicacy if prepared properly—that is, so that they are juicy, not dry. Follow the directions on this page to quickly sauté and stew kidneys, then garnish with a sweet and sour mustard sauce for a very tasty dish. Always buy fresh, clean kidneys from your butcher and prepare them immediately, so they will have a pleasantly piquant smell and taste. Contrary to traditional methods, don't soak kidneys in water, because it weakens their flavor without removing any unpleasant odor.

LAMB KIDNEYS À LA GOURMAND

4 lamb kidneys
5 shallots
2 cloves garlic
1 each red and green bell pepper
2 tomatoes
2 tablespoons oil
6 tablespoons (75 mL) each red Bordeaux and beef or veal stock
3 tablespoons each sherry and heavy cream
1 teaspoon salt
1/2 teaspoon pepper
1 tablespoon paprika

Prepare kidneys following instructions and photographs. Dice shallots and garlic. Quarter, seed, and dice bell peppers. Peel, quarter, seed, and dice tomatoes. Cook kidneys as shown in the photographs and serve immediately, with mashed potatoes and a green salad tossed with vinaigrette.

1 **Cut kidneys open.** Cut kidneys in half horizontally; remove any tendons and blood vessels.

4 **Sauté kidneys.** First, dice shallots and garlic and sauté over medium heat until transparent. Add kidneys and sauté for 3 minutes.

2 **Remove the white portions** with a pointed knife or scissors. Hold blood vessels and clip right at the base. Rinse kidneys and pat dry.

5 **Add bell peppers** and tomatoes and stir to mix. Add red wine and sherry, pouring them in at the edge of the pan so the contents remain hot, and cook for 3 minutes.

3 **Chop kidneys.** Place kidneys on a wooden board cut side down and, using a sharp knife, cut into 1/4-inch (3/4-cm) slices. Dust with flour if desired.

6 **Mix sherry and cream,** spoon into the pan, and stir to mix. Bring to a boil, remove from heat, and season to taste with salt, pepper and paprika.

Sauté veal kidneys quickly; don't let them cook in their own juices or they will become tough and dry. To sauté kidneys, heat skillet until it is very hot, then add oil or butter. Add kidneys, being careful not to crowd the pan. Quickly sauté until lightly browned and remove from pan. Deglaze the pan with wine, meat stock, cream, and herbs for a flavorful sauce. Reheat kidneys in the sauce, being careful not to let it boil. Whole fried or broiled kidneys are cooked when the juices run clear.

VEAL KIDNEYS WRAPPED IN BACON

2 veal kidneys, about 1 pound (450 g) each
salt and pepper
4 slices bacon
2 onions
10 ounces (300 g) mushrooms
1 tablespoon oil
2 tablespoons (30 g) butter
½ cup (125 mL) beef stock
½ cup (125 mL) crème fraîche
¼ cup (60 mL) dry sherry

Cut kidneys in half horizontally. With a pointed knife or scissors, trim the white parts at the core. Rinse kidneys under cold water and pat dry with paper towels. Sprinkle the cut surfaces with ¼ teaspoon each salt and pepper. Wrap kidneys in bacon strips, tie with kitchen string, and tie kidney halves together.

Chop onions. Clean and slice mushrooms. Heat oil in a large pot or Dutch oven over medium-high heat, add kidneys, and fry for 10 minutes, turning occasionally. Transfer kidneys to a warm platter and cover. Melt butter in same pot, add mushrooms, sauté for 2 minutes. Add onions and sauté for 1 minute. Pour in stock, crème fraîche, and sherry, quickly bring to a boil, and season to taste with salt and pepper. Add kidneys with their juices and reheat for 2 minutes. Arrange on warm plates and serve with rice and a green salad tossed with vinaigrette.

Always use the freshest possible kidneys and liver, and serve on preheated plates. Left: Veal Kidneys Wrapped in Lettuce. Right: Calf's Liver with Ham and Sage.

VEAL KIDNEYS WRAPPED IN LETTUCE

2 veal kidneys, about 1 pound (450 g) each
salt and white pepper
3 tablespoons (40 g) butter
1 large head leaf lettuce
1 quart (1 L) full-flavored beef stock
1 tablespoon brandy
1 cup (240 mL) heavy cream
1 tablespoon medium-hot prepared mustard
juice of 1/2 lemon

Cut kidneys horizontally just to the core and remove all white portions with scissors or a pointed knife. Rinse kidneys under cold water, pat thoroughly dry, and sprinkle 1/4 teaspoon salt and 1/4 teaspoon pepper over cut surfaces. Brown butter in a skillet over medium-high heat, add kidneys, and fry for 5 minutes, turning several times. Remove from heat and reserve, saving any browned bits or liquid in the pan. Rinse and separate lettuce leaves. Arrange 8 leaves each on 2 wet cotton towels. Place kidneys on top, wrap in leaves, then wrap tightly in the 2 towels and tie closed. Heat stock, add the 2 "parcels," and simmer for 10 minutes.

For the sauce, add brandy to skillet in which kidneys were fried and heat briefly. Add cream, mustard, and lemon juice and boil until sauce is slightly thickened. Season to taste with salt and pepper. Unwrap kidneys from towels and slice. Serve immediately with sauce, butter-sautéed mushrooms, and rice.

Calf's liver is particularly tender and tasty. Serve it quickly sautéed in butter over high heat so it is still pink on the inside and the juices run red when pierced.

Pork liver is better for pâtés and liver dumplings. Beef liver is less tender and contains many nerves and blood vessels which must be removed, so cut it into bite-size pieces rather than frying it whole. Always add salt to liver *after* it has been fried, because salt draws out moisture and the liver will be dry if salt is added before cooking. If desired, dust the liver with flour before cooking to seal in the juices.

CALF'S LIVER WITH HAM AND SAGE

4 slices calf's liver, about 6 ounces (150 g) each
4 thin slices cured ham
4 sage leaves
3 tablespoons (40 g) butter
1/2 teaspoon salt
1/4 teaspoon pepper

Remove any membranes from liver with a sharp paring knife. Arrange ham and sage leaves on liver and attach with wooden toothpicks. Melt butter in a skillet over medium heat until golden brown. Place liver in pan ham side up and fry for 3 minutes. Turn and fry for an additional 2 minutes. Turn again, season with salt and pepper, and transfer to warm plates. Serve with buttered fettuccini garnished with chopped fresh parsley and a cucumber salad with creamy sweet and sour dressing.

LIVER RAGOUT WITH HERBS

1 1/2 pounds (675 g) beef liver
1 tablespoon finely chopped fresh parsley
1 teaspoon finely crushed dried thyme
1 onion
1 slice white bread, crusts removed
3 tablespoons (40 g) butter
1/2 teaspoon salt
1/4 teaspoon pepper
1 cup (240 mL) beef stock
1/2 cup (125 mL) dry white wine

Cut liver into 1/4-inch (3/4-cm) strips and remove any membranes and nerves with a sharp paring knife. Sprinkle strips with parsley and thyme. Dice onion and bread. Melt butter in a skillet over medium heat until golden brown. Sauté liver for 3 minutes. Transfer liver to a warm plate, season with salt and pepper, and keep warm in a low oven. Add onion and bread to skillet and sauté until golden. Pour in stock and wine and cook until sauce thickens slightly. Add liver, simmer for 2 minutes, season to taste, and serve with mashed or boiled potatoes and a green salad tossed with vinaigrette.

This inviting dish is juicy roulades wrapped in Chinese cabbage and served with a clear tomato sauce. Potatoes boiled in their jackets and tossed with caraway seed go well with this dish.

ROULADES WRAPPED IN CABBAGE LEAVES

1 cup (240 mL) milk
¼ cup (40 g) raw rice
5½ ounces (150 g) each beef, lamb, and pork
1 slice unsmoked bacon or blanched smoked bacon
2 onions
salt and pepper
1 clove garlic
3 tablespoons chopped fresh parsley
1 egg
⅛ teaspoon each dried oregano and basil
13 large Chinese cabbage leaves
butter
1 cup (240 mL) full-flavored beef stock or heavy cream seasoned with salt and pepper
1¾ pounds (800 g) fresh tomatoes, peeled

Bring milk to boil, reduce heat to low, add rice, cover, and cook for 30 minutes. Grind meat, bacon, and onion as shown in photographs; mix with 1 teaspoon salt and ¼ teaspoon pepper. Finely chop garlic and parsley and add to meat mixture with egg and dried herbs. (Do not grind garlic in meat grinder because its taste is hard to get rid of.) Form roulades as shown in photographs, layer in a baking dish, and bake, according to directions. Dot with butter; turn and dot with additional butter if you want roulades to brown on both sides. When the roulades are cooked, carefully pour off liquid into saucepan and cook on top of the stove until reduced to desired sauce consistency. Seed and dice tomatoes, add to sauce, and heat briefly. Season to taste with salt, pepper, and finely chopped fresh parsley or basil. Regular green or Savoy cabbage can be substituted for Chinese cabbage; blanch the leaves a bit longer and cut out the ribs. Roulades rolled in cabbage leaves can be frozen.

If you create your own stuffing with ground meat, try tender lamb or chicken and add organ meats and bacon for variety. For an elegant use of leftover meats, sausages, and vegetables add them to your stuffing mixtures.

GROUND MEATS

Ground beef round is very lean. You may mix it with ground pork for additional flavor and moistness. If you have a meat grinder, you can control the mixture and add other ingredients while grinding the meats. Grinding your own meat is economical and it guarantees freshness—which is important, because ground meat spoils quickly.

Add whole or mashed potatoes, or grains that have been soaked in water to soften them, grinding them right along with the meat. These are tasty alternatives to rice and they help keep meat stuffing mixtures light. They also provide pleasing variation in standard recipes for meatballs and meat loaves.

1 **Grind meats,** bacon, and onion in meat grinder.

2 **Combine ground meat mixture,** cooked rice, garlic, parsley, egg, and dried herbs.

3 **Mix the stuffing** with dough hook or by hand.

4 **To prepare Chinese cabbage,** blanch cabbage leaves and rinse in cold water until cool. Trim the thick part of the ribs as shown.

5 **Place meat stuffing on leaves.** Using a tablespoon, form 12 balls of equal size and place them near the stem ends of the cabbage leaves.

6 **Roll up leaves.** Shape roulades beginning at the stem ends and rolling up ⅔ the length of the leaf, leaving the sides open as shown.

7 **Seal the roulades.** Fold the sides towards the center and finish rolling. This will seal the roulades and hold them together without the need for string.

8 **Layer roulades in baking dish.** Generously butter a baking dish large enough to hold the roulades side by side without overlapping.

9 **Pour in meat broth** until roulades are half covered. Preheat oven to 350°F (175°C) and bake on center rack for 40 minutes, or until meat is fully cooked.

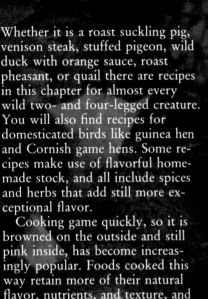

Whether it is a roast suckling pig, venison steak, stuffed pigeon, wild duck with orange sauce, roast pheasant, or quail there are recipes in this chapter for almost every wild two- and four-legged creature. You will also find recipes for domesticated birds like guinea hen and Cornish game hens. Some recipes make use of flavorful homemade stock, and all include spices and herbs that add still more exceptional flavor.

Cooking game quickly, so it is browned on the outside and still pink inside, has become increasingly popular. Foods cooked this way retain more of their natural flavor, nutrients, and texture, and the meat literally melts in your mouth. Larding lean game has become a technique of the past. Now we use flavored oils and bacon, wrapping the meat to prevent it from drying out. Cooking time for poultry has decreased as well, making it tastier and much more juicy. The great French chef Fernand Point once said, "I try to turn every meal into a miracle." Let's try to follow his example!

GAME AND POULTRY

LARGE GAME

The loin from young game is a good cut for roasts. Do not use a larding needle on the meat, because this causes it to lose precious juices. Marinate deer, elk, and boar meat with oil, or cover with bacon strips so it won't dry out during cooking. Always sear the meat over high heat first, then reduce the temperature to 300°F (150°C).

Depending on your taste you may cook meat for a short time, so it is pink and juicy inside, or cook it longer until the meat is tender and comes easily off the bones. This takes about 30 minutes per pound and the meat should be basted.

Rare roasts require about 10 minutes per pound cooking time. When they are cooked, season with salt, wrap in aluminum foil, and let them rest in the oven with the heat turned off so that the meat reaches an even temperature throughout and retains its juices.

BRAISED LEG OF BOAR

1³/₄ pounds (800 g) leg of boar, boned
3 slices bacon
salt and pepper
¹/₂ teaspoon curry powder
¹/₂ cup (125 mL) dry Riesling
¹/₂ cup (175 mL) game stock
1 small apple
¹/₂ medium celery root
¹/₄ cup (60 mL) crème fraîche

Roll the boar meat to form an evenly shaped roast and tie securely with kitchen string. Finely dice bacon and fry until crisp in a roasting pan over high heat. Add the roast and sear on all sides. Season with salt, pepper, and curry powder. Pour in wine and stock at the edge of the pan. Cover pan, reduce heat to low, and braise meat for 1 hour, turning occasionally. Remove from heat and let rest in a warm place. Meanwhile, peel and dice apple and celery root. Add to sauce and boil vigorously for 10 minutes. Whisk in crème fraîche and season to taste. Serve with sautéed mushrooms (preferably a wild type, such as chanterelles), cranberry sauce, and Home-Fried Potatoes.

Game—as a roast, steak, or goulash— tastes great and is lean and easy to digest. Here we show a leg of wild boar garnished with stuffed oranges.

ACCOMPANIMENTS

For Chestnut purée, slit each chestnut with a sharp knife. Place in a preheated 425°F (225°C) oven and roast until the shells crack open, about 15 to 20 minutes. Or you may deep-fry the chestnuts in 350°F (170°C) oil. Peel both inner and outer skins from chestnuts, using a towel to handle them if necessary. Bring salted water to a boil with a little celery root, add chestnuts, reduce heat to low, and cook for 45 minutes. Purée in a strainer or blender, adding some cooking liquid if necessary. Whip with cream or butter.

To prepare glazed chestnuts, toss peeled chestnuts over low heat in 2 tablespoons (30 g) each butter and sugar per pound (450 g) until they are hot and shiny.

Remove core and thick ribs from red cabbage and slice leaves thinly. For each pound of cabbage use 1 medium onion, sliced, and the 1¹/₂ tablespoons goose fat. Sauté cabbage and onion rings in lard until translucent. Pour in 1 tablespoon vinegar and ¹/₄ cup (60 mL) each red wine and meat stock. Season with 1 teaspoon salt, ¹/₄ teaspoon pepper, ¹/₈ teaspoon ground cloves, and 1 bay leaf. Cover and cook for 1 hour over medium heat. Discard bay leaf. Grate in 1 apple and add red currant jelly to taste.

Sauté fresh chanterelles, garlic, and parsley in browned butter for 2 minutes; season to taste.

VINTNER'S ELK LOIN

1 2½-pound (1¼-kg) rack of elk
8 juniper berries
½ bay leaf
10 peppercorns
½ teaspoon dried whole thyme
2 whole cloves
2 tablespoons olive oil
For the stock:
1 small onion
1 medium carrot
¼ medium celery root
1 small tomato
2 tablespoons oil
1 cup (100g) chopped mushrooms
2 cups (450 mL) dry red wine
2 tablespoons sherry vinegar
For the sauce:
2 tablespoons currant jelly
4 tablespoons (60 g) chilled butter
¾ cup (100 g) chopped walnuts
1 cup (100 g) peeled grapes

Carefully remove any skin from meat, then cut meat from bones, reserving bones for stock. Finely crush spices with a mortar and pestle, combine half of them with olive oil, and rub all over meat. Wrap meat in aluminum foil and refrigerate for up to 2 days. Remove from refrigerator 1 hour before roasting. Open the foil. Prepare a game stock according to the recipe on page 15, using the elk bones (cut in pieces), the remaining spices, the stock ingredients listed above, and the remaining ingredients from the basic stock recipe. Reduce stock to ½ cup, remove from heat, and reserve. To serve, reheat stock with jelly and gradually whisk in cold butter, salt, and pepper. Add walnuts and grapes to sauce and heat through.

Place the meat in a very hot heavy skillet and sear over high heat for 2 minutes. Turn, reduce heat to low, and continue cooking for 6 to 8 minutes, covered, turning once. Let rest for a few minutes, then slice diagonally, arrange on plates, and nap with sauce. Serve with potato balls (see Index).

LEG OF VENISON HUNTER STYLE

2¼ pounds (1 kg) leg of venison
½ teaspoon each dried rosemary, marjoram, thyme, and pepper
4 juniper berries, 1 bay leaf
2 tablespoons oil, salt
4 slices bacon
½ cup (50 g) diced onion
1 cup (240 mL) dry red wine
For the sauce:
½ cup (125 mL) game stock
½ cup (125 mL) heavy cream
2 tablespoons jellied cranberry sauce

Remove any membranes from meat, using a sharp paring knife. Crush herbs, pepper, juniper berries, and bay leaf in a mortar and pestle until very fine, mix with oil, and rub all over meat. Place bacon strips on top and secure with kitchen string. Heat roasting pan in a 475°F (250°C) oven, place meat in pan, and sear for 10 minutes adding diced onion after 5 minutes. Pour in red wine, sprinkle meat with salt and reduce oven to 300°F (150°C). Roast for 25 minutes for medium-rare or up to 1 hour for well done, basting every 10 minutes to keep juicy. Meanwhile, reduce game stock and cream by half. Whisk in cooking juices from roast, scraping pan to loosen any browned bits, and heat through. Add cranberry sauce, strain finished sauce, and season to taste.

Prepare potato "pears" according to the recipe for Potato Balls (see Index). Shape mixture into 1¼-inch (3-cm) pear shapes and insert 1 whole clove into each "pear" to simulate blossom end.

Core apples with an apple corer and bake for 30 minutes in the roasting pan with meat. Prepare ¾ cup (175 g) puréed chestnuts (see Index) and combine with ½ cup (125 mL) heavy cream, whipped to soft peaks, and 2 tablespoons orange liqueur. Sweeten with sugar to taste. Stuff apples with chestnut mixture and use as garnish.

TURKEY AND DUCK

Turkey and duck are domestic birds, but they can be prepared much in the same manner as game. Roast or stew whole birds, or prepare a dish with just part, such as the breast.

TURKEY BREAST IN PORTUGUESE SAUCE

1 1½-pound (675-g) turkey breast
2 tablespoons (30 g) butter, softened
½ teaspoon each hot prepared mustard and salt
¼ teaspoon each dried sage, basil, and white pepper
For the sauce:
1 tablespoon oil
½ small onion, diced
½ cup (125 mL) dry white wine
1 clove garlic
1½ pounds (675 g) fresh tomatoes
1 tablespoon chopped fresh parsley
salt and pepper

Remove skin from turkey breast if desired. Combine butter with mustard, salt, herbs and pepper, mix well, and rub all over turkey breast. Cover and set aside for 1 hour. Just before serving, place breast in a very hot skillet, reduce heat to low, and fry breast for 12 minutes, or until it feels as springy as a medium-rare steak. Remove from heat, cover, and let rest 10 minutes before slicing.

Meanwhile, heat oil in a saucepan and sauté onion until transparent. Add wine and garlic and cook until almost all the liquid has evaporated. Peel, seed, and chop tomatoes, add to sauce, and cook for 2 minutes, then whisk in any juices from turkey breast. Add parsley and season to taste with salt and pepper. Cut meat into thin slices and serve with the sauce, accompanied by beans tossed in butter and potato balls (see Index).

ROAST DUCK IN CREAM SAUCE

1 young duck, about 3½ pounds (1½ kg)
½ cup (125 mL) beef stock
½ cup (125 mL) dry red wine
salt and pepper
½ cup (125 mL) heavy cream
1 teaspoon cornstarch

Have the duck cleaned and ready to cook. Rinse it (do not dry) and place breast down in a roasting pan that is just large enough to hold it. Preheat oven to 400°F (200°C) and roast duck for 1 hour, turning it over after 10 minutes to brown breast. Heat stock with wine in a saucepan. Season to taste with salt and pepper and pour over duck after it has browned. Reduce heat to 300°F (150°C), cover duck, and roast until done, basting frequently with stock so duck remains

Bring small pieces of fowl, like duck and turkey breast, to the table on preheated serving plates so they can be eaten as fresh and hot as possible.

moist. Remove duck from oven and keep covered so it stays hot. Skim fat from cooking juices. Mix cream and cornstarch in a saucepan, add hot cooking juices, and bring to boil. Season to taste and pour into a sauceboat. If you prefer pink breast meat, carve the duck right after it has browned. Return legs to oven and roast an additional 20 minutes. Remove from oven, return breast and wings to roasting pan, pour hot stock over them, and reheat for 5 minutes. Save all extra bones to make stock.

Poach peaches in white wine (see Index). Serve hot, filled with currant jelly or cranberry sauce.

Prepare almond-coated Potato Balls (see Index), shaping the mixture into ovals about the thickness of your thumb.

Pigeons with a moist stuffing are a delicacy. If you can't find pigeon, substitute game hens.

SMALL GAME

The breast meat from wild and domesticated birds is as lean as steak and is prepared in much the same way. Pigeons, quail, and other small game birds are very tender and just enough for 1 serving, as shown in the following recipe for stuffed pigeon.

STUFFED PIGEONS

4 pigeons, ready for frying
1 generous pound (500 g) Brussels sprouts
2 shallots, sliced
1 clove garlic, minced
3½ tablespoons (50 g) butter
1 egg
¼ cup (60 mL) heavy cream
salt, pepper, and freshly grated nutmeg
½ cup (125 mL) veal stock
1 teaspoon chopped fresh parsley

Rinse pigeons and pat dry, making sure the cavities are completely dry as well. Blanch Brussels sprouts in 2 quarts (2 L) vigorously boiling water for 7 minutes, drain, and rinse with cold water until cool. Drain, and pat dry, then chop finely or grind in processor or meat grinder. Sauté shallots and garlic in 1½ tablespoons (20 g) butter until transparent, add chopped Brussels sprouts, and cook for 2 minutes, stirring constantly. Remove from heat and let cool. Add egg and cream, mix well, and season to taste with salt, pepper, and nutmeg. Salt and pepper pigeons inside and out, stuff with vegetable mixture, and close the openings with skewers. Melt remaining 2 tablespoons (30 g) butter in large skillet over medium heat until it foams. Place pigeons in skillet and brown on all sides for 5 minutes, then transfer to ovenproof dish. Mix juices from pigeons with veal stock, reduce to thicken slightly, and spoon over pigeons. Preheat oven to 300°F (150°C), place pigeons on center rack, and roast for 20 minutes. Remove from oven and cut pigeons in half lengthwise with a heavy knife. Place paper cuffs around ends of drumsticks to make them easier to handle. Whisk roasting juices until smooth, add parsley, and season to taste. Pour juices over pigeons and serve with potato cakes (see Index).

Wildfowl has become much more rare and expensive than it used to be. Some wildfowl are legally protected against hunting, but wild duck, pheasant, and domesticated quail are plentiful and we can savor them with enjoyment. These precious birds should be handled carefully and treated with respect. In the following recipes we recommend methods for preparing young birds, which are easily recognizable by their flexible breastbones.

STEWED PHEASANT WITH TENDER VEGETABLES

For 2 servings

1 young pheasant, about 2¼ pounds (1 kg)
flour
4 slices lean bacon
2 carrots, peeled
1 small onion
½ teaspoon each salt and pepper
1 sprig each fresh thyme and rosemary
4 juniper berries
1 clove garlic
4 leaves each fresh marjoram and mint
¾ cup (175 mL) hearty red wine
6 tablespoons (75 mL) beef stock
4 ounces (125 g) button mushrooms
1½ tablespoons (20 g) butter
4 green onions

Follow steps illustrated to cut up pheasant. Pat pieces dry and dust with flour, shaking off excess. Dice bacon, carrots, and onion. Fry bacon in skillet, add pheasant, and brown for 10 minutes, turning frequently. Remove from skillet and set aside. Sauté carrots and onion in same skillet, add seasonings, red wine, and stock and cook for 10 minutes. Add pheasant pieces skin side up, cover, and simmer for 10 minutes. Remove breast pieces and continue cooking remaining pieces for 20 minutes longer. Meanwhile, clean mushrooms and sauté in butter. Rinse green onions and cut into 1¼-inch (3-cm) pieces. Add to mushrooms with breast pieces and reheat.

QUAIL WITH MUSHROOMS

For 2 to 4 first-course servings

4 quail, ready to cook
2 tablespoons oil
½ teaspoon dried oregano
¼ teaspoon pepper
1 teaspoon salt
5 shallots
8 ounces (200 g) mushrooms, sliced
¼ cup (60 mL) each dry white wine and heavy cream
1 tablespoon chopped fresh parsley

Place quail on counter breast side up and break breastbone by pushing on it with the ball of your thumb. Make a horizontal cut in the skin between the thighs, bend the thighs inward, and insert through the cut. Mix 1 tablespoon oil with oregano and pepper and rub all over the quail. Set aside for 1 hour. Heat remaining oil in a skillet over medium heat and brown quail for 7 minutes on each side. Sprinkle with salt and transfer to a preheated platter. Add shallots to skillet and sauté for 2 minutes over high heat. Add mushrooms and sauté for 2 minutes. Add white wine, cream, and parsley and cook until slightly thickened. Season to taste and pour over quail. When prepared this way and served with toast, quail make a splendid first course.

WILD DUCK WITH ORANGE SAUCE

2 young wild ducks, about 1¾ pounds (800 g) each
4 slices bacon
2 teaspoons salt
½ teaspoon pepper
1 cup (240 mL) game stock
½ cup (125 mL) orange juice
white part of 3 leeks

Cut up ducks and discard glands from near tail. Arrange bacon slices in a roasting pan and place duck pieces on top skin side down. Roast for 10 minutes in a preheated 400°F (200°C) oven. Turn, sprinkle with salt and pepper, and brown for about 5 more minutes. Remove all pieces except the thighs; reduce heat to 300°F (150°C) and continue roasting thighs an additional 30 minutes. Meanwhile, transfer poultry to an ovenproof dish. Combine game stock and orange juice and reduce by ⅓. Dice leeks. When thighs are cooked, add them to duck pieces in the baking dish. Strain cooking juices from roasting pan into the stock, bring to the boil, and season to taste. Add leeks and spoon sauce over duck. Place in oven for 5 minutes to heat through. Serve with mashed potatoes, green salad, and a light rosé or red wine.

Pheasant tastes best in season, which is from about the beginning of October until the middle of January. Wild duck is available during that same season, while quail can be found all year round.

CHICKEN

The best-quality stewing chickens have taut, light-colored skin, plenty of yellow fat and a stocky body. They weigh from 3½ to 6 pounds (1½ to 2½ kg) and the proportion of meat to bone increases with their weight—which is good to know when comparing prices.

TIP

Grind leftover meat, skin, and raw organ meats like liver, heart, and tripe with an equal amount of fresh meat, bind with egg and breadcrumbs, and season to taste with salt, pepper, and freshly grated nutmeg. Shape meatballs using a teaspoon and simmer in chicken broth for 10 minutes.

Cook chicken according to the recipe for Basic Clear Stock (see Index) but change the cooking method as follows: Substitute dry white wine for part of the water. Bring contents of pot to a rapid boil over medium heat, cover, reduce heat, and simmer for 15 minutes. Add salt. If you have an electric stove, let pot stand, covered, on the turned-off electric burner for 2 hours, or until chicken is completely cooked. If you have a gas stove, simmer for 5 additional minutes before the 2-hour steeping.

Cooking the chicken in the traditional manner is faster: Place chicken in boiling water, simmer for 1 hour, remove from water, let cool, and proceed with your recipe. You may also cook the chicken in a water bath, wrapped in aluminum foil; this method results in juicy chicken but barely-flavored cooking liquid. Suspend the foil-wrapped chicken in the water so it doesn't touch the bottom of the pot, and cook for 1 hour.

1 **Fresh, flavorful ingredients** add aroma to meats and stock. Shown here leeks, carrots, celery roots, onion, thyme, lovage, parsley, white wine, salt, and pepper.

2 **The chicken is done** when the legs move easily in their sockets. Lift chicken from the water with a fork. Carve when chicken is cool enough to handle.

3 **Place the chicken on its back.** Pull the legs away from the chicken to break them off, and remove the wings in the same way.

4 **Pull the skin off.** Using your thumb, loosen the skin at the point where it adheres to the meat. The picture shows how to pull the skin away from the breast meat.

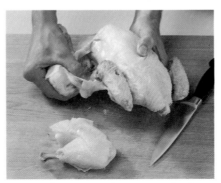

5 **Remove bones from legs.** Remove the hollow bones from the legs and thighs by twisting them out. Holding the meat tightly together, pull out all the small bones.

6 **Remove the breast bone.** With the tip of a sharp knife, loosen the meat from the breastbone and pull it off with your fingers. Remove the wishbone and bone the wings as well.

7 **Slice the meat** when it is cooled, to get nice smooth slices. Cut breast into thin diagonal slices.

Reheat sliced cooked chicken in stock or sauce, being careful not to let it boil, which would dry the meat out. Make sauce from concentrated chicken broth and the ingredients of your choice. Season to taste before serving.

Chicken breast in an herbed velouté sauce is very delicate. Prepare velouté sauce (see index), adding 1 teaspoon each chopped fresh basil, chervil, parsley, and dill, and a pinch of tarragon. Season to taste with freshly grated nutmeg.

Buying a whole chicken is always more economical than buying a cut-up chicken. To thaw a frozen chicken, place it in the refrigerator overnight so it retains its quality and texture. Broiling chickens are particularly tender and juicy when they are cut into pieces and sautéed. The word sauté comes from the French *sauter*, to jump, and it means to stir constantly when searing so food cooks evenly. White meat cooks faster than dark meat, so you will need to remove the breast sooner than the other pieces or it will dry out. After you have removed the breast, add vegetables of your choice such as cucumber, green onions, bell peppers, tender peas, and/or celery root. If desired, pour out the cooking juices and make a sauce with stock or wine and cream.

FAR EAST CHICKEN

1 broiler-fryer about 3¼ pounds (1½ kg)
3 tablespoons each soy sauce and dry sherry
2 teaspoons white wine vinegar or rice vinegar
2 teaspoons sugar
1 teaspoon salt
¼ teaspoon black pepper
¼ teaspoon paprika
1 teaspoon sesame oil
1 large onion, chopped
oil or butter for frying

Cut up chicken and pat dry. In a mixing bowl, combine soy sauce, sherry, vinegar, sugar, salt, pepper, paprika, and sesame oil and mix well. Add onion.

Pour enough oil or butter into a large skillet to cover the bottom. Heat over high heat and sear chicken for 15 minutes, turning frequently. Pour soy sauce mixture over chicken, reduce heat to low, cover, and cook for 10 minutes, basting occasionally. Remove the breast meat; cook remaining chicken for 10 more minutes. Just before serving, return breast to pan to reheat. Serve with steamed rice and a salad.

Carving poultry requires just a few minutes, a cutting board, and a large, sharp, pointed knife. Use your hands to find the joints so you don't cut into the bones. Place chicken (and other poultry) breast side up on a cutting board. Pull legs away from body and cut the skin. Bend legs away from body until the joint pops out of the socket; cut at that point. Press the wings against the body until the shoulder joint becomes visible, then cut toward the body to separate the joint. Cut off the wings. Insert the knife into the body to cut between the ribs. Pull up ribs and cut to separate the back and the breast. Cut the back in half crosswise and the breast in half lengthwise.

CHICKEN WITH OLIVES

1 broiler-fryer, about 3 pounds (1½ kg)
4 ounces (125 g) lean smoked bacon
14 ounces (400 g) small potatoes
1 onion
1 clove garlic
14 ounces (400 g) tomatoes
4 ounces (125 g) mushrooms
3 ounces (100 g) black olives, pitted
¾ cup (175 mL) Cognac or brandy
1 tablespoon butter
salt and pepper

Cut up chicken and pat pieces dry with a paper towel. Finely dice bacon. Peel and quarter potatoes; chop onion and garlic. Peel, seed, and quarter tomatoes. Clean and chop mushrooms.

Fry bacon over high heat in a deep saucepan with lid, stirring frequently, until golden. Add chicken pieces and cook until golden, turning occasionally. After 10 minutes, add potatoes, onion, and garlic and cook for 2 minutes. Add brandy and tomatoes. Reduce heat to low, cover, and cook for 10 minutes. Remove breasts and cook remaining chicken 10 more minutes.

Melt butter in a medium skillet over high heat. Add mushrooms and sauté for 2 minutes, then add chicken with olives. Return breast pieces to pan and heat through. Season with salt and pepper.

Serve Chicken with Olives very hot with a fresh green salad, country bread, and a fruity white wine.

Stir-frying is one of the many cooking techniques we have learned from the Chinese. Cutting ingredients into matchstick-size pieces takes time, though a processor greatly speeds the job. But cooking is very quick, so you save a lot of energy. We chose this recipe for stir-fried chicken because you can alter and vary it as you like.

Try substituting duck meat for chicken and changing the marinade to suit your own taste, using sherry, ginger, or garlic. Good vegetables—which must be impeccably fresh—are root vegetables, mushrooms, bell peppers, peas, cabbage, leeks, and onions.

PREPARING POULTRY FOR STIR-FRYING

Using a heavy knife, cut a meaty stewing or frying chicken in half lengthwise. Remove the meat from the bones using your hands; use a knife only where the meat is attached to the bones. Cut meat into very thin strips with a sharp knife and remove tendons from thighs. Reserve the carcass and scraps for stock. Cut the skin into fine strips as well; season them and fry until crisp. Use as a garnish for a stir-fried dish.

SICHUAN CHICKEN

3 cups chicken meat cut into strips
2 tablespoons light soy sauce
1 teaspoon cornstarch
2 medium carrots, peeled
1 bunch green onions
1 fresh red chili pepper
1/4 cup (60 mL) vegetable oil
1 teaspoon sesame oil

Mix chicken with soy sauce and cornstarch until all strips are coated; cover, and marinate for 30 minutes. Cut carrots and cleaned green onions into matchstick-size strips. Cut chili pepper into thin rings and remove seeds. Heat a heavy skillet over high heat. Pour in half the vegetable oil and add chicken when oil is hot. Stir-fry for 1 to 2 minutes, or until it is golden and fragrant. Remove from skillet immediately. Add remaining vegetable and sesame oil; add carrots and stir-fry for 1 minute. Return the chicken to the skillet and reheat. Add more soy sauce if desired and serve immediately.

Sichuan Chicken was originally stir-fried in a wok over an open fire. The wok's entire surface heats evenly and the heat penetrates the ingredients so quickly that they are cooked in seconds. A large, heavy skillet on your stovetop will work just as well.

Roast duck will be very crisp if you brush the skin with salted water just before it is done. Serve with red cabbage and glazed chestnuts.

VEGETABLES AND POTATOES

We have only begun to realize the full potential of vegetables. No longer do they sit quietly on the sidelines, often ignored or pushed aside. The vegetables of the past were cooked beyond recognition, but the cooking of today has discovered the wonderful flavors and textures of properly cooked vegetables. They are so superb and so easy to prepare that vegetable recipes have been incorporated into the menus of food-conscious people everywhere. A food processor is a big help in preparing vegetables and making purées, timbales and flans, which can be served as appetizers or side dishes. Also in this chapter you will find marvelous potato dishes. As with other vegetables, potatoes should be very fresh and, if peeled, only the thinnest layer of skin should be removed. Never soak them after they have been cut. Steam vegetables only briefly; they should be *al dente*, or crisp-tender. And always use seasonal vegetables. If you follow these rules, your dishes will be a delight—and they'll have the maximum possible flavor

COOKING VEGETABLES

Cooked vegetables will retain their individual flavors perfectly if they are cooked properly. You will get the best results by cooking small quantities of vegetables in a large amount of water, which should return to a vigorous boil right after you add the vegetables so that it takes as little time to cook them as possible. Depending on their variety and texture, this may only take a few seconds or minutes. Leafy vegetables collapse immediately, which means they're done. Tender beans take about 3 minutes, Brussels sprouts 5 minutes. To test, remove and cut open the largest piece. It is done when it is crisp-tender and no longer has a raw taste. The exact cooking time depends on your personal preference; it can be varied from a bit more to a bit less, but vegetables should never be cooked to mushiness.

The single and most important seasoning is salt, which not only brings out specific vegetable flavors but also opens cells in the vegetable, allowing any undesirable properties to cook out. In the case of cabbage, for example, salt helps it lose its bitterness and become more digestible.

Brief cooking time decreases loss of nutrients as well. Serve vegetables immediately after cooking, or cool them in ice water to stop the cooking process and preserve their flavor. (Alternatively, rinse small quantities in a strainer under cold water to cool.) This causes the outer pores to close and the skins to tighten; the vegetables will look more brilliant than when they were raw.

But do not leave them in water! Quickly drain and dry them, then reheat or use them in your recipe.

1 **Place cleaned green beans** in a large pot of boiling salted water (1 tablespoon per quart). Allow 10 cups of vigorously boiling water for every 8 ounces of beans.

2 **Using a slotted skimmer,** drop the cooked vegetables into ice water for a few seconds, then remove and let drain. Cover and refrigerate. Reheat to serve immediately or freeze for later use.

Cooked vegetables—½ to 1 cup (150 to 250 g) per serving—are steamed or tossed in melted butter or cream right before serving. This prevents them from overcooking and enables you to cook them ahead of time and have them crisp the following day. Refrigerate cooked vegetables overnight in a tightly covered container to preserve all nutrients, or freeze them. To use the vegetables, either thaw

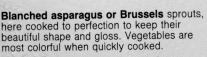

Blanched asparagus or Brussels sprouts, here cooked to perfection to keep their beautiful shape and gloss. Vegetables are most colorful when quickly cooked.

them first or place them in a saucepan filled with water over low heat. Reduce the cooking time so they don't overcook while the water is heating.

Vegetables cooked this way can be served with meat or fish. Or, for a wonderful meal, combine several vegetables and top them with a fried egg. Enhance their appeal by adding Hollandaise or Béarnaise sauce (see Index). Crisp vegetables are also perfect for purées, timbales, flans, gratins, and salads.

Cooking vegetables quickly in boiling salted water is called "blanching." If you plan to freeze vegetables, blanching is necessary to destroy the enzymes that cause deterioration. We also recommend it as a matter of course for strongly flavored vegetables such as fennel, celery, cabbage, turnips, and kale. Blanch these vegetables, then steam, sauté or braise them with butter to enhance their flavors. Following is a list of how best to prepare and cook individual fresh vegetables to enjoy their full flavors.

Artichokes

To serve them whole, see Index. For artichoke bottoms, see directions on following pages.

Asparagus

Peel stalks, starting below the tip. Snap off woody end of stalk and discard. If desired, cook stalks separately from the tips, which cook more quickly.

Beets

Simmer, unpeeled, in water. Cool in cold water then peel.

Bell Peppers

Quarter, remove stems and white membranes, then slice peppers. Braise, steam, or blanch them first for milder flavor.

Broccoli

Separate the florets. Peel and slice the thick stalks; quarter the small ones. Make sure the florets don't fall apart before the stalks are cooked. Either braise or steam after blanching.

Brussels Sprouts

Cut off stems and remove outer leaves. Always blanch Brussels sprouts.

Cabbage and Savoy Cabbage

Remove thick stalks, slice leaves, and braise or blanch before steaming.

Cauliflower

Separate into florets. Discard the core and cut the thick stalks into matchstick-size pieces. Cook florets and stalks separately and blanch before steaming.

Celery Root

Simmer in water, peel, and use as desired. Or slice first and braise or steam.

Cucumber

Cut in half lengthwise, remove seeds, and slice into halfrounds or matchstick-size pieces. Steam or braise. Blanch only if you plan to use them in a stew.

Fennel

Quarter or slice and blanch fennel to reduce the intense anise flavor. Then, if desired, braise or steam.

Green Beans

If they are tender, cook them whole. Cut larger beans into bite-size pieces.

Kale

Remove ribs and blanch kale before cooking or braising.

Kohlrabi

Peel, cut into the size you wish, and braise or steam. If you have young bulbs, pull off the skin starting at the bottom. Finely chop the center leaves and sprinkle over the kohlrabi after they are cooked.

Leeks

Wash leeks and slash lengthwise, then cook whole. Or cut them into rounds and steam or sauté.

Peas

Shell and blanch large peas; don't steam them. Cook the entire pod of sugar or snow peas.

Salsify

Wash thoroughly, peel, and place immediately in cold water. Add a little vinegar and flour to the water to keep this root vegetable white. Quarter the thick stalks, then cut into small pieces to reduce cooking time. Cook in salted water.

Spinach

Wash thoroughly, discard stems, and blanch leaves for a very tasty dish.

Turnips

Slice thinly and braise, then add to your dish.

Zucchini

Zucchini are good steamed or sautéed. Slice small zucchini and braise or blanch.

GRATINS

These baked vegetable dishes are small meals in themselves. You can prepare them in advance, because the vegetables stay crisp and fresh under the protective top layer. Almost all blanched or sautéed vegetables are suitable for gratins; only tomatoes should be used raw, peeled, and seeded. The sides of the gratin dish should be 1¼ to 2 inches (3 to 5 cm) high. Layered vegetables need only be cooked for a short time. They will be full of vitamins and very appealing, with a substantial golden crust.

ASPARAGUS AU GRATIN

1 generous pound (500 g) asparagus
½ teaspoon salt
2 lemon slices
1 sprig parsley
1½ cups (350 mL) water
1½ tablespoons (20 g) each butter and flour
½ cup (125 mL) heavy cream
¼ teaspoon white pepper
3 dashes Worcestershire sauce
⅛ teaspoon freshly grated nutmeg
butter

Peel asparagus, starting below the tips, and snap off the woody stem ends. Add peels, trimmings, salt, lemon slices, and parsley to 1½ cups (350 mL) boiling water and cook for 10 minutes. Line a strainer with a towel and pour the asparagus cooking liquid through, pressing on the solids to extract all liquid. Pour the cooking liquid into a clean large pot and bring to boil. Cut asparagus into 2-inch (5-cm)-long pieces. Add the stalks to cooking liquid and cook for 5 minutes. Add the tips and cook for 5 more minutes. Drain, reserving liquid, and shake dry. In a saucepan melt butter over low heat until it foams. Add flour

and stir for 2 minutes. Pour in asparagus cooking liquid and whisk until smooth. Add cream and cook for 10 minutes, or until thickened. Season with pepper, Worcestershire sauce, nutmeg, and salt, if desired. Layer asparagus in a baking dish, cover with hot sauce, and dot with butter. Bake for 10 minutes in a preheated 400°F (200°C) oven. If the sauce was cold when poured over asparagus, allow an additional 5 minutes cooking time.

CAULIFLOWER AU GRATIN

1 large cauliflower
1 teaspoon fresh lemon juice
salt
½ cup (125 mL) water
3 tablespoons (50 g) butter
½ cup (65 g) flour
3 eggs
½ cup (50 g) grated Emmenthal or Gouda cheese
⅛ teaspoon freshly grated nutmeg

Place cauliflower in a large amount of rapidly boiling water with lemon juice and salt; cauliflower must be completely covered. Cook for 10 minutes. Remove cauliflower and transfer to a strainer to cool. Place in a soufflé dish large enough to leave a 1- to 1¼-inch (2- to 3-cm) space around the cauliflower.

Meanwhile, combine ½ cup water with butter and a pinch of salt in a saucepan and bring to boil. Add the flour all at once and stir with a wooden spoon until the mixture is smooth. Remove from heat. Add 1 beaten egg to flour mixture and blend well. Cool slightly, then add remaining eggs, grated cheese, and nutmeg. Mix well and pour over cauliflower. Bake in preheated 400°F (200°C) oven for 25 minutes, or until golden brown. Serve hot, alone or with cured ham.

LEEKS AU GRATIN

1 generous pound (500 g) leeks, white parts only
1½ tablespoons (20 g) butter
½ teaspoon salt
¼ teaspoon pepper
⅛ teaspoon freshly grated nutmeg
2 egg yolks
½ cup (125 mL) heavy cream

Cut leeks diagonally into ⅜-inch (1-cm) pieces. Melt butter in a deep skillet over low heat. Add leeks and sauté for 2 minutes, then transfer to a baking dish. Combine salt, pepper, and nutmeg with egg yolks and cream and mix until blended. Pour over hot leeks and brown in preheated 350° (175°C) oven for 10 minutes; if the leeks were cold, bake an additional minutes.

More gratins

For carrots, celery root, spinach, or green beans use 1 cup (240 mL) Mornay sauce (see Index). Cover tomatoes, celery stalks, fennel, and chicory with a mixture of 3 eggs and tablespoons each breadcrumbs and freshly grated Parmesan cheese; do with butter and bake.

For white or Savoy cabbage, Brussels sprouts, or bell peppers use 1 cup (240 mL) Béchamel sauce (see Index) or a mixture of 3 eggs, ¾ cup (175 mL) milk, and salt and pepper to taste. Allow 1 to 1½ pounds (500 to 750 g) vegetables for 4 servings.

Asparagus au gratin is a light, tasty treat for lunch or dinner. Serve it with a sparkling white wine to make a complete meal.

FRENCH BEANS

1½ pounds (675 g) green beans
12 ounces (350 g) fresh tomatoes
2 slices (50 g) bacon
1 onion
1½ tablespoons (20 g) butter
1 bunch savory
½ cup (125 mL) beef stock
salt and pepper

Trim the ends from the beans. Cut the beans into julienne strips. Peel, seed, and dice tomatoes. Dice bacon and onion and sauté in butter until golden. Add beans, savory, tomatoes, and stock, bring to a boil, cover, and cook for 10 minutes.

Season to taste with salt and pepper. Stir and taste the beans; if they are still hard, continue cooking until crisp-tender. Serve with marinated herring and boiled potatoes in their jackets.

For variation, cook beans in heavy cream, add plenty of chopped fresh parsley, and mix well. Always cook beans with savory to intensify their flavor. Tie the savory into a bouquet garni so you can easily remove it before serving.

PURÉED VEGETABLES

These purées are particularly attractive side dishes for lightly sautéed meats. Any firm vegetables will do. They are either lightly cooked and then puréed or cooked until very tender and put through a strainer. Just before serving melt butter, add vegetables and then cream, mix well, and season as desired. Garnish with fresh herbs. A simple purée of white beans seasoned with garlic, parsley, salt, and pepper is wonderful with lamb.

Timbales and flans

These are light, airy vegetable specialties. Fill individual molds with vegetables, cook in a waterbath, and unmold. Serve as a side dish or garnish with a sauce and serve as an appetizer. Tender vegetables like spinach and peas need only be blanched, then covered with a seasoned egg and cream mixture. Firmer vegetables such as beans, broccoli, and carrots are best when puréed.

PURÉE OF GREEN BEANS

3 quarts (3 L) water
3 tablespoons salt
1½ pounds (675 g) green beans
1 bunch savory
1½ tablespoons (20 g) butter
¼ cup (60 mL) heavy cream
white pepper
1 teaspoon minced fresh parsley

Bring water to boil with salt in a large pot. Trim beans and add to boiling water with savory. Boil for 3 to 6 minutes, depending on the tenderness of the beans. Drain, quickly cool beans in cold water, and drain again. Chop beans coarsely, then purée in blender. Melt butter over low heat, add bean purée, and cook for 1 minute. Add cream, salt to taste, and pepper and mix well. Garnish with parsley.

Serve delicate, airy Broccoli Timbales with Walnut Sauce as an elegant first course or to accompany choice cuts of meat.

BROCCOLI TIMBALES WITH WALNUT SAUCE

1 12-ounce (350-g) head of broccoli

1 tablespoon (15 g) butter

¼ cup (60 mL) chicken broth

2 eggs

¼ cup (60 mL) heavy cream

salt and white pepper

Walnut Sauce (see below)

Trim broccoli before weighing, then chop coarsely. Melt butter over low heat, add broccoli, and sauté until translucent. Pour in broth, cover, and cook for 5 minutes. Let cool, then purée in a blender, adding eggs, cream, and seasonings. Butter 4 ½-cup (125-mL) molds or ramekins and fill with timbale mixture. Place in a roasting pan and add hot water to come halfway up the sides of the molds. Bake in a preheated 400°F (200°C) oven for 20 to 25 minutes, or until set. Unmold immediately and serve as a first course with sauce.

Walnut Sauce

Shell 6 fresh walnuts, chop meats, and toast in 2 teaspoons butter. Add ¾ cup (175 mL) velouté sauce made with chicken stock (see Index), bring to boil, remove from heat and season to taste with freshly grated nutmeg.

Vegetable flans. Spoon cooked vegetables into a blender with motor running. Here we have ¼ cups (300 g) peeled, diced carrots, sautéed in 1 tablespoon (15 g) butter, then cooked with ¼ cup (60 mL) meat stock. Purée vegetables, add 2 eggs and ⅓ cup (80 mL) heavy cream, and season with pinches of salt, sugar, and freshly grated nutmeg or as desired. Choose Brussels sprouts, rutabagas, Savoy cabbages, celery root, or cauliflower for flans and imbales. Serve with creamy velouté sauce (see Index), seasoned with spices and herbs that complement the vegetables.

Fill molds and sear. Butter ½-cup (125-mL) molds or cups. Fill with vegetables and cook according to directions for Broccoli Timbales. Unmold immediately.

STEAMED, SAUTÉED AND BRAISED VEGETABLES

These are cooking methods that use butter as the chief flavoring medium. Some of the best vegetables to combine with butter are cucumbers and their relatives, leeks, and root vegetables. But the flavor of blanched vegetables can also be intensified when they are prepared with other fats. The choice of fat (butter, oil, or bacon fat) is as important as ingredients like onions or garlic, which, when sautéed first, are perfect companions for many vegetables.

Generally, herbs are used sparingly because they can overpower the vegetables' distinctive flavors. We use parsley and a thyme sprig tied together when steaming and braising, because they enhance the vegetables' own flavors. Use savory to cook beans and cabbage-like vegetables, along with some caraway seed wrapped in a cheesecloth bag to make them more digestible. We prefer flat-leafed Italian parsley because it is more flavorful. Sprinkle plenty of minced garlic over any cooked vegetable to improve its flavor. Always chop herbs finely to release the maximum flavor. To enhance the aroma of many vegetables, sprinkle them with *fines herbes*, a mixture that includes fresh chervil, chives, parsley, and some tarragon. Season with salt and pepper only when the vegetables are nearly cooked. Use a tiny sprinkling of ground mace as well; we prefer it over the somewhat bitter nutmeg, particularly when used with cabbage-like vegetables.

Use mace with carrots, too, or try seasoning them with caraway. You can always intuit what goes together by placing the vegetables and the spice next to each other to see if their aromas are mutually complementary.

FRIED ZUCCHINI

Cover the bottom of a skillet with oil and heat until smoking. Add ½ to 1 small chopped onion and sauté until golden. Add zucchini slices and stir continuously until they are golden and translucent. Season with salt and pepper, toss with Parmesan cheese, and serve. Eggplant can be fried in exactly the same way.

Simmering

Toss raw or blanched vegetables in butter or oil over low heat until they are aromatic and have absorbed all of the fat. Then simmer the vegetables in their own juices or add other liquids, such as a neutral veal stock. Cover vegetables with ⅜ to ¾ inch (1 to 2 cm) liquid, cover, and simmer over low heat until they are *al dente*, stirring occasionally so that vegetables will cook evenly. Remove from the heat immediately and serve as soon as possible, because their freshness and crunchiness won't last long: Cucumbers will turn soft and mushy and other vegetables will fall apart.

Sautéing and frying

Generally, slice vegetables very thinly and cook only in small amounts. Don't cook too many at once, because all slices must touch the bottom of the pan if they are to cook evenly. Whether you sauté or fry raw or blanched vegetables is up to your taste—refer to the list on page 113. Do not chop watery vegetables like zucchini and eggplant into very small pieces; they cook quickly and will disintegrate. Heat oil in a large skillet over high heat until smoky. (If desired add a very small amount of peanut oil. Use just a little because it has a strong flavor, but it tastes great with vegetables.) Add very dry vegetables and stir-fry until they are fragrant and transparent. This brings out the vegetables' best colors and is perfect for cooking Chinese-style dishes.

Braising

Quickly brown vegetables in oil, butter, or bacon fat, then cook them in their own juices or in a liquid such as water or, better yet, veal stock, which improves the taste of virtually any savory dish. Follow the directions on page 118 for simmering vegetables.

Since there are always exceptions to any rule, braise red cabbage the classic way (page 112), until soft, for the best flavor. Most people prefer kale, too, to be cooked until very tender. But there is no reason to drown it in butter or bacon fat.

Cook all other vegetables only until crisp-tender so they retain their vitamins. Do not start cooking them until it is almost time to eat; they should be served fresh and crunchy. Reheated, they taste only half as good (with a few exceptions) and they are only half as good for you. Avoid leftovers and cook only enough for one meal—about 1¼ cups (150 g) vegetables, after trimming, per person.

Following are three recipes for braised and steamed vegetables.

BROCCOLI IN WINE SAUCE

1½-pound (675-g) head of broccoli
2 tablespoons (25 g) butter
2 cloves garlic, minced
¾ cup (175 mL) dry white wine
¾ cup (175 mL) orange juice
1 teaspoon grated orange peel

Blanch broccoli until almost cooked through. Melt butter in a deep skillet over medium-high heat until it foams. Add garlic and sauté for 10 seconds. Pour in white wine and orange juice and cook sauce for about 6 minutes, or until creamy. Add broccoli and toss in sauce for 3 minutes, or until heated through and fully cooked. Serve immediately—try this with lamb chops.

TIP FOR COOKING MUSHROOMS

Salt mushrooms before sautéing because they contain a lot of water. Cover and heat until they exude their juices. Remove and drain well, reserving liquid. Reduce the liquid and add to the mushrooms or save it to flavor other preparations.

CARROTS IN CREAM

8 to 10 medium-size young carrots
1½ tablespoons (20 g) butter
¾ cup (175 mL) heavy cream
salt and pepper
2 egg yolks
2 tablespoons minced mixed fresh herbs

Peel carrots, cut into thin slices, and toss in butter over medium heat for a few minutes. Add cream, season with salt and pepper, and cook uncovered for 5 minutes, stirring occasionally. Blend some of the cream with the egg yolks, remove pan from heat, and add egg mixture to carrots, stirring constantly. Add herbs and adjust seasoning. Serve with steak and potatoes.

BRAISED FENNEL

2 medium fennel bulbs
2 tablespoons (30 g) butter
½ cup (125 mL) veal stock
salt
pinch of sugar
1 teaspoon fresh lemon juice

Rinse fennel and cut into ⅜-inch (1-cm)-wide strips. Blanch for 3 minutes; drain. Chop the fine green stalks. Melt the butter in a saucepan over low heat until lightly browned. Add fennel and sauté for 1 minute. Pour in veal stock, season with salt and sugar, cover, and braise for 2 minutes. Stir in lemon juice and serve immediately. Try braised fennel with broiled pork loin and mashed potatoes.

STEAMED SPINACH

1 generous pound (500 g) spinach
4 green onions
2 tablespoons (30 g) butter
½ cup (100 g) chopped fresh parsley
1 teaspoon salt
pinch of mace (optional)

Rinse, stem, and blanch spinach. Cool, drain, and squeeze with hands to remove excess liquid. Trim onions, halve lengthwise, and slice thinly. Melt butter in a saucepan over low heat until it foams, add onions and parsley, cover, and cook until onions are soft, about 10 minutes. Add spinach and mix well. Season with salt and mace, if desired. Heat through and serve immediately with an omelet or with fried calf's liver.

SICILIAN VEGETABLE STEW

1 large eggplant
salt
2 small zucchini
4 medium baking potatoes
2 to 3 stalks celery
1 large yellow onion
1½ pounds (675 g) fresh tomatoes
¼ cup (60 mL) olive oil
1 red bell pepper
12 fresh basil leaves

Cut eggplant into ⅜-inch (1-cm) pieces, mix with 1 tablespoon salt, and set aside for 30 minutes to drain. Pat dry with a paper towel. Cut zucchini and potatoes into ⅜-inch (1-cm) pieces. Peel the tough strings from the celery stalks and cut stalks crosswise into ⅛-inch (½-cm) slices. Slice onion. Quarter tomatoes and remove seeds. Purée in a blender and strain to remove the skins, if desired. Heat olive oil in a large saucepan over medium-high heat. Add eggplant first, then zucchini and celery, and stir for 2 minutes, or until golden. Remove from saucepan and reserve. Cook potatoes for 5 minutes, or until golden; add onions and brown quickly. Add red pepper and puréed tomatoes, cover, reduce heat, and simmer for 10 minutes. Add reserved vegetables, cover, and simmer for 6 to 8 minutes, or until done. Mix well and season with salt. Chop basil and add to stew. Serve immediately.

Sicilian Vegetable Stew is a light meal in itself. For a more substantial meal, serve it with simple cheese toast: Butter a slice of country bread and top with a thick slice of Gruyère, Emmenthal, or other cheese; broil until the cheese is melted.

GERMAN-STYLE BRAISED CUCUMBERS

2¼ pounds (1 kg) English cucumbers
2 tablespoons vinegar
salt
1 slice lean bacon
1 onion
1 cup (240 mL) beef stock
2 tablespoons sugar
½ teaspoon pepper
1½ tablespoons (20 g) butter, softened
1½ tablespoons flour

Peel cucumber and cut in half lengthwise. Remove seeds and cut cucumber into ⅛-inch (½-cm) slices. Combine vinegar and 1 teaspoon salt, mix with cucumber, and set aside for 1 hour. Finely dice bacon and onion. Fry bacon until crisp, remove from skillet, add onion, and sauté in bacon drippings until golden. Drain cucumber and add to onion with stock, sugar, and pepper. Cover and simmer for 10 minutes. Combine butter and flour, add to vegetables, and stir. Simmer for 10 more minutes. Sprinkle with bacon bits and serve.

Tender, juicy peas, shown here with shallots and lettuce, are available year round in your grocers' freezer.

FRENCH-STYLE PEAS

5 small shallots
2½ tablespoons (40 g) butter
1 teaspoon salt
½ teaspoon sugar
½ cup (125 mL) water
4 sprigs parsley
1 small head of lettuce
1 pound (450 g) young shelled peas

Sauté shallots in butter over low heat until transparent. Season with salt and sugar, add water and parsley, cover, and cook for 10 minutes. Discard outer leaves from lettuce; quarter the heart of the lettuce and tie it together with string. Add to shallots, cover with peas, and simmer for 10 minutes. Remove parsley sprigs and string from lettuce, toss all vegetables, and season to taste.

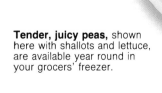

The recipes on these pages include the best examples of crisp sautéed and deep-fried potatoes. All potato dishes will turn out perfectly if the butter or oil is so hot that it sizzles when you add the potatoes. They should be very dry, even when you are using potatoes that have been precooked. Boil potatoes a day ahead and refrigerate them overnight for easier, smoother slicing. Chilled potatoes will also absorb less fat.

HOME-FRIED POTATOES

| 2¼ pounds (1 kg) boiling potatoes |
| 4 slices lean bacon |
| 2 tablespoons chopped onion |
| 2 tablespoons oil |
| 1 teaspoon salt |
| ½ teaspoon black pepper |
| 4 small firm tomatoes |

Peel and thinly slice potatoes by hand, with mandoline, or in processor. (If desired, scrub potatoes carefully and leave the skins on.) Pat dry with a paper towel and wrap in the towel to prevent discoloration. Dice bacon and fry in a large, heavy skillet over medium heat until golden. Remove bacon and reserve. Sauté onions briefly and set aside. Pour oil into skillet, heat for several minutes, and add potatoes. Sprinkle with salt and pepper, cover, and cook for 10 to 15 minutes. Do not turn potatoes until they are browned on the bottom; when they are, stir occasionally until done. Meanwhile, peel and slice tomatoes. Combine tomatoes, onion, and bacon bits with potatoes in skillet. Mix thoroughly, cover, and cook for 3 to 4 minutes, or until the potatoes are crunchy and roasted on all sides. Serve with cold cuts, tartar sauce, and a fresh green salad. Or, for a good, quick meal, try them with sour cream and herbs or pickled herring.

POTATO BALLS

| 1¾ pounds (800 g) baking potatoes |
| ½ teaspoon caraway seed |
| 2 tablespoons heavy cream |
| 2 egg yolks |
| ⅛ teaspoon freshly grated nutmeg |
| 1 teaspoon salt |
| ¼ teaspoon pepper |
| flour |
| 1 egg, beaten |
| ½ cup (60 g) chopped almonds |
| oil for deep frying |

Cover potatoes with water, add caraway seed, and boil for 20 minutes. Rinse under cold water, peel, and press through a potato ricer. Combine cream, egg yolks, and seasonings and add to hot potatoes to form a smooth dough. Wrap in foil and refrigerate overnight.

Flour your hands and roll cold potatoes into small balls, about ¾ inch (2 cm) in diameter. Roll balls first in beaten egg, then in chopped almonds. Arrange side by side on a platter and refrigerate for 1 hour to dry and harden the coating a bit, so it adheres to the potato balls as they cook.

Heat oil in a large pot or deep fryer over medium-high heat to about 375°F (190°C). Test the oil with a chunk of bread—it should sizzle immediately when placed in the fat. Add the potato balls a few at a time to prevent oil from cooling down. Deep-fry potato balls in 2 or 3 batches until golden brown. Drain on paper towels and place in a preheated serving bowl. Serve immediately or keep hot in a low oven. Use the same mixture for potato croquettes, which can be rolled in breadcrumbs. Or shape the dough into a long roll, refrigerate it overnight, and slice in ⅜-inch (1-cm)-thick rounds. Use less fat to fry potato cakes in a skillet. Flavor the dough as desired. You may add grated cheese, chopped fresh herbs, garlic, or onions, whatever goes with the meat you are serving.

French Fries are also deep-fried. Cut ⅜-inch (1-cm)-thick French fries from firm raw potatoes, either by hand or in processor fitted with the French-fry disc. Rinse under cold water and dry thoroughly. Deep-fry small batches for 10 minutes each in 375°F (190°C) oil. Remove and sprinkle with salt. Drain on a paper towel, then wrap with the towel to keep hot. This will make very crisp French fries. You may also fry thick or thin potato slices which require a shorter cooking time.

Potato dishes are nourishing and substantial. Front: a hearty farmer's breakfast with bacon. Back: Potato Balls coated with sliced almonds, delicious with delicate meat dishes.

POTATOES AU GRATIN

For 4 to 6 servings
2¼ pounds (1 kg) small boiling potatoes
1 clove garlic
8 tablespoons (125 g) butter, softened
2 eggs
1⅔ cups (400 mL) milk
1 tablespoon heavy cream
salt and pepper
butter

3 **Layer the potatoes.** Arrange the slices as shown in the photograph, beginning at one end and overlapping the slices.

1 **Slice potatoes.** Peel and pat dry, then thickly slice them by hand or in processor.

4 **Pour in egg and milk mixture.** Beat eggs, add milk and cream, mix well, and season with salt and pepper. Heat over low heat for 15 minutes, then pour over potatoes.

2 **Butter the baking dish.** First rub the baking dish with a halved garlic clove, then brush with butter.

5 **The gratin is done** when it is golden brown. Bake in a 350°F (180°C) oven on the center rack for about 40 minutes. Dot with butter just before serving.

Potatoes are delicious when carefully prepared, which they deserve—they're high in protein, and the protein is complemented by milk. Potatoes contain important B-vitamins and enough vitamins A and C to meet a substantial part of our daily requirement. They are also rich in minerals such as potassium, which, among other things, helps reduce water in the body. Nutritional values vary only slightly among varieties of potatoes, so they are usually selected for their cooking characteristics only: For example, salad potatoes are firm, baking potatoes starchy. Select potatoes according to your own personal taste.

For boiled potatoes, use a firm white- or red-skinned variety. Leave small potatoes whole; quarter larger ones. Allow 1 tablespoon salt per 1 quart water. Start the potatoes in cold water, bring quickly to a boil, and simmer for 20 minutes. Drain and steam briefly. Potatoes cooked this way are traditionally peeled, but peel them as thinly as possible to retain the valuable nutrients that are found right under the skin. For potatoes boiled in their jackets to be served as a side dish, select uniform-size boiling potatoes. Place them in cold water with some caraway seed, bring to a boil, and simmer until done. Test by inserting a knife into a potato; it will slip off easily if potato is cooked. Remove from heat, peel potatoes, and place in a preheated serving bowl. Steam cold potatoes, or toss in hot butter to reheat, and serve hot.

Use starchy potatoes for mashed potatoes, potato soup, dumplings, and pancakes as well as for potato balls, croquettes, and French fries, if you prefer them soft.

For potato salads and fried potatoes, boil potatoes in their skins. Always cook them a day ahead, rinse under cold water, peel, and spread out to cool completely so they slice smoothly.

Fry sliced or diced potatoes in hot

oil or butter over medium-high heat until they are browned on the bottom. Turn and finish frying, being careful when you turn them that they don't fall apart.

Season with salt, pepper and chopped onion and add some marjoram or thyme during the last few minutes of cooking. Oil, butter, and bacon drippings are all suitable for fried potatoes.

For potato salad, pour well-seasoned meat stock over sliced potatoes, toss, and let stand until they absorb the stock. If necessary, drain potatoes, then make a dressing of your choice. Try a sauce made of heavy cream mixed with wine, vinegar, onion, salt, pepper, a pinch of sugar, and a lot of chopped fresh parsley. A vinaigrette dressing (see Index), used warm or lukewarm, makes a very light potato salad. According to your taste and preference, try adding other ingredients such as finely chopped pickles, chopped egg, sliced tomatoes, bacon bits, or diced cooked celery root.

For baked potatoes, select a type with a high starch content. Cut medium-size potatoes in half lengthwise, season the cut surface as desired, and place on a baking sheet. Bake in a 350°F (180°C) oven for 25 minutes. Large (1-pound/400-g) potatoes, wrapped in aluminum foil, take about 1¼ hours in the oven. If you cook them first on top of the stove for 10 minutes, you'll save energy and decrease the baking time by half.

PURÉED POTATOES

2¼ pounds (1 kg) baking potatoes

salt

about 1 cup (240 mL) milk or cream

¼ teaspoon freshly grated nutmeg

1½ to 3 tablespoons (20 to 40 g) butter

Peel potatoes; cut large ones in half or in quarters so all pieces are the same size and will finish cooking at the same time. Cover potatoes with cold salted water and bring to boil over medium heat. Reduce heat and simmer for 20 minutes. Drain, return to low heat, and toss.

In a mixing bowl, mash potatoes with a potato masher. Beat with a whisk or electric mixer set at medium speed until creamy.

Slowly add hot milk or cream until purée has the desired consistency. Season with nutmeg.

Finally, add butter and mix well. The better quality butter you use, the less you'll need.

Always make plenty of mashed potatoes—people eat a lot of them when they are prepared as shown here! If desired, sprinkle with chopped fresh parsley, toasted breadcrumbs or nuts, or sautéed onion rings.

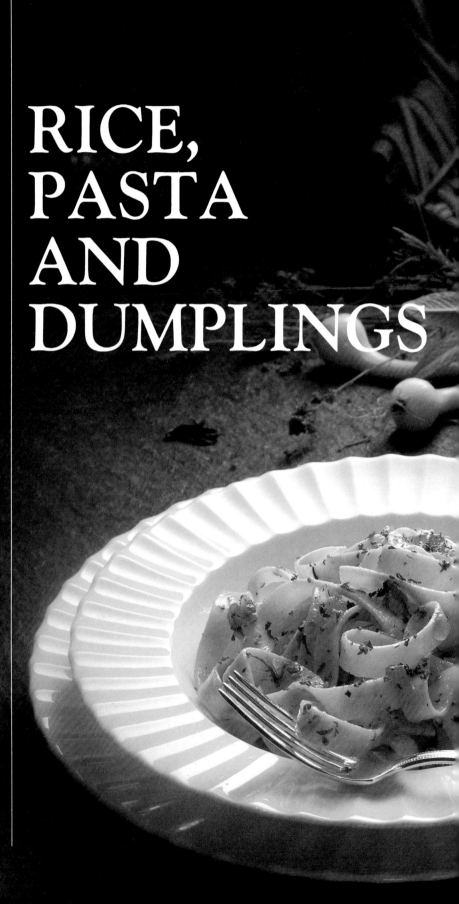

Pasta originated in rice country, but, rice is at home in pasta country. We're talking about China and Italy, who fight a continuous battle for the honor of having invented pasta. Ancient sources show that rice has been cultivated in China since 2800 B.C. at least—and it is still the most important food product for at least 1 billion people. It's no surprise that there is a Chinese saying, "a meal without rice is like a pretty girl with one eye." We want to go beyond rice and pasta history and concern ourselves with savory preparations of both. They are terrific to experiment with, because both have a relatively neutral flavor and harmonize well with a variety of ingredients. Here we offer you risotto in several variations, a super Brazilian rice dish prepared with tender lobster, and a number of pasta sauce recipes beginning with *pesto alla Genovese*, the delicious and popular cheese and basil sauce. We have included some lesser known and surprising combinations, too.

Lastly we give you a couple of recipes for dumplings, inclding one that is made by wrapping the mixture in a napkin and boiling it, much as you would a steamed pudding.

RICE, PASTA AND DUMPLINGS

ALL ABOUT RICE

High-quality white rice has the husk removed, but should be unpolished and still have its silvery skin, which contains so many important minerals and vitamins. We suggest long-grain rice for savory dishes. Or try converted rice, which does not stick together after cooking because of a special parboiling procedure that forces nutrients into the rice before it is polished. Brown rice, still containing the germ, has retained all its vitamins, minerals, and fiber. It requires much longer cooking—about 45 to 50 minutes, several times that of white rice. Wild rice, with its nutty taste, is a special delicacy, even when mixed with white rice. It too needs much longer cooking than white rice.

For 4 servings you will need about 1 cup (200 g) raw rice if it is to be served as a side dish or 2 cups if served as a main dish. Pour rice into 2 quarts (2 L) boiling water, add 1½ teaspoons salt, and a splash of oil (oil prevents the rice from boiling over). Stir once, bring to a boil, and cook over low heat for 18 minutes. Drain, toss with butter, and serve immediately, or make ahead and reheat in a double boiler.

Braised rice is healthier than rice cooked according to other methods because you don't discard any cooking water. Sauté 1 cup (200 g) raw rice alone or in butter over low heat until transparent, stirring constantly; do not let it brown. Pour in 2 cups (2 L) stock or water, either hot or cold, and cook for 20 minutes over low heat, covered tightly to keep the steam in. Make a simple risotto with butter, olive oil, and onion. Add other flavorful ingredients such as vegetables, mushrooms, and meat, all sautéed separately and mixed with the rice at the last minute, to serve as a full meal.

RISOTTO MILANESE

3½ tablespoons (30 g) butter
¼ cup (30 g) chopped onion
2 tablespoons diced beef marrow
1 clove garlic, diced
1¼ cups (250 g) Italian arborio rice
½ cup (125 mL) dry white wine or meat stock
3 cups (700 mL) chicken stock
¼ teaspoon saffron (powder or threads)
⅓ cup (45 g) freshly grated Parmesan cheese

3 **Pour in wine** or meat stock and cook until rice has absorbed it completely.

1 **Sauté onion and beef marrow.** Melt 2 tablespoons butter in a large saucepan over low heat. Add onion and beef marrow, stir, and cook until transparent. Add garlic.

4 **Add chicken broth** a little at a time, stirring and cooking over low heat until rice has absorbed all the liquid before adding more. Soak saffron in a little stock and add.

2 **Sprinkle in rice** and cook, stirring until transparent.

5 **Remove from heat** and mix with the remaining butter and Parmesan cheese.

BRAZILIAN-STYLE RICE

For 8 servings

1 chicken, approximately 2½ pounds (1¼ kg)
12 ounces (350 g) pickled pigs' feet
6 tablespoons (100 mL) olive oil
hot pepper sauce
salt
2 onions
1 clove garlic
1 small can (8 ounces/225 g) tomatoes
1 tablespoon tomato paste
1 tablespoon paprika
1 teaspoon powdered saffron
¼ teaspoon ground red pepper
2 cups (450 mL) chicken stock
½ cup (125 mL) dry white wine
2 cups (400 g) raw long-grain rice
12 ounces (350 g) raw shelled seafood (lobster, crab, or shrimp)
4 ounces (120 g) smoked sausage
8 cooked artichoke bottoms, halved
12 ounces (350 g) shelled young peas

Cut chicken into 8 pieces. Dice pigs' feet into ⅛-inch (½-cm) pieces. Combine oil, ½ teaspoon pepper sauce, and 1 teaspoon salt, add chicken and pork, mix, and marinate for 30 minutes. Finely chop onions and garlic and have remaining ingredients ready. Heat a large heavy skillet over high heat and sauté meats for 5 minutes, or until they are golden on all sides. Add onions and garlic and sauté for 1 minute. Add canned tomatoes, tomato paste, and spices and mix well. Slowly pour in stock and wine at the edge of the pan so ingredients in pan stay hot. Cover and simmer for 20 minutes.

Meanwhile, pour rice into 2 quarts (2 L) boiling water, cook for 12 minutes, and drain. Add to the sauce and place remaining ingredients on top: seafood, sliced sausage, artichoke bottoms, and peas. Cover skillet and steam for 10 minutes. Season to taste and serve.

PASTA

Homemade pasta can become a hobby. Try it once and you will discover how easy it is and how wonderful fresh pasta tastes. Use durum semolina flour for the most refined pasta, and whole-wheat flour for nutritious, flavorful, and filling pasta. You may omit the eggs in your pasta dough and replace them with additional oil and warm water. It is possible to make pasta without a machine, but it is more fun with a manual one, and no effort at all with an electric machine.

BASIC PASTA DOUGH

2⅓ cups (300 g) flour
3 eggs
1 to 2 tablespoons oil
1 teaspoon salt

Sift flour onto a board, make a well in the center, and fill with remaining ingredients. Mix contents of well with fork until completely blended, then gradually mix in flour. Knead dough until satiny and elastic. If you have a food processor or heavy-duty mixer,

1 **On a floured board,** roll out dough very thinly, then fold the sheet of dough in thirds like a business letter.

2 **Using a sharp knife,** cut pasta into thin ribbons. Handle the dough carefully so the strips don't stick together.

3 **Separate the strips** and spread them on a towel. Cook them immediately in a large amount of boiling salted water with a bit of oil added to it, or let the pasta dry completely, then cover tightly and store in a dry place.

130

combine all ingredients in work bowl and "knead" dough on slow, then medium speed. Either way, cover dough with a towel to prevent it from forming a crust and set aside for 1 hour or longer. Roll out dough and use it as you like. We will give you some ideas on the following pages.

WHOLEWHEAT PASTA

1 pound (450 g) wholewheat berries or 2¼ cups wholewheat flour	
1 tablespoon soy flour	
2 eggs	
1 teaspoon salt	
3 tablespoons oil	
5 tablespoons (75 mL) warm water	

Grind wheat berries in a home mill, reserving about 1 cup bran to use for another purpose, or use wholewheat flour. Mix and knead ingredients by hand or with a processor or heavy-duty mixer. Roll dough into a ball and brush lightly with oil so the surface doesn't dry out. Place a warmed bowl upside down over dough and set aside for 1 hour. Roll dough out and cut into noodles of desired width.

2 **Sift flour,** reserving bran, which does not swell enough to keep the dough together. Use only the flour (gluten and white part of wheat) that falls through the sifter.

3 **Add water.** Combine flour and remaining ingredients except water in a mixing bowl. Water should be lukewarm to activate the gluten in the flour.

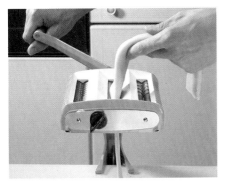

1 **Rolling the dough.** After you have kneaded the dough, feed it through your pasta machine several times, changing the rollers to smaller settings each time, until pasta has desired thickness.

2 **Cut strips** after the dough has been left to dry a bit but is still flexible. Feed through rollers to make either wide or narrow noodles.

1 **Grind wheat.** Follow directions for your machine and grind at moderate speed.

4 **Knead dough** with a dough hook, slowly at first to mix ingredients, then at a higher speed to obtain a smooth, elastic dough.

Pasta mixed with a flavorful sauce or *pesto* makes a delightful, quick meal. The following recipes should stimulate your own ideas, including how to successfully and elegantly incorporate leftovers into your pasta dishes. Always have a piece of Parmesan cheese on hand to grate fresh each time you use it.

FETTUCCINE AL PESTO

For the pesto:
1¼ teaspoons salt
5 peeled cloves garlic
⅓ cup (40 g) pine nuts
½ cup (120 g) fresh basil leaves
½ cup (50 g) freshly grated aged Pecorino cheese
¾ cup (80 g) freshly grated Parmesan cheese
¼ teaspoon pepper
1 cup (240 mL) olive oil
For the pasta:
1 pound (450 g) fettuccine or other flat pasta
salt and oil

In a large mortar and pestle sprinkle salt over garlic and pine nuts and crush to form a paste. Slice basil leaves into strips, add to mortar, and crush as well. Add cheeses and pepper and slowly blend in oil. If desired, thin the pesto with a bit of pasta cooking liquid just before serving. If you prefer milder pesto, omit the Pecorino cheese. For a more pungent mixture add 3 to 4 anchovies.

You may make pesto in a food processor, including grating the cheese with the fine grating blade. Always use freshly grated cheese; it has much more flavor.

Fettuccine are flat, ribbony noodles that are particularly delicious when homemade, though good-quality noodles are available commercially as well.

You may substitute spaghetti for the fettuccine to make *spaghetti al pesto.* Cook the pasta with salt and oil (see below), drain, and return to pot. Toss with enough pesto to coat the pasta evenly

HOW TO COOK PERFECT PASTA

For 4 servings, boil 2 quarts (2 L) water with 2 tablespoons salt in a large pot. Add 1 pound (450 g) pasta and a little oil, which will prevent the water from boiling over. Stir pasta once to separate it, then boil uncovered until tender but still firm at the center, or *al dente.* To test, remove a noodle from the pot and bite into it.

Fresh pasta is done after 1 to 4 minutes. Commercial, dried pasta—the best is made with durum wheat—needs about 10 minutes cooking time. When pasta is cooked, lift it from the water with a fork or a slotted spoon, drain well, and serve. Or drain, rinse under warm water, toss in melted or browned butter, and reheat.

Vermicelli with Prosciutto

Melt 3½ tablespoons (50 g) butter. Cut 6 ounces (150 g) very thinly sliced prosciutto into very fine julienne. Season with black pepper and heat in the butter but do not cook, which would make ham dry and tough. Toss with freshly cooked vermicelli.

Green Pasta with Anchovy Paste

Soak 3½ ounces (100 g) anchovies and ½ cup (100 g) capers in water to cover for 1 hour. Drain and pat dry. Place on a board with 2 cloves garlic and 3 ounces (100 g) pitted black olives and mince together, or purée in a blender. Add ½ cup (125 mL) olive oil and 6 tablespoons minced fresh parsley, mix well, and season with black pepper. Serve with cooked pasta.

Narrow Ribbon Pasta with Mushrooms

Clean and trim 10 ounces (300 g) fresh mushrooms and slice thinly. Melt butter in a large skillet until it foams. Add mushrooms and minced garlic to taste, toss for 1 minute, add a bit of heavy cream, and bring to boil. Season with salt, pepper, and finely chopped red bell pepper, if desired. Toss with cooked pasta.

Ribbon Noodles with Poppyseeds

Sauté 2 tablespoons poppyseed and ⅔ cup (60 g) sliced almonds in 2½ tablespoons (30 g) butter or chicken fat. Toss with cooked ribbon pasta and season to taste with salt and pepper.

Pasta and Cheese

Grate 2 ounces (60 g) each Gruyère, Emmenthal, Parmesan, and a mild, buttery cheese of your choice. Toss cooked pasta in 3½ tablespoons (50 g) butter and add cheeses, salt, and pepper. Pour into a soufflé dish and heat in a 400°F (200°C) oven for 5 to 10 minutes, or until cheese is melted.

Fettuccine al Pesto is one of the most distinctive of all pasta treatments.

PASTA SAUCES

Pasta served with sauce is a meal in itself. The sauce should be carefully seasoned and not too spicy, so it enhances the pasta flavor and doesn't overpower it. Serve pasta dishes with a fresh salad for a nutritious meal.

SPAGHETTI ALLA CARBONARA

1 pound (450 g) spaghetti
2 whole eggs
2 egg yolks
1/2 cup (50 g) freshly grated Parmesan cheese
4 ounces (120 g) prosciutto
1/2 cup (125 mL) heavy cream
1 tablespoon butter
1 teaspoon salt
1/4 teaspoon pepper

Cook spaghetti and drain. Meanwhile beat eggs and yolks and mix with half the Parmesan cheese. Finely chop ham and sauté in a large skillet over medium heat. Add cream, butter, salt, and pepper and bring to a boil. Toss noodles in sauce to reheat. Stir in egg and cheese mixture and heat gently until thickened, being careful not to let sauce boil or it will curdle. Serve sprinkled with remaining Parmesan cheese.

RAW TOMATO SAUCE

1¾ pounds (800 g) fresh tomatoes
1 bunch basil
3 cloves garlic
6 tablespoons (100 mL) olive oil
salt and pepper

Peel, seed, and dice tomatoes. Mince basil leaves. Halve garlic cloves lengthwise and remove any green sprout inside. Mince in garlic press or with a sharp knife, mix with tomatoes and basil, then add oil and mix well. Season to taste with salt and pepper, cover, and refrigerate for 30 minutes. Toss with hot pasta and serve.

MEAT SAUCE ALLA BOLOGNESE

1½ ounces (40 g) prosciutto or cooked ham
2 tablespoons (25 g) butter
8 ounces (200 g) lean ground beef
1 cup (240 mL) fresh tomato sauce (see Index)
1 slice lemon peel
2 tablespoons heavy cream
salt and pepper
1/8 teaspoon freshly grated nutmeg
freshly grated Parmesan cheese

Dice ham as finely as possible. Melt butter in a Dutch oven or deep-sided skillet over high heat until golden. Add ham and ground beef and brown slightly, stirring constantly. Reduce heat, add tomato sauce, stir, and bring to boil. Add lemon peel and simmer for 30 minutes. Remove lemon peel. Stir cream into sauce and season with salt, pepper, and nutmeg. Serve with spaghetti (or your choice of pasta) and top with freshly grated Parmesan cheese.

COLD CHIVE SAUCE

1 hard dinner roll
2 hard-cooked egg yolks
1 raw egg yolk
1/2 cup (125 mL) oil
6 tablespoons chopped fresh chives
2 tablespoons white wine vinegar
salt and sugar

Trim the crust from the roll and discard. Soak the roll in cold water until soft, then squeeze out excess liquid. Press cooked egg yolks through a strainer into a large bowl, add soaked roll, and mix with raw egg yolk. Slowly whisk in oil. Add chives and vinegar and season to taste with salt and sugar. This sauce can also be made in a blender.

Spaghetti alla Bolognese will whet your appetite for other quick pasta dishes. The sauce should be thick, as shown here, and not runny, so it softly coats the pasta.

135

CANNELLONI

1 onion, chopped

1 carrot, peeled and chopped

2 stalks celery, chopped

10 ounces (300 g) mushrooms, diced

4 tablespoons (60 mL) oil

1 pound (450 g) ground beef

1 teaspoon salt

1 teaspoon chopped fresh marjoram

1 egg

Basic Pasta Dough (see Index)

½ cup (125 mL) heavy cream

¾ cup (80 g) grated Tilsit cheese

2½ tablespoons (40 g) butter

Heat 2 tablespoons oil in a large skillet. Add beef; brown lightly on all sides. Transfer to a bowl. Add 2 more tablespoons oil to skillet and sauté onion, carrot, and celery until onion is translucent. Add mushrooms and sauté for 2 minutes. Add sautéed vegetables to ground beef, then add seasonings and egg, mix well, and season to taste. Thinly roll out pasta dough and cut into 4-inch (12-cm) squares. Let dry briefly, then cook in boiling water, drain, and arrange next to each other on work surface. Distribute stuffing mixture evenly among the pasta squares, roll up, and arrange in a buttered dish. Cover with cream and cheese and dot with butter. Bake in preheated 400°F (200°C) oven for 20 minutes, or until golden.

136

LASAGNA VERDE BOLOGNESE

6 ounces (150 g) spinach

salt

2⅓ cups (300 g) flour

3 eggs

2 tablespoons oil

Meat Sauce alla Bolognese (see Index)

Béchamel sauce (see Index)

¾ cup (80 g) freshly grated Parmesan cheese

Clean and trim stems from spinach and cook in boiling salted water for 3 minutes. Drain, rinse under cold water, and pat dry. Press spinach through a fine sieve and combine with flour, eggs, oil, and salt to make a smooth dough. If necessary, adjust the amount of flour or oil to make dough firmer or softer. Cover and set aside to rest for 1 hour, then roll out pasta very thin. Cut into 13×9-inch (33×23-cm) pieces and boil in salted water until *al dente*. Rinse the pasta under cold water and pat dry. In a 13×9-inch (33×23-cm) baking dish layer the meat sauce, pasta, and Béchamel sauce, in that order, until all the ingredients are used, being sure to end with Béchamel. Sprinkle with Parmesan cheese and bake in a preheated 400°F (200°C) oven for 20 minutes or until golden. Be careful that the cheese does not get too brown or it will taste bitter.

RAVIOLI STUFFED WITH HERBED CHEESE

12 ounces (350 g) ricotta cheese

1 egg yolk

¼ cup chopped fresh herbs (parsley, basil, sage, rosemary)

salt and pepper

Basic Pasta Dough (see Index)

1 egg white, lightly beaten

2½ tablespoons (40 g) butter

freshly grated Parmesan cheese

Fresh Tomato Sauce (see Index)

Combine ricotta, egg yolk, and herbs, mix well, and season with salt and pepper. Roll out half the pasta dough and mark out 1⅝-inch (4-cm) squares with the back of a knife blade. Drop 1 teaspoon ricotta mixture in the center of each square and brush edges of dough around filling with beaten egg white. Roll out second half of the dough, carefully place on top, and press dough together between mounds of filling. Prick any air bubbles with a needle. Using a pastry wheel, cut out squares for ravioli and cook in boiling salted water for 12 minutes. Drain. Melt butter in a large saucepan, add ravioli, and toss quickly. Serve with grated cheese and tomato sauce.

SPINACH GNOCCHI

1½ pounds (675 g) spinach
salt
5 tablespoons (80 g) butter
8 ounces (200 g) ricotta cheese
¾ cup (100 g) freshly grated Parmesan cheese
pepper
freshly grated nutmeg
2 eggs
about ¾ cup (100 g) flour

Clean and rinse spinach, trim stems, and cook leaves briefly in boiling salted water. Drain, rinse under cold water, and pat dry. Chop finely and mix with 1½ tablespoons hot melted butter. In a mixing bowl, combine spinach, ricotta, 1½ ounces (40 g) grated Parmesan, eggs, salt, pepper, and nutmeg and mix well. Add enough flour to make a soft, smooth dough and refrigerate for 1 hour. Bring salted water to a boil in a large pot and drop in dough by rounded teaspoonfuls. Simmer for 7 minutes, being careful not to let water boil. Gnocchi are done when they feel firm. Remove with a slotted spoon, drain, and place in a buttered baking dish. Cover with remaining cheese and butter and broil until cheese is melted.

SPAETZLE

2⅓ cups (300 g) flour
3 eggs
scant ½ cup (120 mL) water
½ teaspoon salt
2½ tablespoons (40 g) butter

Combine flour, eggs, water, and salt and mix dough as shown in photographs. Place dough on a cutting board and scrape it off into the simmering water as shown, or press dough through a large-hole colander or spaetzle press. Always drop directly into the pot, and cook only small batches at a time. Remove cooked spaetzle with a slotted spoon, drain, and toss in melted or browned butter. If you are making them to serve later, rinse cooked spaetzle under cold water, spread on a tray, cover, and refrigerate. Be careful that spaetzle neither stick together nor dry out. Toss in hot butter just before serving.

1 **In a mixing bowl,** combine flour, eggs, water, and salt. Slowly knead with dough hook until all the flour is incorporated.

2 **Knead dough** until it is smooth and light, either by hand or in a mixer on medium speed.

3 **Scrape spaetzle** from cutting board. Place some dough on a wet board and, using a knife, scrape strips of dough into simmering, salted water.

4 **Spaetzle are done** when they rise to the surface of the water. Remove with a slotted spoon. Cook in several small batches, draining in a colander as they are cooked.

DUMPLINGS

These are popular with hearty roasts and gravy. Dumplings are usually made from a basic recipe, then varied as desired. Traditional dumplings are easy to make, particularly if you use a processor to grate the potatoes.

MUSHROOMS IN CREAM SAUCE

1 generous (500 g) mushrooms
3½ tablespoons (50 g) butter
2 large shallots, finely diced
1 tablespoon flour
2 cups (450 ml) heavy cream
dash of meat glaze or 1 bouillon cube (see Index)
salt and pepper
¼ cup minced fresh parsley

Carefully sort through mushrooms (you may use any type of mushroom) and slice ⅛ inch (½ cm) thick. Rinse mushrooms only if they are sandy. In a large skillet melt butter over high heat until it foams. Add mushrooms and sauté for 1 to 2 minutes. Remove from skillet and drain, reserving liquid. Return liquid to skillet. Add shallots and flour, mix well, and cook for minute. Add cream and meat glaze and whisk until sauce thickens. Return mushrooms to skillet and mix well. Heat through, season with salt and pepper, toss with parsley, and serve immediately.

Napkin Dumplings with mushrooms in cream sauce are a dream! Serve with a chilled dry white wine. If desired, add fried bacon bits to dough, shape into little dumplings, and cook for 20 minutes.

NAPKIN DUMPLINGS

8 day-old dinner rolls

1 cup (240 mL) lukewarm milk

6 eggs, separated

6½ tablespoons (100 g) butter

1 teaspoon salt

⅛ teaspoon freshly grated nutmeg

pepper (optional)

¼ cup (20 g) minced fresh parsley

1 tablespoon minced fresh basil

napkin 32 inches (80 cm) square

appr. 3 quarts (3 L) salted water

butter or bacon fat

1 **Dice rolls.** Using a serrated knife, cut rolls into strips, then into small cubes.

2 **Pour in lukewarm milk,** increasing the amount if rolls are very hard and dry. Cover and set aside for milk to be absorbed.

3 **Beat egg yolks** and 5 tablespoons (80 g) butter in a mixing bowl until creamy. Add salt, nutmeg, and pepper, if desired.

4 **Mix dough.** Add minced herbs and egg yolk mixture to bread and milk. Sauté onion in 1½ tablespoons (20 g) butter until tender, add to bread and egg yolk mixture, and blend well with a rubber spatula.

5 **Add egg whites.** Meanwhile, beat egg whites until stiff. Carefully fold them into the dough using a wooden spoon.

6 **Wrap and tie dumpling.** Scald the napkin or towel and wring it dry. Shape dough into a log and place on napkin. Fold napkin over dough loosely, allowing room for the dumpling to expand, and tie ends.

7 **Cook dumpling.** Attach the wrapped dumpling, seam side up, to a wooden spoon with kitchen string and suspend in rapidly boiling salted water. Cover and boil gently for 1 hour.

8 **When dumpling is cooked,** unwrap and cut into thick slices, which will be tender and light. Fry in butter or bacon fat until golden and crusty.

SIMPLE DESSERTS

Beloved sweets. They are the grand finale to a fine meal and the long awaited conclusion to daily dinners. A good meal without dessert is like an unfinished culinary symphony. In today's fine restaurants, desserts are offered by the dozen, often brought to the table on a cart. They are all superb—just like the recipes in this chapter! Their preparation takes time and effort but it isn't in vain. Carefully savored bites, sparkling eyes, and satisfied faces make it all worthwhile. An interesting observation about desserts—next to children, men have the biggest sweet tooth. And it doesn't matter what you offer—puddings, fruit salads, sherbets or parfaits, soufflés or omelets, as long as they are made with the best ingredients available. You will find all the recipes on the following pages. And you'll enjoy the challenge of devising imaginative variations, too.

CREAMS, CUSTARDS, AND PUDDINGS

Cooked vanilla custard, often called *crème anglaise* in culinary parlance, is essentially a traditional vanilla sauce taken a step further. This luscious mixture is a great accompaniment to many desserts and is the basis for others, including the universally beloved Bavarian cream and many high-quality ice creams.

Chilled custard tastes great by itself or poured over fruit puddings, compotes, or coffee and chocolate mixtures. Do not refrigerate custards more than 2 days; if you do refrigerate them, whip again just before serving. If desired, fold in some whipped cream to lighten the custard.

BASIC VANILLA CUSTARD
(*Crème Anglaise*)

6 egg yolks
1/2 cup (100 g) sugar
2 cups (450 mL) milk
1/4 vanilla bean

Carefully separate eggs; there must be no white clinging to the yolk. Combine sugar and egg yolks and whisk, or beat slowly with an electric mixer, until the sugar is completely dissolved. Continue according to photographs and instructions. To thicken the sauce, pour mixture into a saucepan and cook over low heat, stirring constantly and running the whisk or spoon along the bottom of the pot to prevent custard from sticking. Remove from heat when the sauce thickens enough to coat a wooden spoon. Immediately place saucepan in ice water and stir occasionally until sauce is cool to prevent a film forming on top. Strain to remove any lumps.

Be very careful not to let the custard boil; the egg yolks will curdle and the custard will be ruined.

VANILLA CREAM

This smooth molded cream is among the most popular desserts becaue it is very easy to prepare. The egg yolk enriches the basic cornstarch pudding, which is also known as "flummery" or *blancmange*.

1/2 cup (100 g) sugar
1/4 cup (40 g) cornstarch
4 egg yolks
2 cups (450 mL) milk
1/2 vanilla bean
powdered sugar

In a small bowl, combine half the sugar and the cornstarch. Carefully separate egg yolks from whites (which if left behind will make the mixture lumpy). Combine egg yolks and 1 cup

1 Combine egg yolk and sugar. Separate eggs very carefully, making sure there is no white with the yolks. Place in a mixing bowl, add sugar, and whisk.

2 Whisk egg yolk mixture. Whisk or blend on low speed of mixer until the sugar is completely dissolved, about 10 minutes. Do not whip or beat vigorously.

3 Pour in vanilla milk. Combine milk and vanilla bean and bring just to a boil. Pour directly into yolk mixture, whisking constantly.

4 Heating sauce. Pour sauce into a saucepan and cook, stirring constantly, until thick enough to coat the back of a spoon.

142

(240 mL) milk with sugar/starch mixture and mix until completely smooth.

Pour remaining milk into a saucepan and sprinkle evenly with remaining sugar, which will sink to the bottom of the pan and prevent the milk from sticking. Add vanilla bean and slowly bring milk to boil over low heat. Do not stir milk during the heating process.

Stir egg and cornstarch mixture again to keep cornstarch from settling. Pour slowly and evenly into boiling milk, stirring constantly in a circular motion to prevent mixture from sticking. Continue stirring until all the ingredients are completely blended and the cream bubbles and thickens. Remove from heat immediately and pour into the molds of your choice, which have been rinsed with cold water. Refrigerate and unmold when chilled. If you want to use the cream as the basis for other recipes, pour it into a bowl and refrigerate. In either case, sift powdered sugar over the top to prevent a skin from forming on the surface. If you want it to maintain a spreadable consistency, place the saucepan of hot vanilla cream in a bowl filled with ice water to cool, or press the chilled pudding through a strainer to soften it.

This can be used wherever you need a creamy filling—in a fruit tart, for example, or another creamy dessert. You can also use this vanilla cream thickened with cornstarch to lighten buttercreams, and fold it into whipped cream to make a filling for layer cakes. Do not make vanilla cream more than 2 days before you plan to use it.

Molded Chocolate Cream with vanilla sauce and fresh raspberries—a dessert that delights adults and children alike.

MOLDED CHOCOLATE CREAM

1 envelope unflavored gelatin
¼ cup (60 mL) cold water
½ cup (100 g) sugar
⅓ cup (50 g) cornstarch
2 egg yolks
2 cups (45 mL) milk
½ vanilla bean
2 ounces (60 g) semisweet chocolate
4 1-cup (240-mL) molds or cups
powdered sugar

Sprinkle gelatin over ¼ cup water in a heatproof cup and let stand until softened, about 3 to 5 minutes. Place cup in a saucepan of gently simmering water until the gelatin is dissolved.

Combine sugar, cornstarch, egg yolks (with no hint of whites), and some of the milk and mix well. Bring the remaining milk to boil with the vanilla bean in a saucepan. Meanwhile, melt chocolate in a double boiler; stir into the hot milk. Slowly pour in the cornstarch mixture, whisking constantly and being sure to run whisk along the bottom of the pan so mixture doesn't stick. Cook until mixture bubbles and thickens. Remove from heat and add dissolved gelatin, mixing well. Rinse out molds or cups with cold water and fill with the hot cream. Dust with powdered sugar, cover, and refrigerate for approximately 2 hours, or until firm. Unmold and serve with a vanilla or fruit sauce.

TIP

Make buttercream using a whisk or a mixer on medium speed. Adding about ¾ cup (150 g) sugar to 2½ tablespoons (35 g) softened unsalted butter and mix until the sugar is completely dissolved. Cool. Stir Vanilla Cream or Chocolate Cream over ice water until it is the same temperature as the buttercream and add to buttercream 1 tablespoon at a time, mixing well.

BAVARIAN CREAM

1 cup (240 mL) milk
½ vanilla bean
2 egg yolks
¼ cup (50 g) sugar
2 envelopes unflavored gelatin
⅓ cup (80 mL) cold water
1 cup (240 mL) heavy cream

Prepare a basic Vanilla Cream (page 142) from milk, vanilla, egg yolks, sugar, and gelatin dissolved in water. Stir until gelatin is completely incorporated and strain to remove any lumps. For a lighter, more airy Bavarian that will not be unmolded, reduce the amount of gelatin to 1⅓ envelopes. Place the bowl of Bavarian cream in ice water to cool and thicken, stirring occasionally. Whip the cream until stiff. When Bavarian cream is thickened but still runny, remove from ice water and immediately fold in the whipped cream. Spoon into dessert glasses, individual molds, or a 3-cup (700-mL) mold.

Tap molds on the countertop to remove air bubbles, then chill for at least 2 hours. If unmolding, dip mold briefly in hot water and turn cream out onto plate. Serve with a fruit sauce or stewed fruits.

2 **Fold in whipped cream.** The vanilla cream must not be too thick, thin, or warm, or the whipped cream will liquefy.

3 **Bavarian cream** is the ideal consistency when it is thick and smooth and runs easily off a spoon. Immediately fill molds or dessert glasses; the Bavarian cream will firm up quickly.

Chocolate Surprise Bavarian Cream

Prepare a basic Vanilla Cream (page 142) using 4 egg yolks, ¾ cup (150 g) sugar, 1¼ cups (300 mL) milk, and 1 vanilla bean. Add 1 envelope unflavored gelatin, softened in ¼ cup water and dissolved in a pan of simmering water. Mix well. Whip 1¼ cups (300 mL) heavy cream until stiff and fold into vanilla cream to make a Bavarian cream. Divide ⅓ of the Bavarian cream mixture among eight ½-cup (125-mL) molds or dessert glasses. While it cools, melt 3 ounces (80 g) semisweet chocolate in a double boiler, let cool to lukewarm, and add with 1½ tablespoons Benedictine or brandy to the remaining Bavarian cream. Fill a pastry bag with chocolate mixture. Dip the tip ⅜ inch (1 cm) into the vanilla Bavarian cream already in the molds or glasses and fill the centers with the chocolate Bavarian cream mixture.

1 **Stir until cold over ice water.** Slowly stir the basic cream mixture with gelatin over a bowl filled with ice cubes until mixture is thickened. Remove immediately. Meanwhile, whip the cream until stiff.

4 **To serve,** briefly dip mold in hot water and unmold cream on a plate. The Bavarian cream shown here is served with a raspberry sauce.

FRUIT SAUCES AND COMPOTES

Fruit sauces can be made in many different ways. Nearly any fruit is suitable; try berries, apricots, peaches, and plums, as well as exotic fruit such as mango or kiwi. The riper the fruit, the less sugar you need to add when puréeing it. Some fruits, among them oranges and plums, are usually cooked first, though you will need to add sugar to cooked fruit. We recommend using fresh seasonal fruits. In an emergency, use good jams or jellies mixed with wine, fruit juice, or liqueur as flavorings. Add your own ideas and imagination to the following recipes to create sauces. (These recipes all yield 4 to 6 servings.)

Orange Sauce

Peel the colored rind from 1 orange. Cut into very fine julienne, blanch in boiling water, drain, and rinse under cold water. Strain ¾ cup (175 mL) freshly squeezed orange juice into a medium saucepan, add ½ cup (90 g) sugar and orange peel, and boil for 3 to 4 minutes. Stir in 1½ tablespoons Grand Marnier (or any other orange liqueur). Let cool before serving.

Raspberry Sauce

Purée 8 ounces (200 g) ripe raspberries in blender and strain to remove seeds. In a medium saucepan combine 6 tablespoons (70 g) sugar, ⅓ cup (75 mL) red Burgundy, and the peel of 1 lemon and bring to boil. Add raspberry purée and cook for 3 to 4 minutes. Remove and discard lemon peel and serve sauce hot or cold.

Apricot Sauce

Blanch 3 to 4 very ripe large apricots, peel, halve and remove pits. Purée apricots in blender and add 2 tablespoons fresh lemon juice, 1 tablespoon apricot liqueur, and 2 teaspoons brandy. Sweeten with a bit of powdered sugar, if desired.

Cranberry Sauce

Boil ⅓ cup (65 g) sugar with ⅓ cup (75 mL) water to form a syrup. Add 3 cups (300 g) very ripe cranberries and cook for 5 minutes. Strain and flavor with 1 tablespoon rum and a pinch of cinnamon. Cool. Stir ⅓ crème fraîche into sauce just before serving.

Pineapple Sauce

Purée the flesh of 1 medium pineapple in blender. Add ⅔ cup (125 g) sugar to 6 tablespoons (100 mL) water and bring to boil. Add ½ vanilla bean and ⅔ of the purée and boil for an additional 2 minutes. Stir in 1 tablespoon Cognac or brandy and the remaining purée. Let cool and serve.

Strawberry Sauce

Purée 1½ cups very ripe strawberries and strain. Melt ½ cup (125 mL) orange marmalade in a small saucepan over low heat. Remove from heat and stir in 1 tablespoon rum. Let cool, then add to purée and mix well.

Garnish Chocolate Bavarian Cream with whipped cream and grated chocolate and serve with a fruit sauce. Here it is served with Raspberry Sauce, Apricot Sauce, and Zabaglione.

LIME CREAM

1½ envelopes unflavored gelatin
¼ cup (60 mL) cold water
¾ cup (150 g) sugar
⅓ cup (75 mL) milk
3 egg yolks
1½ cups (350 mL) heavy cream
½ cup (125 mL) fresh lime juice
1 tablespoon orange liqueur

Sprinkle gelatin over ¼ cup water in a heatproof cup and let stand until softened, about 3 to 5 minutes. Place cup in a saucepan of gently simmering water until the gelatin is dissolved.

Combine sugar, milk, and egg yolks and, using a whisk or mixer, whisk until sugar is completely dissolved and mixture is smooth. Pour into a stainless steel bowl (or the top of a double boiler), place in a water bath over simmering water, and cook for 5 minutes, or until thickened. Add gelatin and mix well. Set bowl in a larger bowl filled with ice water. Whip cream until stiff and fold into egg mixture when it is cool and thick. Combine lime juice and orange liqueur and stir into cream. Chill.

WINE CREAM

2 envelopes unflavored gelatin
⅓ cup (80 mL) cold water
1 cup (240 mL) milk
½ cup (110 g) sugar
3 egg yolks
½ cup (125 mL) white wine
1 tablespoon brandy
grated peel and juice of ½ lemon
1 cup (240 mL) heavy cream

Sprinkle gelatin over ⅓ cup water in a heatproof cup and let stand until softened, about 3 to 5 minutes. Place cup in a saucepan of gently simmering water until the gelatin is completely dissolved.

Combine milk, sugar, and egg yolks and prepare as for Vanilla Cream (page 142). In a medium bowl blend gelatin into hot cream mixture and place bowl in ice water. Add wine, brandy, and grated lemon peel and juice. Whip cream until stiff. Stir wine mixture until thickened, fold in whipped cream, and spoon into dessert glasses. Refrigerate until ready to serve.

PASSIONFRUIT CREAM

4 to 6 passionfruit
1 generous pound (500 g) raspberries
1 envelope unflavored gelatin
¼ cup (60 mL) cold water
1 cup (240 mL) heavy cream
4 to 5 tablespoons sugar
3 egg yolks
1 tablespoon dark rum

Cut passionfruit in half, scrape out pulp, and strain into the top of a double boiler. Rinse raspberries only if necessary; carefully pat dry. Fill 4 to 6 dessert glasses with raspberries and refrigerate. Sprinkle gelatin over ¼ cup water in a heatproof cup and let stand until softened, about 3 to 5 minutes. Place cup in pan of simmering water until gelatin dissolves.

Whip cream and refrigerate. Place passionfruit pulp over simmering water, add sugar and egg yolks, and whisk for 3 to 5 minutes, or until foamy. Add gelatin and mix. Transfer bowl to larger bowl of ice water and beat for 2 to 3 minutes, or until cool. Stir in rum and cream. Spoon over berries.

MOUSSE AU CHOCOLAT

8 ounces (240 g) bittersweet or semisweet chocolate
1/4 cup (60 mL) strong coffee, preferably espresso
5 eggs, separated
1/2 cup (50 g) sugar
1 teaspoon vanilla
1/2 cup (125 mL) heavy cream
heavy cream, plain or whipped (garnish)

Break chocolate into chunks and melt in a double boiler over warm water. Stir in coffee, remove from heat, and let cool until chocolate is lukewarm. Beat egg whites until stiff, sprinkling in 1/4 cup of the sugar as they begin to thicken. Refrigerate. Combine egg yolks, remaining sugar, and vanilla and beat until foamy and sugar is dissolved. Whip cream until stiff. Add egg yolk mixture to the lukewarm chocolate and mix well. Fold in whipped cream, then carefully fold in egg whites. Cover mousse and refrigerate until firm. Serve with either whipped or plain cream.

LEMON CHEESE CREAM

3 eggs, separated
3/4 cup (150 g) sugar
finely grated peel and juice of 2 lemons
1/4 cup (60 mL) white wine
8 ounces (240 g) cream cheese, softened
1 cup (240 mL) heavy cream

Combine egg yolks and 1/2 cup (100 g) of the sugar in heavy-bottomed saucepan. Add the lemon peel, lemon juice, and white wine. Whisk over low heat until mixture is foamy and slightly thickened. Place pan in ice water and let cool, stirring occasionally. Meanwhile, beat cream cheese until fluffy and whip cream until stiff. Whip egg whites (using a whisk or mixer set at high speed) until foamy. Slowly add sugar and continue beating until stiff. Combine egg yolk mixture and cheese and mix well. Fold in whipped cream and egg whites. Spoon into dessert glasses and chill briefly before serving.

ZABAGLIONE

1/2 cup plus 2 tablespoons (120 g) sugar
4 egg yolks
1 whole egg
1/3 cup (80 mL) Marsala

Using a whisk or a mixer set at low speed combine sugar, egg yolks, and egg and stir until sugar is dissolved, but do not let mixture become foamy. Pour into a stainless steel bowl (or the top of a double boiler) and place over barely simmering water; the water must not touch the bottom of the bowl. Gradually add Marsala, whisking constantly until mixture is doubled in volume and reaches temperature of 115°F (45°C) on a candy thermometer. Immediately spoon into 4 dessert glasses and serve.

For variation, substitute white wine, champagne, or sherry for the Marsala. If you would like to serve this cold, whisk the zabaglione over ice until chilled; this will keep it from deflating.

PEACHES IN RED WINE

4 large peaches
2 cups (450 mL) red Bordeaux
¼ cup (60 g) sugar
½ cinnamon stick
1 tablespoon Cognac or brandy

Blanch peaches by placing them on a slotted ladle and dipping them into boiling water (see picture). Peel peaches, cut in half and remove pits. Combine wine, sugar, and cinnamon stick and bring to boil. Reduce heat, add peaches, and simmer for 5 minutes. Remove peaches and reserve. Boil wine and sugar mixture vigorously for 5 minutes, add Cognac or brandy, and return peaches to mixture. Cover and let cool. You may also poach plums and cherries in red wine according to this traditional recipe. Or try apples, pears, and gooseberries poached in white wine—they're great! Dried fruits such as plums, apricots, figs, or apples are a delicacy, too, when

1 Peel peaches. Dip peaches into boiling water and rinse under cold water so skin is easy to remove. Use the same method for peeling apricots and plums.

2 Poach fruit. Cook peaches in a simmering mixture of red wine with sugar and cinnamon. Remove them, reduce the wine mixture, add Cognac, and return peaches to pan.

simmered in red wine with honey, cinnamon, and whole cloves. Try wine with these fine compotes instead of the more usual water.

Poached fruits and compotes should be cooked very briefly to preserve their vitamins and enhance their flavors. Cook them gently in a syrup, flavored to your taste so they retain their shapes. The fruit should look as good as it tastes.

GERMAN FRUIT PUDDING

1 pound (450 g) fresh red currants (or substitute pitted ripe cherries)
8 ounces (200 g) raspberries
2 cups (450 mL) water
4 ounces (100 g) fresh gooseberries
²/₃ cup (120 g) sugar
6 tablespoons (60 g) cornstarch
10 ounces (300 g) fresh berries (raspberries, strawberries, or cherries)

Remove stems from currants and place currants in a medium saucepan. Add raspberries, cover, and bring to a boil. Remove from heat and let stand for 10 minutes. Strain the fruits, using a dough scraper to push as much fruit through the strainer as possible. Add enough water to the fruit juice to make 1 quart, add gooseberries and sugar, and bring to boil. Mix cornstarch with cold water, pour into hot fruit juice, and let boil briefly, stirring constantly. Cool pudding until lukewarm, gently stir in fresh berries, cover, and refrigerate until firm. Serve with fresh milk, cream, or vanilla sauce.

MELON BASKETS WITH COMPOTE

1¾ pounds (800 g) mixed fresh seasonal fruit (apricots, pears, currants, apples, cherries, peaches, kiwis, plums)
3 cups (700 mL) water
½ cup (100 g) sugar
1 cinnamon stick
3 to 4 whole cloves
peel of 1 lemon
1 small round watermelon

Rinse fruit and cut into equal-size pieces. Remove pits from cherries; leave gooseberries and currants whole.

Blanch apricots, peaches, and plums, peel and remove pits. Peel apples and pears, core, and cut into quarters. Peel kiwis. Combine water, sugar, cinnamon, cloves, and lemon peel in a medium saucepan and boil for 10 minutes. Add fruit and cook for 2 to 3 minutes. Remove from heat. Cover and let cool in liquid. Cut one end from the melon, scoop out the pulp and seeds, and decoratively cut the edge with a knife. Fill the melon "basket" with compote, cover, and refrigerate. If desired, add seeded melon pieces to chilled compote.

FROZEN DESSERTS

Frozen desserts are some of the most refreshing conclusions to a meal. Mold these in a loaf pan so you can serve them easily. You may create a number of different frozen variations, depending on which flavor you choose as the dominant one.

FROZEN VANILLA CREAM

For 10 servings
6 egg yolks
1 cup (200 g) sugar
1 cup (240 mL) milk
1 vanilla bean
1⅓ cups (300 mL) heavy cream
6-cup (1½-L) mold or loaf pan

This dessert consists of a basic vanilla cream with whipped cream added. Prepare the basic cream according to the instructions on page 142; then, using a whisk or mixer set on medium speed, beat hot cream for 15 minutes until cool and fluffy. Whip cream until stiff and carefully fold into the vanilla cream. Fill a chilled pan or mold with mixture and freeze for at least 3 hours. To unmold, dip pan in warm water and turn out onto a platter. Slice and serve with fresh fruits and sauces (see Index).

Frozen Espresso Mousse

Made with ¼ cup (30 g) ground espresso beans. Bring milk to boil, pour over coffee, and let stand for 5 minutes. Strain through cheesecloth. Let coffee-flavored milk cool, then use it in place of plain milk in the recipe for Frozen Vanilla Cream above. Flavor with Cognac or brandy. Serve with fresh kiwi slices and whipped cream.

Sherbets used to be made only from juices, wine, or champagne, but now we like to use fresh fruits that have been quickly puréed in a blender and strained to remove seeds and peel. A sugar syrup, flavored to perfection with ginger, cinnamon, or citrus peel, provides the right flavor and texture. Use powdered sugar in the sugar syrup because it dissolves quickly. You may vary the amount of sugar in your sherbets, or mix them with sweetened whipped egg whites or whipped cream. Sherbets will be especially light and creamy if you use an ice cream maker, but your freezer works well too, as we will show you here.

NECTARINE SHERBET

For about 8 servings
1 cup (200 g) sugar
½ cinnamon stick
2 bitter almonds or a few drops of almond extract
1⅓ cups (300 mL) water
1 generous pound (500 g) nectarines, pitted, peeled, and puréed
juice of 1 lemon or lime

Granités look like crushed ice. They are called *Granité* in French and *Granita* in Italian, and they are similar to the Persian *sharbate*, the original sherbet. Freeze wine, champagne, or the juice from tart fruits that have been only moderately sweetened. Because of the small amount of sugar, ice crystals form in the granité. They can be either fine or coarse, depending on how often you stir the mixture.

1 **Freeze sherbet.** Mix puréed fruits and flavored sugar syrup, freeze, and stir after 30 minutes.

2 **Stir again** when the sherbet begins to set at the edges. The more you stir, the longer it takes to solidify but the smoother your sherbet will be.

RED WINE GRANITÉ

For about 8 servings

³⁄₄ cup plus 2 tablespoons (180 g) sugar

³⁄₄ cup (175 mL) water

juice of 1 lime or lemon

juice of 1 orange

several mint leaves

1 bottle (750 mL) red Burgundy

whipped cream and fresh mint leaves (optional garnishes)

In a medium saucepan, combine sugar, water, citrus juices, and mint leaves and boil for 3 minutes. Cool. Add wine, stir, and pour mixture into a flat dish. Remove mint leaves and place pan in freezer, stirring granité once an hour until it reaches the desired consistency. Fill chilled glasses with granité and garnish with whipped cream and mint leaves or serve with fresh seasonal fruit.

Granité can either be coarse or fine: You can serve it as soon as it begins to freeze at the edges, or keep stirring the crystals back into the liquid center and wait until it is entirely crystallized.

HOT DESSERTS

DESSERT OMELET

For 2 to 4 servings
2 egg yolks
½ teaspoon grated lemon peel
½ vanilla bean
4 egg whites
6 tablespoons (80 g) sugar
¼ cup (30 g) flour
2 tablespoons (25 g) butter, browned and hot
1½ tablespoons (20 g) butter for frying
fruit salad or compote for filling
powdered sugar

Preheat oven to 400°F (200°C). Combine egg yolks, lemon peel, and vanilla and mix well. Whip egg whites until stiff with a whisk or mixer. Gradually add sugar and beat to form stiff peaks. Fold in egg yolk mixture, then sifted flour. Pour in hot browned butter and mix well.

Melt butter in an ovenproof skillet or omelet pan over medium heat. Pour in batter and smooth top with a spatula or dough scraper. Cook for 1 to 2

2 **Add flour.** Sift flour over batter and fold in carefully, then fold in the melted butter. Melt butter for frying in a skillet or omelet pan.

3 **Smooth out batter** after it has been poured into the skillet. You may cook the omelet, covered, on top of the stove or in the oven.

1 **Mix egg yolks and whites.** Using a wooden spoon or spatula, fold egg yolk mixture into stiffly beaten egg whites.

4 **Fold the omelet in half,** using a spatula, after it has been filled with fruit as shown. This omelet is filled with kiwis and strawberries flavored with orange liqueur.

minutes, or until golden on the bottom, then place in oven and bake for 10 minutes. Fill with fruit salad or fruit compote and dust with powdered sugar.

Warm desserts are very versatile because you can change the flavors easily during the preparation, and you can combine them with many toppings. Vanilla ice cream is delicious with the following recipe.

BAKED CHOCOLATE PUDDING

For 6 to 8 servings
powdered sugar
4 ounces (120 g) semisweet chocolate
6 egg yolks
1 teaspoon vanilla
½ cup (100 g) sugar
1 cup (100 g) finely grated almonds
6 tablespoons (50 g) fine breadcrumbs
vanilla ice cream, whipped cream, or hot chocolate sauce (garnish)

Butter a 2-cup (½-L) covered pudding mold and dust with powdered sugar. Preheat oven to 350°F (170°C). Melt chocolate over simmering water. Add egg yolks, vanilla, and half the sugar and whisk until foamy. Combine almonds and breadcrumbs. Beat egg whites until almost stiff, then slowly add remaining sugar and continue whisking until stiff peaks form. Stir ¼ of the whipped egg whites into the chocolate mixture with the almonds and breadcrumbs. Fold in the remaining egg whites. Pour immediately into the prepared mold and cover tightly. Set mold in a roasting pan and pour in enough hot water to come halfway up the side of the mold. Place pan on the bottom rack of the oven. Bake for 40 minutes and serve hot, topped with lightly whipped cream or hot chocolate sauce.

LIME SOUFFLÉ

For 4 servings
¾ cup (175 mL) milk
⅓ cup (50 g) flour
3½ tablespoons (50 g) butter
juice of 2 limes
grated peel of 1 lime
1 tablespoon lemon or orange liqueur
5 egg whites
4 egg yolks
⅓ cup (70 g) sugar
powdered sugar

Evenly butter a 5-cup (1¼-L) soufflé dish and sprinkle with sugar. Preheat oven to 400°F (200°C) and heat a water bath to 185°F (80°C) in oven.

Bring milk to boil. Knead flour and butter together and stir small portions into the milk until the mixture is smooth. Blend in lime juice, lime peel, and liqueur. Remove from heat and beat in 1 egg white. Pour mixture into a bowl and let cool to lukewarm. Gradually whisk in 4 egg yolks to make a silky cream. Combine 4 egg whites and sugar and beat slowly at first, then faster until stiff peaks form. Stir ¼ of the beaten egg whites into the soufflé mixture, then carefully fold in remaining whites. Immediately transfer to the soufflé dish and place the dish in a roasting pan that contains enough water to come halfway up the sides of the dish. Bake soufflé for 40 minutes. Remove from oven, dust with powdered sugar, and serve immediately. Even the most perfect soufflé will collapse soon after it is removed from the oven; this won't affect its taste, but it will affect its appearance!

You can vary lime soufflé easily—try using lemon, orange, or vanilla, for example. The baking dish must have smooth, straight sides so the soufflé will rise evenly. Fill the dish to no more than ½ inch (1½ cm) of the rim so the soufflé won't overflow.

153

We want to state right from the start that baking has never been as easy as it is today, thanks to modern kitchen equipment. Take it from one who has stirred grandmother's cake batter over and over again—by hand, with a lot of elbow grease—and who now realizes that machines do a great job of stirring, kneading, and mixing doughs. It's no exaggeration to say that practically all the work done is done for you when making cakes, cookies, pastries, meringues, and even yeast doughs. But if you prefer to mix and knead your doughs by hand, go ahead—grandmother's method still works well for classic doughs.

This chapter introduces classic doughs and invites you to vary them and create your own. We show you how to make such specialties as *Japonais*, based on a classic meringue that is filled with grated nuts and a smooth coffee buttercream. And we will show you how to make *Bûche de Noël*, a richly garnished French Christmas cake. The cake part of the Bûche de Noël is so good on its own that it doesn't really need any fillings or garnishes. But it's human nature to try to improve on perfection, and bakers are no exception.

BAKING WITH CLASSIC DOUGHS

QUICK CAKE LOAVES

3¾ cups (500 g) flour
1 tablespoon baking powder
1 cup (250 g) unsalted butter or margarine, softened
1¼ cups (250 g) sugar
4 eggs
¾ cup (175 mL) milk
finely grated peel of 1 lemon
pinch of salt
fine breadcrumbs (optional)
powdered sugar or frosting

1 **In the large bowl** of an electric mixer, combine all ingredients: First sift in flour and baking powder, then add softened butter, sugar, eggs, milk, lemon peel, and salt.

2 **Mix for 3 minutes** on high speed, scraping sides of bowl frequently.

Preheat oven to 400°F (200°C). Prepare the batter as shown in the photographs. Butter two 1-quart (1-L) loaf pans and dust with fine bread-crumbs. Better yet, line pans with parchment paper so cakes will come out easily—and you can leave the paper on the cakes to prevent them from drying out. Fill pans just over half full with batter and place on the bottom oven rack. Bake for 1 hour, or until a skewer inserted in the center comes out clean. Let cool for 10 minutes in pan before unmolding, then dust with powdered sugar or cover with frosting.

3 **Pour batter into a loaf pan** lined with parchment paper. To measure the paper, trace the pan's outline on the paper and cut with scissors.

MARGARETENKUCHEN

For the batter:
fine breadcrumbs
1 cup (250 g) butter
4 ounces (100 g) almond paste or marzipan
³⁄₄ cup (140 g) sugar
¹⁄₂ teaspoon vanilla
6 eggs separated
1 cup (120 g) flour
¹⁄₂ cup (80 g) cornstarch
For the glaze:
¹⁄₂ cup (150 g) apricot jam, melted and strained
1¹⁄₃ cups (180 g) powdered sugar
1 tablespoon rum or fresh lemon juice
sliced toasted almonds (optional)

Butter a 10-inch (25-cm) springform pan and refrigerate briefly to firm the butter. Dust pan with fine breadcrumbs, rotating the pan to cover the entire surface; discard excess crumbs.

On a cutting board, knead butter, almond paste, and ¹⁄₃ of the sugar into a soft dough. Place in a mixing bowl, add vanilla, and mix at medium speed, adding egg yolks one at a time. With clean beaters, whip egg whites at medium speed to soft peaks. Add remaining sugar and beat at high speed until stiff. Gently fold ¹⁄₃ of the egg whites into the batter. Sift flour and cornstarch over batter and fold in, then gently fold in remaining egg whites. Preheat oven to 350°F (190°C).

Carefully pour batter into prepared pan and smooth top so it will rise evenly. Place on the center rack and bake for 50 to 60 minutes, or until golden. Remove from oven and let cool for 10 minutes in pan, then unmold and brush with strained hot apricot jam. Combine powdered sugar and rum or lemon juice, mix well, and brush over glaze. If desired, sprinkle toasted almond slices around the base of the cake, as shown.

MARBLE CAKE

1 cup (250 g) unsalted butter or margarine, softened
1¹⁄₄ cups (250 g) sugar
4 eggs
1³⁄₄ cups (500 g) flour
¹⁄₂ cup (50 g) grated almonds
1 tablespoon baking powder
5 tablespoons (75 mL) milk
2 ounces (60 g) semisweet chocolate, grated
5 tablespoons (40 g) cocoa powder
2 tablespoons rum

Prepare batter as shown in photographs (page 156), or mix it by hand: Combine softened butter and 1 cup (200 g) sugar in a mixing bowl and beat until creamy. Add eggs one at a time and mix well. Combine flour with almonds and baking powder. Add flour mixture to egg mixture with 1 tablespoon milk. Combine remaining 4 tablespoons milk, ¹⁄₄ cup (50 g) sugar, chocolate, cocoa, and rum and mix well, then blend in ¹⁄₃ of the white cake batter.

Butter a 10-inch (25-cm) tube pan and pour in half of the white batter, then pour in the chocolate batter and cover with remaining white batter. Marble the cake by swirling through batters with a fork. Preheat oven to 350°F (180°C) and bake cake for 1 hour and 20 minutes, or until tester inserted in center comes out clean. Remove from oven and unmold cake onto rack immediately.

157

SPONGE CAKE LAYERS

For a layered fresh fruit cake
5 eggs, separated
½ cup (100 g) sugar
2 tablespoons (25 g) sugar
pinch of salt
½ teaspoon vanilla
¾ cup (100 g) flour
¾ cup (100 g) cornstarch

Prepare batter in a mixer as shown or by hand, using a whisk. Preheat oven and bake sponge cake. Remove from oven, unmold, and let stand overnight. The following day, cut the cake into three layers; it will be easier to handle than when freshly baked.

Filling for a Chocolate-Raspberry Cake

Pick through 10 ounces (250 g) fresh raspberries (set the prettiest aside for garnish). Whip 3 cups (700 mL) heavy cream with ¼ cup (50 g) sugar until stiff. Have ready 2 ounces (60 g) semi-sweet chocolate, 1 tablespoon orange liqueur, and 6 tablespoons (60 g) powdered sugar for the chocolate cream, and some cocoa for dusting the cake. Follow the photographs and instructions for details.

2 **Whip egg whites until stiff.** Begin beating egg whites at medium speed and slowly add ½ cup (100 g) sugar. Increase speed and beat until sugar is dissolved and egg whites are stiff.

3 **Beat egg yolks.** Whisk but do not beat egg yolks, 2 tablespoons sugar, and salt. Add vanilla.

5 **Stir some egg whites** into egg yolk cream. Remove whisks from egg whites and blend the egg white clinging to beaters with the egg yolk mixture.

6 **Blend the egg mixtures** by folding the remaining egg whites into the egg yolk mixture using a spatula or wooden spoon.

1 **Prepare pan.** Cover bottom of 10-inch (24-cm) springform pan with a square of parchment paper, then lock the ring around it to hold the paper in place. Butter the paper only, not the sides of the pan. Cut off excess paper with scissors.

4 **The egg whites are fully beaten** when they are silky, shiny, and stiff enough to cut with a knife. If you whip them by hand, use powdered sugar instead of granulated sugar, because it dissolves more quickly.

7 **Gradually sift flour** and cornstarch over egg mixture and carefully fold it in.

8 **Smooth batter** after it has been poured into the springform pan, using a scraper.

11 **Cut layers** with a knife, if desired, but the blade must be longer than the cake's diameter. Cut carefully, with a sawing motion.

14 **Spread cream over cake.** Spread some cream on top and sides of cake and refrigerate briefly. Then spread ⅔ of remaining cream over cake and make a pattern with a decorating comb.

9 **Bake cake immediately.** Place in a preheated 400°F (200°C) oven and bake for 35 minutes. Remove from oven and let cool in pan.

12 **Spread chocolate cream** on the bottom layer: Melt chocolate, add liqueur and 3 tablespoons powdered sugar, and whip until thick and smooth. Mix with ⅓ of the whipped cream.

15 **Garnish the cake.** Sift cocoa over top of tart. Fill a pastry bag with remaining whipped cream and, using a star tip, pipe rosettes around the top of the tart. Garnish with the reserved raspberries.

10 **Cut layers** with strong thread. Wrap thread around the cake ⅓ of the way down from the top, cross the ends, and pull the thread slowly through. Repeat.

13 **For the raspberry cream** toss berries with 3 tablespoons powdered sugar and mix with ⅓ of the whipped cream, crushing berries slightly. Spread mixture between layers.

16 **The cake is done** and should be eaten the day it is assembled. Cover (the cream will quickly absorb any foreign flavors) and refrigerate until ready to serve.

159

SWISS ROLL

6 egg yolks
½ cup (90 g) sugar
pinch of salt
grated lemon peel
4 egg whites
¾ cup (90 g) flour
3 tablespoons (45 g) butter, melted and cooled (optional)

Preheat oven to 450°F (230°C). Combine egg yolks with 1 tablespoon sugar, salt, and a bit of lemon peel and stir but do not beat. Prepare batter following photographs and instructions. If desired, mix 3 tablespoons melted butter into batter just before pouring it into the pan; this will make the cake richer but less fluffy. Place cake pan on the center oven rack and check after 6 minutes; cake is baked when it springs back when lightly pressed with finger. Do not overbake, or cake will dry out and may break during rolling.

1 **Beat egg whites.** Begin beating egg whites at medium speed, gradually add remaining sugar, and increase speed until egg whites are stiff and can be cut with a knife.

2 **Add egg yolk mixture.** Using a wooden spoon or spatula, carefully fold egg yolk mixture—made with egg yolks, sugar, salt, and lemon peel—into egg whites.

3 **Mix in flour.** Gradually sift the flour onto the batter and fold in.

4 **Pour batter into jelly roll pan.** Line pan with parchment paper and brush with softened butter, then pour in batter, using a rubber spatula to get all the batter from the bowl

5 **Spread batter evenly** with spatula. Bake in a preheated 450°F (230°C) oven for 10 minutes at the most; check after 6 minutes to see if cake is firm.

6 **Unmold cake** onto a moist kitchen towel when it is golden and springs back at the touch of a finger. Immediately remove paper and, if desired, brush top of cake with jam.

7 **Roll the cake** using the towel as an aid. Lift the roll with the towel and transfer it to a plate. Cover with towel and let cool.

Bûche de Noël is to the French Christmas what plum pudding is to England's. The whole family can help decorate the log-shaped cake.

BÛCHE DE NOËL

Bûche de Noël, or Christmas log cake, is a French holiday tradition. The "log" of light cake, has dark "annual rings." These rings are always made of buttercream flavored with either coffee or nuts. The cake is garnished with blossoms, leaves, and "mushrooms" made from marzipan and/or chocolate. Or, as shown here, cream flowers, leaves, and stems are piped onto the cake and sprinkled with chopped pistachios, and the cake is garnished with chocolate coins and candied cherries.

1 Swiss Roll (page 160)
For the filling:
3/4 cup (140 g) sugar
1/4 cup (40 g) cornstarch
3 egg yolks
2 cups (450 mL) milk
1 teaspoon vanilla
powdered sugar
5 ounces (130 g) semisweet chocolate
1 1/2 cups (350 g) unsalted butter, softened

Prepare Swiss roll as shown on the previous page, unmold on a moist towel, and cover with a second moist towel to keep cake soft so it doesn't break when rolled. The cake must be completely cool before it can be filled and rolled.

Combine sugar, cornstarch, egg yolks, milk, and vanilla to make a basic vanilla cream as shown on page 142. Dust with powdered sugar (to prevent a skin from forming on the surface) and cool. When cool, strain the cream and whisk until smooth and creamy. Break chocolate into pieces and melt in a double boiler. Cool over ice water, stirring occasionally. In a mixing bowl, cream softened butter at medium speed until fluffy and very light. Gradually add chocolate and basic cream mixture to butter and mix well. Spread half the buttercream evenly over the cake, leaving about 3/4 inch (2 cm) uncovered along the edge. Roll cake, using the towel to help you. Place the roll on a board, frost with a thin layer of buttercream, and transfer to a plate. Fill a pastry bag fitted with a small star tip with buttercream and pipe straight lines lengthwise along the roll. Use your imagination to garnish the "log." Our photograph shows "stumps" made of cake roll trimmings that have been cut off at an angle.

CHOCOLATE ROLL

4 ounces (120 g) semisweet chocolate
8 egg whites
3/4 cup plus 1 1/2 tablespoons (180 g) sugar
1 1/2 teaspoons vanilla
1/2 cup (60 g) flour

Prepare this cake as for Swiss Roll (page 160). Melt chocolate in a double boiler; cool. Whip egg whites until stiff; beat in sugar and vanilla. Add chocolate (batter will lose much of its volume). Gently fold in flour. Spoon batter into a pastry bag fitted with a round tip and pipe straight lines of cake batter into a jelly roll pan lined with buttered parchment paper. Bake in a preheated 400°F (200°C) oven for 10 to 12 minutes. Cool for 5 to 10 minutes, then unmold onto a sheet of wax paper. Cool completely, spread with desired filling—try raspberry jam or vanilla or coffee buttercream flavored with kirsch—and roll up.

MERINGUES

For 6 large or 30 small meringues

1 cup (240 mL) egg whites (about 8)

1¼ cups (250 g) superfine sugar

1½ cups (200 g) powdered sugar

¼ cup (30 g) cornstarch

Follow instructions and photographs to prepare the meringue. Use a pastry bag to pipe meringues onto wax paper or parchment paper. (Spoons won't work; the meringue mixture is too sticky.) Bake in a 250°F (120°C) oven for 3 hours, then turn oven off and leave meringues in oven to dry overnight. To remove meringues from wax paper, lift and moisten the underside with water. Wait a few minutes and meringues will come off easily.

Meringues stay tender and crisp for a long time if stored in a completely dry container. Make them ahead of time to have on hand, making sure they are stored airtight. Vary the flavor of the meringue by adding such ingredients as coffee or chocolate. The following variation, with almonds or hazelnuts, is renowned.

Meringue at its finest. As shown here, the meringue has been piped onto the baking sheet using a pastry bag with star tip. Meringues are dried rather than baked. Place in 250°F (120°C) oven, turn oven off after 3 hours, and leave meringues to dry overnight. They make wonderful desserts—try them with apple halves poached in wine and topped with vanilla sauce.

1 **Beat egg whites** until white and fluffy, using a whisk or a mixer at medium speed.

2 **Gradually add sugar,** reducing speed to low. When all sugar is added, increase speed to high.

3 **Continue beating** at medium or high speed until sugar is completely dissolved, egg whites are shiny, and the beaters leave a "track" in them.

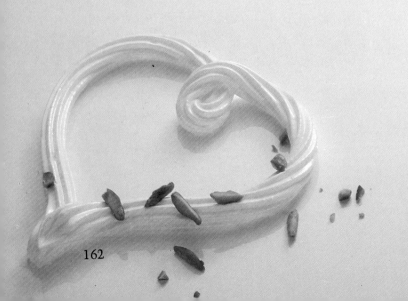

162

4 **Sift powdered sugar** and cornstarch onto wax paper. Add to egg whites, mixing wth spatula until completely smooth and free of lumps.

5 **Fill pastry bag.** Fold the top of pastry bag out and, using a scraper, fill bag with meringue. Shake bag so meringue settles at the tip. Close bag and twist.

6 **Pipe meringue,** holding the bag in one hand and pressing while guiding the bag with the other hand.

JAPONAIS

For 6 meringues, each 10 inches (25 cm) in diameter

10 egg whites

1½ cups (320 g) sugar

1¾ cups (250 g) grated toasted almonds or hazelnuts

6 tablespoons (50 g) flour

¾ cup (100 g) powdered sugar

1 teaspoon vanilla

Coffee Buttercream (see next recipe)

ground toasted almonds or hazelnuts (garnish)

Beat egg whites and sugar until stiff, as shown in the photographs. Combine nuts with flour and powdered sugar and fold into egg whites with vanilla. Pipe or spread meringue onto a parchment paper-covered baking sheet and bake in a 350°F (160°C) oven about 30 minutes or until golden, leaving the oven door open slightly so steam will escape. (The baking temperature may seem high for meringues, but it will make them particularly crisp and flavorful.)

For traditional *Japonais*, spread ⅓ of the coffee cream on each of 2 meringue layers, fluted side up, and place one on top of the other. Place the third layer on top of the other two, flat side up. Cut the sides so they are flush and straight, and evenly spread the remaining buttercream over the top and sides of cake. Sprinkle with ground toasted almonds or hazelnuts and press them in with a knife so they stick.

COFFEE BUTTERCREAM FILLING

¼ cup (30 g) ground coffee

1 cup (240 mL) milk

2 tablespoons cornstarch

2 egg yolks

⅓ cup (70 g) sugar

2 tablespoons powdered sugar

¾ cup (175 g) unsalted butter, softened

Pour ¾ cup (175 mL) boiling milk over coffee, let steep for 5 minutes, then strain through cheesecloth and squeeze coffee grounds completely. Discard grounds. Use this "coffee milk" to make the basic cream on page 142; sprinkle with powdered sugar and let cool. Cream butter and blend in the coffee-flavored basic cream a spoonful at a time. For best results, have the butter and coffee mixture at the same temperature.

163

SHORT PASTRY

For two 10-inch crusts

3 cups (380 g) flour

¾ cup plus 1½ tablespoons (200 g) butter, softened

1 cup (130 g) powdered sugar

1 egg

pinch of salt

vanilla or grated lemon peel (optional)

Sift flour onto a board and make a well in the center. To the well add softened butter (cut into chunks), powdered sugar, egg, salt and, if desired, vanilla or grated lemon peel. Blend these ingredients by hand or with 2 forks, then use a large knife to chop the mixture into coarse crumbs. (Or use a heavy-duty mixer with a dough hook to prepare the dough— see photographs.) Briefly knead mixture into a smooth dough and shape into a ball. Wrap with foil and refrigerate for 1 hour. Roll out the dough on a lightly floured board or marble slab. Wrap the dough around the rolling pin and unroll it into a 10-inch (25-cm) springform pan. Press evenly into pan and prick several times with a fork to prevent air bubbles from forming during baking. For "blind" baking, cover dough with waxed paper and fill with dried beans, rice, or pie weights to keep dough from losing its shape. Bake in a preheated 375°F (190°C) oven for 10 minutes.

LINZERTORTE

1¼ cups (160 g) powdered sugar

1 cup (250 g) butter, softened

2 egg yolks

2 tablespoons milk

1 teaspoon vanilla

½ teaspoon cinnamon

pinch of ground cloves

1⅔ cups (240 g) ground roasted almonds

1½ cups (180 g) flour

1 large round baking wafer (Oblate), optional

1 egg yolk, beaten with a little cream or milk (glaze)

⅔ cup (200 g) raspberry jam

sliced almonds (garnish)

Make dough either by hand, starting with flour and almonds blended together, or knead in a mixer. Continue

To make dough in a mixer, knead softened butter, sugar, and spices for 2 minutes. Add egg and knead for 3 to 4 minutes to make a smooth dough. Turn off machine, add flour, and mix in at low speed. Increase speed to medium and knead dough to a coarse crumb.

Linzertorte is raspberry tart with spices and ground almonds.

164

1 **In a mixing bowl** combine powdered sugar, butter, egg yolks, milk, vanilla, and spices and mix at medium speed to form a smooth dough. Add half of the almonds and mix well.

2 **Combine remaining almonds** with flour. Add to mixture in bowl and mix at slow speed until incorporated, then continue to mix at medium speed.

3 **Shape dough into a ball,** wrap, and refrigerate for 1 hour. Roll out half the dough and place in 10-inch (26-cm) springform.

as shown in photographs. If you don't have a large wafer (available in European delis), substitute with small ones or use none at all. Bake dough in 400°F (200°C) oven for 10 minutes, reduce heat to 325°F (160°C), and bake for 1 hour and 5 minutes more.

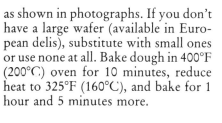

4 **Place** *Oblate* **on top** of dough. Leave ⅜ inch (1 cm) around edge and brush with egg yolk glaze.

5 **Roll some of the dough** into a thin 32-inch (82-cm) rope and lay it around the outside edge of the torte as shown, pressing gently.

6 **Spread jam evenly** over entire surface of dough (or wafer), using a flexible spatula.

7 **Make a lattice.** Roll remaining dough into ⅜-inch (1-cm)-thick ropes and arrange a lattice on top. Brush with egg glaze and sprinkle edge with almonds.

1 **Scald dough.** In a saucepan, combine water, butter, and salt and bring to boil. Add sifted flour all at once and stir with a wooden spoon until dough forms a smooth ball.

2 **Add eggs** to the cooled mixture one at a time and mix well. Use either a wooden spoon or a mixer with a dough hook.

3 **Shape rosettes.** Fill a pastry bag fitted with a star tip with dough and pipe large rosettes onto a buttered baking sheet, leaving enough space between for them to expand to several times their size.

CREAM PUFFS

1 cup (240 mL) water
6 tablespoons (100 g) butter
pinch of salt
2 cups (250 g) flour, sifted
5 to 6 eggs
1 teaspoon vanilla
powdered sugar

Cream puffs are made from a special cooked dough. Combine water, butter, and salt in a saucepan and bring to boil. Add flour and stir briskly until dough forms a ball. Let dough cool, then add eggs one at a time, beating well after each addition, until dough is resilient, shiny, and firm enough to be piped through a pastry bag or shaped as desired. Pipe large rosettes onto a buttered baking sheet and bake as described under picture 4. When cool, cut rosettes in half horizontally and fill with whipped cream, then dust with powdered sugar to make classic cream puffs.

4 **Bake cream puffs.** Preheat oven to 425°F (220°C). Place baking sheet on the center oven rack and pour a cup of water on the bottom of the oven—cream puffs need steam during baking. Immediately close oven door and do not open for 15 to 20 minutes. Remove from oven when golden and transfer cream puffs to a cooling rack.

1 **Brush wax paper** with a thin layer of butter. Refrigerate briefly so butter hardens.

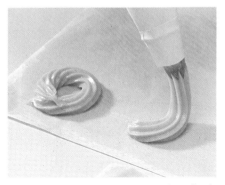

2 **Pipe rings using pastry bag** fitted with a large star tip. Make rings of equal size and leave plenty of space between them.

3 **Place in hot oil.** Pick up paper with doughnuts on it, turn it over, and lower the rings into the hot oil so that the butter on the paper melts and the doughnuts slip right off into the fat.

FEATHERLIGHT DOUGHNUTS

1 cup (240 mL) milk
6 tablespoons (100 g) butter
pinch of salt
1 teaspoon sugar
1¾ cups (230 g) flour
5 to 7 eggs
oil for deep-frying
powdered sugar

Make dough as for cream puffs (see previous recipe), cover with a moist towel to prevent a skin forming, and cool. Stir in eggs one at a time until dough is soft but keeps its shape when piped through a pastry bag. Pour 2 inches (6 cm) of oil into a shallow pan and heat to 350°F (170°C). Pipe rings of dough as shown here and deep fry. (Or drop dough by tablespoonfuls into hot oil.) Fry as shown in picture 4. Remove from fat and set on a cooling rack, dust with powdered sugar, and serve hot.

4 **Fry doughnuts** in a shallow pan or deep-fat fryer at 350°F (175°C). Fry the first side with the pan covered, turn doughnuts with a long-handled fork, and finish frying uncovered. Remove from oil with a slotted spoon.

YEAST DOUGHS

Yeast dough is good for both sweet and savory baked goods. All-purpose flour is excellent; wholewheat flour gives the dough more flavor but makes it heavier as well. Yeast doughs are always a success if you protect them against drafts and let them rise at room temperature.

BASIC YEAST DOUGH

3¾ cups (500 g) flour
1 cup (240 mL) lukewarm milk
1 ounce (30 g) fresh yeast or 1 envelope dry yeast
5 tablespoons (60 g) sugar
4 tablespoons (60 g) butter, melted and cooled
2 eggs
1 teaspoon salt

Prepare dough as shown in photographs and shape as desired. Yeast doughs are very versatile—you can make either filled or plain cakes, rolls, and small pastries with them.

2 **The yeast has risen enough** when it has doubled in volume and the flour on top cracks. Combine sugar, butter, eggs, and salt, blend well, and stir into yeast mixture.

4 **Shape dough into a ball,** dust with flour, and let rise in a covered bowl for 30 to 60 minutes, depending on room temperature.

3 **Knead the dough** until it is resilient and no longer sticks to the sides of the bowl. Begin kneading at low speed until all the flour is incorporated, then continue at medium speed.

5 **The dough has risen enough** when it is doubled in size. If you like a fine crumb, knead dough again, cover, and let rise an additional 30 to 60 minutes.

1 **Place flour in a mixing bowl.** Make a well in the center, add milk and crumbled yeast, and mix them together. Dust milk and yeast with flour, cover, and let stand for 15 minutes.

POPPYSEED STOLLEN

1 recipe Basic Yeast Dough (see previous recipe)

10 ounces (300 g) ground poppyseed

2 cups (450 mL) milk

½ cup (100 g) sugar

¼ cup (40 g) cornstarch

1 egg yolk

2 tablespoons (30 g) butter, softened

Mix dough as shown on previous page and let rise. Combine ground poppyseed with ¾ of the milk and bring to boil. Remove from heat and let soak for 10 minutes. Combine remaining milk, sugar, cornstarch, egg yolk, and softened butter and mix well. Add to poppyseed mixture and boil briefly, stirring constantly. Remove from heat and cool. Roll out yeast dough into a 12×16-inch (30×40-cm) rectangle. Spread with poppyseed filling and roll up dough from both sides towards the center. Butter a baking sheet, place stollen on sheet, and let rise until doubled in bulk. Bake in 425°F (220°C) oven for 15 minutes, reduce temperature to 400°F (200°C), and bake an additional 45 to 50 minutes.

QUICK YEAST DOUGH

Combine all ingredients in a heavy-duty mixer. Knead first at low speed until all flour is incorporated, then continue at medium speed until the dough is resilient and comes away from the sides of the bowl. Let dough rise longer than for regular bread; the resulting bread will be light and airy.

Braid the yeast dough and bake. Only a firm, resilient dough is suitable for braiding and shaping. To braid, roll dough into 3 strands of equal length that are thinner at the ends than in the middle. Place next to each other on a board and braid, starting at the center and working towards the end near you—then place an outer strand over the center one, turn loaf 180 degrees, and continue the braid to the other end. Press the end pieces tightly together so they don't come apart during baking. Cover braid and let rise until doubled in size. Brush with beaten egg, sprinkle with coarse sugar, and bake in a 400°F (210°C) oven for 30 minutes, or until golden.

A stirred yeast dough is made with more butter and eggs than other doughs. It is very soft and runny, almost like a batter, and it needs to be baked in a pan or a mold. Two typical products of this type of yeast dough are Gugelhupf and Savarin.

GUGELHUPF

3³/₄ cups (500 g) flour
1¹/₂ tablespoons (35 g) fresh yeast
¹/₂ cup (125 mL) lukewarm milk
10 tablespoons (150 g) butter, softened
¹/₂ cup (100 g) sugar
¹/₂ teaspoon salt
4 eggs
³/₄ cup (80 g) raisins
1 tablespoon rum
¹/₂ cup (50 g) chopped almonds
¹/₂ cup (50 g) finely chopped candied orange peel
fine breadcrumbs
powdered sugar

This favorite coffeecake is made from a basic recipe which may be altered by adding more raisins, currants, and/or other finely chopped dried fruits. Or dust the mold with chopped almonds or other nuts instead of breadcrumbs. Use a 9-inch (22-cm) tube pan. Preheat oven to 400°F (200°C), let the dough rise in the mold, and bake for 45 minutes. If Gugelhupf becomes too brown, cover with foil. To test for doneness, insert a skewer in center of Gugelhupf—if it comes out clean, the cake is done. Let cool briefly, unmold, cool completely, and dust with powdered sugar.

1 **To prepare sponge,** sift flour into a mixing bowl. Crumble yeast into the center and mix with some of the flour and the lukewarm milk. Dust yeast mixture with flour, cover, and let rest for 15 minutes.

2 **Add other ingredients.** Combine softened butter, sugar, salt, and 1 egg in a mixing bowl and mix at medium speed. Soak raisins in rum for 1 hour before using.

3 **Beat butter mixture** at high speed and add eggs one at a time. Continue beating until mixture is doubled in volume.

4 **Stir yeast dough.** Add sponge and flour to the butter mixture and mix in slowly with dough hook. Increase speed to medium and knead until dough is satiny and has some air bubbles.

5 **Cover dough and let rise** until doubled in size. Add raisins, almonds, and candied orange peel and mix well with a wooden spoon.

6 **Spread dough in a 9-inch (22-cm) tube pan** that has been buttered and dusted with breadcrumbs. Cover and let rise again until doubled in size.

Savarins are yeast cakes that are soaked in a flavorful sweet syrup after baking. The syrup may be flavored with liqueurs, spirits, or spices. You may also vary the dough by adding candied lemon and/or orange peel and raisins, according to your taste and imagination. This soaked yeast cake was named for the great French gastronome, Brillat-Savarin; today it is a classic dessert throughout the world. Large Savarins are baked in special 6-inch (15-cm) ring molds and single serving Savarins are baked in 4-inch (10-cm) molds. But any ring mold may be used to bake a Savarin. Savarins freeze well too. When freshly baked, let cool until lukewarm, wrap tightly, and freeze. Generally, any yeast cake similar to the ones in this chapter, containing raisins and dried fruit and baked in a fluted mold, can be turned into a Savarin.

SAVARIN WITH GRAPES AND STRAWBERRIES

For the dough:
2³/4 cups (350 g) flour
1 envelope dry yeast
6 tablespoons (80 mL) lukewarm milk
10 tablespoons (150 g) butter, melted
4 eggs
3 tablespoons sugar
½ teaspoon salt
½ teaspoon grated lemon peel
For the syrup:
1 cup (240 mL) water
6 tablespoons (80 g) sugar
1 thin piece of orange peel
2 tablespoons honey
2 tablespoons brandy or Cognac
1 teaspoon fresh lemon juice
For the glaze:
¹/3 cup (100 g) apricot jam

For the filling:
8 ounces (200 g) grapes
½ cup (125 mL) water
6 tablespoons (80 g) sugar
½ teaspoon vanilla
2 tablespoons brandy or Cognac
8 ounces (200 g) small strawberries
½ cup (125 mL) heavy cream, whipped until stiff

Make a sponge as shown in picture 1 and let rise. Blend lukewarm butter, eggs, sugar, salt, and lemon peel and pour into flour mixture. Knead by hand or with a dough hook at medium speed until dough is very resilient. Let rise again. Butter a ring mold, dust with flour, and fill halfway—at most—with the dough. Let rise again until doubled, then bake in a 400°F (200°C) oven for 25 to 30 minutes. Test for doneness with a skewer. For the syrup, combine water, sugar, and orange peel and bring to boil. Set aside to cool to lukewarm, then mix in honey and remove orange peel. Add brandy and lemon juice and mix well. Melt apricot jam and strain. Invert Savarin onto cooling rack placed over a bowl. Pour syrup over Savarin until it is well soaked, then brush with hot apricot jam glaze. Serve warm—try it with a wine sauce—or cold with compote or fresh fruit and whipped cream.

For the filling, peel the grapes and soak them in a syrup made from water, sugar, and vanilla. Add brandy and strawberries, mix gently, and set aside for 10 minutes. Fill center of Savarin with this mixture and garnish with whipped cream.

"To starve and to splurge is equally bad. To savor is everything." It wouldn't be a bad idea to adopt these words of the great epicure Brillat-Savarin who experienced heavenly delight in savoring sweets. Just look at this mouthwatering Black Forest cake. Dessert lovers will go into ecstacy over it, and with good reason, because it is among the most famous of European baked creations. And it is not even hard to make: It's a chocolate layer cake, filled with sour cherries and whipped cream lightly flavored with kirsch. A sweet poem that tempts the palate—and the other cakes in this chapter are equally delicious.

The buttercream layer cake has been a favorite for holidays and at special parties for more than a century. Our love for layer cakes developed in the 19th century, when pastry chefs took pride in creating masterpieces. Their recipes have endured over the years and found their way into everyday cookbooks as well as into the repertoires of great pastry chefs.

Let us stimulate your creativity. Follow these recipes first, then experiment—a sure path to mastery.

FANCY CAKES AND TORTES

BUTTERCREAM HAZELNUT CAKE

1 recipe Sponge Cake Layers (see Index)
For the buttercream:
1 recipe basic Vanilla Cream (see Index)
1 cup (250 g) butter, softened
½ cup (80 g) powdered sugar
2 ounces (50 g) Nutella (chocolate hazelnut paste, available at gourmet shops)
¾ cup (90 g) shelled hazelnuts
For the syrup:
3 tablespoons sugar
2 tablespoons water
1 tablespoon amaretto
semisweet chocolate (garnish)
42 toasted husked hazelnuts (garnish)

The day before, bake the sponge layers and let stand overnight to firm before cutting. Prepare the vanilla cream as well.

To make vanilla buttercream, combine butter, powdered sugar, and the prepared vanilla cream in a mixing bowl and blend well.

Melt the Nutella in a double boiler. Remove from heat and let cool until it starts to solidify. Toast hazelnuts in a 400°F (200°C) oven until the skins crack, then shake nuts in a strainer to remove skins. Grind the hazelnuts in small batches, using a manual nut grinder, food processor, or blender. Add ground nuts and Nutella to buttercream and mix well. Bring sugar and water to a boil, let cool, and add amaretto. Cut sponge cake into 3 layers (see page 159). Soak each layer with the amaretto syrup and spread ¼ of the buttercream on each, then stack the layers. Spread all but a few table-spoons of the remaining buttercream evenly on top and sides of cake, using a metal spatula. Reserve remaining buttercream for garnish.

Follow the photographs and the instructions for garnishing the torte.

3 **Add ground hazelnuts** at low speed, then add melted, cooled Nutella and mix briefly. Spread mixture on cake layers.

1 **Cream butter until fluffy.** Add powdered sugar and mix at low speed, then increase speed to high and whip until mixture is fluffy and has significantly increased in volume.

4 **Scrape thin shavings** of cool, firm chocolate over cake using the sharp edge of a knife blade.

2 **Add vanilla cream** by tablespoons, mixing at medium speed. It should be at the same temperature as the butter.

5 **The cake is done** when it is evenly covered with chocolate shavings. Use a pastry bag with a plain tip to pipe dots of reserved buttercream around the edge of the cake. Place a whole hazelnut in the center of each dot.

ALMOND CHERRY TORTE

2 layers of Japonais *made with almonds (see Index)*	
4 eggs, 2 egg yolks	
²/₃ cup (125 g) sugar	
³/₄ cup (90 g) flour	
¹/₃ cup (40 g) cornstarch	
4¹/₂ tablespoons (70 g) butter, melted and cooled to lukewarm	

For the filling and syrup:

¹/₂ recipe buttercream (see previous recipe)	
6 tablespoons (100 mL) kirsch	
¹/₃ cup (70 g) sugar	
¹/₄ cup water	

For the garnish:

¹/₂ cup (50 g) sliced toasted almonds	
powdered sugar	
12 candied cherries	

Bake two 10-inch (26-cm) almond *Japonais* layers. Prepare sponge cake layer in 10-inch (26-cm) springform pan using eggs, yolks, sugar, flour, cornstarch, and melted butter, following directions for sponge cake layers on page 158. Prepare buttercream, adding 1 tablespoon kirsch at the end. Bring sugar and water to a boil, cool, and mix with remaining kirsch. Pour over the cake. Assemble the cake as shown and decorate.

1 **Spread ¹/₃ of the buttercream** evenly over the first *Japonais* layer, using a metal spatula. Place the cake, baked the day before, carefully on top.

2 **Soak with a kirsch-flavored syrup,** spreading with a pastry-brush.

3 **Spread remaining buttercream** on top and sides of cake, then top with second *Japonais* layer. Press almond slices along the sides and sift powdered sugar over the top. Garnish with cherries.

175

HOW TO WHIP CREAM

The cream should have a 30 percent butterfat content, and it should be at least two days old. Fresh, lower-fat cream does not reach the desired volume and it will separate and liquefy quickly once beaten. The older the cream, the better it whips; it stays stiff and reaches 2 to 3 times its volume. You can store heavy cream for 10 days or more at 40°F (5°C), covered tightly, before it begins to sour. Whipped cream easily absorbs flavors, so keep it tightly covered and away from strong-smelling foods. Try mixing the cream with freshly mashed fruit to enhance its flavor. Always chill utensils used for whipping cream, including the bowl, and we recommend using a stainless steel bowl. Combine cream and sugar (3 tablespoons sugar to 2 cups [450 mL] heavy cream) in a chilled bowl (photograph 1). Beat at high speed until thickened (picture 2). Reduce speed to medium and beat until cream is stiff and firm (picture 3). Use immediately if possible.

BLACK FOREST CAKE
(see photograph on page 172)

For the cake:
5 eggs
¾ cup (150 g) sugar
¾ cup (100 g) flour
6½ tablespoons (60 g) cornstarch
⅓ cup (50 g) cocoa powder
3½ tablespoons (50 g) butter
For the filling and garnish:
1 1-pound (450-g)-can tart cherries
1 cup (240 mL) cherry juice
pinch of cinnamon
2½ teaspoons cornstarch
7 tablespons (100 g) sugar
1 tablespoon water
¼ cup (60 g) kirsch
3 cups (700 mL) heavy cream
semisweet chocolate

The day before, prepare cake, following directions on page 158, adding cocoa to the flour mixture, and blending in melted butter at the end.

Drain cherries, reserving the juice. Bring juice and cinnamon to a boil. Mix cornstarch with a bit of water and add to juice. Bring to boil, remove from heat, and add cherries, reserving the nicest ones for garnish. Let cool.

Divide the cake into 3 layers. Bring 2 tablespoons sugar to a boil with the water, remove from heat, and mix in kirsch. Whip cream and 5 tablespoons (60 g) sugar until stiff. Fill a pastry bag fitted with a star tip with ⅓ of the cream. Spread a thin layer of cream on the bottom layer, pipe 4 rings of cream on top, and fill the gaps with the cherry mixture. Top with the second layer, sprinkle evenly with half the kirsch syrup, and cover with cream. Top with the third layer, soak with remaining kirsch syrup, and pipe 16 cream rosettes around the edges of the cake. Place 1 cherry in the center of each rosette. Shave chocolate over top.

FLAKY RASPBERRY TORTE

For the layers:

4½ tablespoons (70 g) butter

¼ teaspoon salt

1 teaspoon sugar

1 tablespoon water

1½ cups (200 g) flour

5 eggs

For the filling:

10 ounces (300 g) fresh raspberries

6 tablespoons (50 g) powdered sugar

1 tablespoon framboise

1 quart (1 L) heavy cream

6 tablespoons (80 g) sugar

powdered sugar

Prepare dough for layers following the directions on page 166 for cream puffs, but spread on baking sheet as shown. Bake 5 layers individually in a 450°F (230°C) oven until dough is golden and crisp. Remove from oven and let cool. Continue as shown under photograph 2.

Save 16 nice raspberries for garnish. Toss the remainder with powdered sugar and framboise, cover, and refrigerate for 30 minutes. Whip cream with sugar until stiff. Fold ⅔ of the whip-

Flaky Raspberry Torte is a very light cream cake; it should be eaten soon after it is assembled because it loses its crispness very quickly.

ped cream quickly and thoroughly into the raspberry mixture. Spread half of the raspberry cream evenly over each of 2 layers (photograph 3). Place the third layer on top, spread ¾ of the remaining cream evenly over top and sides of torte, and sprinkle with coarse crumbs made from 2 crushed cake layers. Fill a pastry bag fitted with a star tip with the remaining cream and pipe 16 rosettes around the edge of the torte. Place 1 raspberry on each rosette and dust entire surface with powdered sugar. Serve torte no more than 2 to 3 hours after it has been assembled.

1 Make thin layers. Butter a baking sheet and dust with flour. Mark a circle 10 inches (26 cm) in diameter in center of sheet and spread ⅕ of the dough evenly over the circle. Bake and repeat for 4 additional layers.

2 Chop crumbs. Reserve the 3 nicest layers for the tart, trimming the edges so they are perfectly round. Chop the remaining 2 layers and all scraps into crumbs by first cutting them into strips, then cutting strips into fine pieces.

3 Fill torte. Spread raspberry cream evenly over 2 layers and assemble with the third layer on top. If you like, substitute other flavorful berries for raspberries—try small strawberries.

177

As far back as 1418 the apple tart was a common Lenten dish in Europe. It was spiced with cinnamon, which blends perfectly with the fruit. Since then the apple tart has multiplied, so to speak. Countless recipes for baking with apples have been developed, along with recipes for all the other fruits growing in Mother Nature's garden.

No matter the variety, fresh fruits are wonderful for baking. They are best in season, but the season for fruits—and the cakes made with them—can be extended by separately freezing an entire baked sheet cake and the fruit. When you are ready to enjoy it, combine them for the final dessert.

Baking has become a popular hobby and it has never been as easy to do as it is now.

BAKING WITH FRUIT

Simple cakes topped with fresh seasonal fruits are perfect Sunday desserts. The recipes on the following pages show how you can improve delicious plain cakes with new ideas. Try cherries, blackberries, plums, and apples for summery delights.

BLUEBERRY CAKE

Prepare a yeast dough according to the recipe for apricot cake (see Index), using 2⅓ cups (300 g) flour.

1 quart (1 kg) blueberries
2⅔ cups (350 g) flour
1 cup (200 g) sugar
½ teaspoon cinnamon
¾ cup (200 g) butter, melted

Roll out yeast dough; place on a greased rimmed baking sheet and prick several times with a fork to prevent air bubbles from forming. Distribute blueberries evenly over entire surface of dough. Combine flour, sugar, cinnamon, and melted butter in a bowl and knead into crumbs with your fingers. Sprinkle over blueberries, then let cake rise to double its height. Preheat oven to 425°F (220°C) and bake blueberry cake on the center rack for 30 minutes, or until dough is cooked through.

RHUBARB CAKE

Short Pastry (see Index), made with 3 cups (380 g) flour
1 cup plus 3 tablespoons (150 g) ground almonds
½ cup (75 g) fine breadcrumbs
4½ pounds (2 kg) rhubarb
¾ cup (150 g) sugar
½ teaspoon cinnamon
4 egg whites
1 cup (200 g) sugar

Roll out pastry, place on a rimmed baking sheet, and prick several times with a fork to prevent air bubbles from forming. Preheat oven to 400°F (200°C) and bake pastry for 10 minutes. Lightly toast almonds, mix with breadcrumbs, and sprinkle over dough. Cut rhubarb into ⅜-inch (1-cm) slices and distribute them evenly over the cake. Sprinkle with ¾ cup (150 g) sugar, mixed with cinnamon.

Bake on the center oven rack for 30 minutes. Beat egg whites until stiff, slowly add remaining sugar and continue beating until stiff and glossy. Spread over cake or pipe an egg white lattice over cake using a pastry bag. Place the cake on top oven rack and bake for 10 more minutes, or until meringue is golden.

APRICOT CAKE

2⅓ cups (300 g) flour
2 tablespoons dry yeast
½ cup (125 mL) milk
2½ tablespoons butter
1 egg yolk
3 tablespoons sugar
pinch of salt
1 teaspoon grated lemon peel
For the filling:
¼ cup (50 g) sugar
⅓ cup (45 g) cornstarch
2 egg yolks
2 cups (450 mL) milk
1 teaspoon vanilla
8 ounces (200 g) almond paste or marzipan
For the topping:
2¾ pounds (1¼ kg) apricots
⅔ cup (80 g) ground blanched almonds
½ cup (150 g) apricot jam

Prepare dough according to directions on page 158 and place on a rimmed baking sheet as shown here. For the filling, prepare a vanilla cream (see page 142) using the ingredients listed above. Add the almond paste to the filling, mix well (photograph 3), and spread over the dough. Arrange apricot halves over cream as shown, sprinkle with almonds, and bake. Heat apricot jam, strain, and brush over cake.

1 **Roll out the dough.** On a floured board, roll dough out to the same size as the baking sheet. Roll up dough starting from the small side.

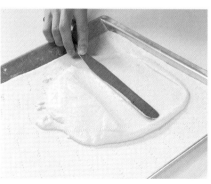

4 **Spread filling over dough,** going right to the edges and the corners. A spatula or dough scraper works well.

2 **Butter a baking sheet** and unroll dough on sheet, pressing tightly against edges and rim.

5 **Arrange apricots on filling.** Dip fresh apricots briefly in boiling water, remove skin, cut in half, and remove pits. Carefully arrange apricots on cream cut side down.

3 **Combine almond paste** with 2 tablespoons of the vanilla cream and blend in mixer at low speed. Increase the speed and add remaining vanilla cream a spoonful at a time.

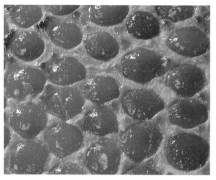

6 **The cake is done** when it has baked for 25 minutes. Place on the center rack in a preheated 400°F (200°C) oven. Apricot cake should be eaten as soon as possible after baking.

RASPBERRY TARTLETS

Short Pastry (see Index), using 1½ cups (190 g) flour

Vanilla Cream (see Index), using 1 cup (240 mL) milk

6½ ounces (180 g) almond paste or marzipan

1 tablespoon framboise

1 generous pound (500 g) raspberries

powdered sugar

Prepare pastry and bake in eight 4-inch (10-cm) tartlet pans in a preheated 375°F (190°C) oven for 10 minutes. Let cool for 5 minutes, then unmold and cool completely. Mix vanilla cream, almond paste, and framboise. Fill tart shells as shown. Depending on the season, you may garnish tarts with blackberries, blueberries, small strawberries, sliced kiwis, or chopped figs instead of raspberries; use the freshest, ripest fruits available.

2 **Line molds.** Wrap the pastry around rolling pin and unroll into molds. Press dough into molds with your thumb and trim off any excess.

5 **Spread cream in tartlets.** Divide cream equally among the shells and spread it evenly, being sure to go right to the edges so the fruit doesn't soak the crust.

3 **Fill molds with beans,** rice, or pie weights to maintain the pastry's shape—but first prick the pastry several times to prevent air bubbles forming, and place wax paper on pastry under the weights.

6 **Fill with raspberries.** Arrange fresh, clean fruits next to each other on the cream, then sift powdered sugar evenly over tartlets.

1 **Roll out pastry.** Divide chilled pastry into 2-ounce (60-g) pieces, knead briefly until smooth, shape into balls, and roll into 6-inch (15-cm) rounds on a floured surface.

4 **Remove weights** after baking and peel paper off, using a pointed knife.

7 **The raspberry tarts are ready to serve** after they have been broiled just long enough to lightly caramelize the sugar.

ORANGE MERINGUE TARTLETS

Short Pastry (see Index), using 1½ cups (190 g) flour

For the filling:

juice and grated peel of 1 lime

1 cup (240 mL) fresh orange juice

14 tablespoons (200 g) butter, softened

½ cup (120 g) sugar

4 egg yolks

1 tablespoon cornstarch

grated peel of 1 orange

For the meringue and garnish:

4 egg whites

½ cup (120 g) sugar

½ cup (50 g) sliced toasted almonds

1 large orange, peeled and sectioned

Line eight 4-inch (10-cm) tartlet pans with pastry, cover with wax paper, and fill with rice, dried beans, or pie weights for blind baking. (You can use the weights or beans repeatedly.) Lightly brown tartlets in preheated 375°F (190°C) oven for about 10 minutes; cool. Remove weights and wax paper and carefully unmold tart

2 **Extract juice** of both fruits with an electric juicer for quick results and an optimum amount of liquid. You may need the juice of more than 1 orange to make 1 cup.

3 **Cook the filling.** In a saucepan combine juice, peel, butter, sugar, egg yolks, and cornstarch and whisk over low heat until boiling. Let cool over ice water, stirring.

5 **When tarts are ready,** garnish them with toasted almond slices and orange sections.

shells. Prepare filling according to instructions accompanying the photographs. Remove from heat, place in a bowl of ice water, and stir until cool, which should take just a few minutes; this will prevent a film from forming on top. Spread filling into cooled tartlet shells. Whip egg whites and sugar to a meringue (see page 162) and spoon over cream or pipe through a pastry bag fitted with a star tip. Broil briefly until meringue is golden. Serve tartlets on the same day. If you prefer, make one 10-inch (26-cm) tart instead of individual tarts.

Making Short Pastry Ahead of Time

Pastry will stay fresh for 8 to 10 days if tightly wrapped in foil and refrigerated, or you may freeze it for up to 3 months. Partially bake pastry shells before freezing them; to use frozen shells, let them thaw and bake again in a hot oven until the butter flavor has fully developed and the shells are golden.

1 **For the filling,** grate the lime and orange peels after you have rinsed fruit well under hot water. You may substitute lemon for the lime, if desired.

4 **Pipe or spread meringue** on tarts after they have been filled. Bake or broil until meringue is golden.

183

Many fruits develop their fullest flavor and aroma only when they are cooked or baked, as the following recipes show.

CURRANT MERINGUE TART

Short Pastry (see Index), using 1½ cups (190 g) flour
1 recipe Swiss roll (see Index)
6 tablespoons (120 g) currant jelly
1 generous pound (500 g) red currants or sour cherries
6 egg whites
1 cup (210 g) sugar
¼ cup (20 g) toasted almond slices

Prepare pastry as shown on page 164, roll out, and fit into a 10-inch (26-cm) tart pan. Prick pastry with a fork and bake in a 375°F (190°C) oven for 20 minutes, or until crisp.

Prepare Swiss roll batter as shown on page 160, but divide between 2 buttered 10-inch cake pans. Bake in a preheated 450°F (230°C) oven for 10 minutes.

Spread half of the jelly on short pastry, place 1 cake layer on top, cover with remaining jam, and add the second cake layer. Firmly press layers together.

Stem currants, reserving 12 to 16 clusters for garnish. For meringue, beat egg whites, slowly add sugar, and continue beating until stiff. Fold half of the meringue into the currants and spread mixture over the top of the tart. Spread all but 2 to 3 tablespoons of remaining meringue on top and sides of cake, and decorate the sides by pulling the meringue towards the top using a decorating comb. Fill a pastry bag with the remaining meringue and garnish the top of the tart with meringue rosettes. Sprinkle sides with almond slices and bake in a preheated 475°F (250°C) oven until the tips of the meringue are golden. Remove from oven, let cool, garnish with currants, and serve.

PLUM TART

½ recipe for Short Pastry (see Index), using ¾ cup (100 g) flour
3 envelopes unflavored gelatin
½ cup (125 mL) cold water
½ cup (100 g) sugar
3 tablespoons water
2¼ pounds (1 kg) pitted plums
3 tablespoons cornstarch
½ cup (125 mL) heavy cream

Prepare half a recipe of short pastry. Line a 9-inch (23-cm) springform pan with pastry, prick with a fork, line with wax paper, and fill with dried beans, rice, or pie weights. Place on the center rack of a preheated 375°F (190°C) oven and bake for 10 minutes. Remove weights and paper and bake pastry for an additional 10 minutes, or until golden.

Soften gelatin in ½ cup (125 mL) cold water in a heatproof cup then place cup in simmering water until gelatin is dissolved. Combine sugar, 3 tablespoons water, and plums and bring to a boil to fully develop the flavor of the plums. Mix cornstarch with a bit of water to make a thin paste, add plums, stir well, and bring to boil. Add gelatin, remove from heat, and place in a bowl of ice water to speed the cooling process, stirring occasionally until mixture thickens. Pour into pastry shell, spread evenly, and refrigerate until firm. Whip cream and use to garnish tart.

TARTE TATIN

For the pastry:
1¼ cups (150 g) flour
5 tablespoons (80 g) butter
2 teaspoons powdered sugar
1 egg yolk
½ teaspoon salt
3 to 4 tablespoons water
For the filling:
5 tablespoons (80 g) butter
¾ cup (150 g) sugar
2¾ pounds (1¼ kg) tart baking apples

Prepare short pastry as shown on page 164, chill, knead, and roll out so it is a bit larger than a 9-inch (24-cm) pie pan.

Spread pie pan with 5 tablespoons (80 g) butter and sprinkle with the sugar, rotating the pan to coat evenly. Refrigerate until butter is firm. Peel, quarter, and core apples. Stand apple quarters tightly together in pan. Wrap pastry around a floured rolling pin and lay it over apples. Press the edges of dough to the pan's rim to seal in apples. Prick the pastry several times with a fork to allow steam to escape during baking. Preheat oven to 425°F (220°C), place pan on center rack, and bake for 45 minutes. Do not unmold tart immediately or you will lose the juices, but don't wait longer than 5 to 8 minutes because the caramelized sugar will harden and stick to the pan.

July is the season for tart, refreshing red currants. These transparent red berries deserve to be used in a masterpiece like the tart shown here.

SELECTED PASTRIES

If you look up the melodious French word *pâtisserie* you will find the definition "confectionery, cakes, and pastry." But somehow it seems inadequate to call the repertoire of magnificent French creations just "cakes and pastries." They are more like works of artistic craftsmanship, filled with the best butter, cream, apricot jam, and delicately garnished fondant. They are a visual delight and pure joy for the palate. *Pâtisserie* served with coffee or espresso makes the gourmand's world perfect.

The pastries in this chapter are the best of the best. They will spoil your family and friends all year round.

CREAM POCKETS

1 recipe for Swiss roll (see Index)

2½ tablespoons butter, softened

filling (see suggestions below)

powdered sugar

Line 3 baking sheets with parchment paper and, with a pencil, mark 18 to 20 circles on each; circles should be 4½ inches (12 cm) in diameter and spaced ¾ inch (2 cm) apart. Preheat oven to 425°F (220°C). Prepare cake according to directions, carefully folding in the softened butter at the end. Fill a pastry bag with the batter and pipe it into the marked circles, beginning at the outside and working in a spiral toward the center. Bake for 10 minutes, or until light golden, being careful not to let circles brown at the edges or they will break when you fill them. Remove from oven and invert the cake circles, still attached to the paper, onto another piece of parchment or wax paper. Remove paper from circles and fill them as desired. Dust with powdered sugar before serving. Filling suggestion: purée 12 ounces (350 g) fresh fruit (try raspberries or strawberries), mix with 1½ envelopes dissolved unflavored gelatin, sweeten to taste with sugar. Let cool, then fold in cream.

Here, small cake circles are filled with vanilla cream and with strawberry cream. You may omit the gelatin from the fruit and cream mixture if you plan to serve the "pockets" immediately.

PETITS FOURS

For 35

13 ounces (360 g) almond paste

6 egg yolks

1 teaspoon grated lemon peel

½ cup (120 g) sugar

5 egg whites

1 cup minus 2 tablespoons (120 g) flour

½ cup (150 g) apricot jam

½ cup (70 g) powdered sugar

1 generous pound (500 g) fondant (cooked sugar frosting)

1 tablespoon rum

Line 2 rimmed baking sheets with parchment paper. Preheat oven to 425°F (220°C). In a large mixing bowl combine 3 ounces almond paste, egg yolks, lemon peel and ¼ cup (60 g) sugar and mix well. Beat egg whites until very stiff, slowly adding remaining sugar. Fold egg yolk mixture into egg whites. Gradually sift flour over mixture and fold in. Spread evenly on baking sheets and bake for 8 to 10 minutes, but do not let cakes brown. Unmold immediately and continue as shown in photographs.

Knead remaining almond paste into a ball and roll out on a board dusted with powdered sugar to prevent it from sticking, then lay it on top of the cake. Place a board or baking sheet on top to help layers hold together. If desired, tint fondant with food coloring or fruit juice, or brush with an egg white glaze and garnish with sugar dragees and candied fruit. This is a classic confection that may be filled with cream or flavored with liqueur.

1 **Spread apricot jam.** Turn first cake layer out on wax paper. Melt apricot jam, strain, and spread ⅓ of it on cake.

2 **Turn second layer out** on top of the first layer and remove paper. Spread with half the remaining apricot jam and place on a clean baking sheet.

3 **Cover with almond paste.** Knead 10 ounces almond paste with powdered sugar and roll out to the size of the baking sheet. Wrap around the rolling pin and unroll over cake.

Egg White Glaze

Combine 1 egg white,
2 teaspoons fresh lemon juice,
and 1 cup plus 2 tablespoons
sifted powdered sugar and whisk
until mixture is smooth and
white. Thicken with more
powdered sugar if necessary.
cover with a moist towel until
ready to garnish petits fours.

4 **Cut petits fours.** Cover the cake with wax paper and place a light weight (a thick baking sheet is good) on top. Let stand for 24 hours. Cut cake into 1⅝-inch (4-cm) squares as shown.

5 **Glaze top.** Brush strained apricot jam thinly over squares and let dry. Melt fondant in a double boiler—do not let it get warmer than 100°F (35°C).

6 **Cover with fondant.** Add rum to fondant and stir well. Dip petits fours into fondant upside down, then place on a rack to harden.

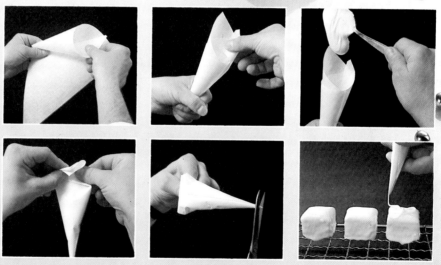

HOW TO DECORATE WITH A PASTRY BAG

Make a bag by cutting a piece of parchment paper in half diagonally. 1. With the thumb and index finger of your left hand, grasp the paper in the middle of the long side. With your right hand, fold paper in wards toward the left. Continue bringing paper around, keeping hold of the bag's tip. 2. Fold the projecting end of the paper towards the inside to close and secure the bag. 3. Fill the bag with a small amount of glaze—be sure to keep the rim of the bag clean. 4. Squeeze the air out of the bag und close it by folding it from one side to the other, as shown. 5. Cut the tip of the bag to desired size. 6. Press with your right hand and guide pastry bag with your left hand to decorate petits fours and special cakes. If desired, you may also garnish pastries with sugar pearls and pieces of candied fruit.

COOKIES

The Christmas cookie season begins in November. The selection of international favorites is enormous, but we will restrict our recipes to just a few. Wonderfully soft ring cookies and bars will certainly inspire you to make more holiday cookies.

CHOCOLATE NUT BARS

¾ cup (180 g) butter, softened
¾ cup (100 g) sifted powdered sugar
1 egg
½ teaspoon vanilla
3½ ounces (80 g) semisweet chocolate, melted and cooled
2⅓ cups (300 g) flour
½ cup (70 g) finely ground hazelnuts
For the coating and topping:
8 ounces (200 g) semisweet chocolate, melted and cooled
chopped hazelnuts and pistachios

Combine butter, sugar, egg, and vanilla and mix well, either with a spoon or in a mixer with a dough hook. Blend in chocolate. Add flour and nuts and mix to make a soft dough. Place dough in pastry bag or spritz gun fitted with a star tip and pipe bars onto a baking sheet. Bake nut bars in a 375°F (190°C) oven for 10 to 12 minutes, or until golden. Remove from oven and let cool. Dip half of each bar in chocolate and sprinkle with chopped nuts.

RING COOKIES

1¼ cups (300 g) butter, softened
1¾ cups (250 g) powdered sugar
1 cup (125 g) cornstarch
1 tablespoon milk
3½ cups (500 g) flour
1 teaspoon grated lemon peel
pinch of salt
For the coating and topping:
8 ounces (200 g) semisweet chocolate, melted
½ cup (50 g) sliced toasted almonds

Combine butter and sugar in a mixing bowl and blend with a spoon or the dough hook attachment of your mixer at low speed. Add remaining ingredients in order listed. Shape equal-size rings on a baking sheet with a pastry bag or spritz gun. Bake in a preheated 375°F (190°C) oven for 10 to 12 minutes, or until light golden. Dip half of each ring in melted chocolate, then sprinkle with toasted almond slices.

MERINGUE CHRISTMAS TREE ORNAMENTS

⅔ cup (150 g) egg whites (about 5)
1½ cups (200 g) powdered sugar, sifted
2 drops each red and yellow food coloring
To decorate:
colored sugar sprinkles
sugar flowers
gold or silver sugar dragees
chopped pistachios
melted semisweet chocolate

Place egg whites in a stainless steel bowl, add sifted powdered sugar and beat for 1 minute at high speed. Place the bowl over a pan filled with 140°F (60°C) water and whisk until egg white mixture is at 110 to 120°F (45° to 50°C). Return bowl to mixer and mix at medium speed until cooled. Divide meringue into 3 portions. Add red food coloring to one portion, yellow food coloring to the second, and leave the third portion white. Line 2 baking sheets with parchment paper. Fill a pastry bag with the pink mixture and pipe desired designs onto a baking sheet. Repeat with remaining meringue mixtures. Decorate all 3 portions with sugar sprinkles, chopped pistachios, and any other desired garnishes. Place in a 125°F (50°C) oven, leave the door propped slightly open, and dry ornaments overnight. The following day, decorate with dots of melted chocolate.

Homemade Christmas tree ornaments are easier to make than you think. When finished, hang them from the tree with gold thread.

SAVORY BAKING

"Santé, Salute, Prost"—whether French, Italian, or German, in this chapter we have collected the most delicious, hearty baked goods from throughout Europe. They all go well with a glass of dry, fruity white wine: savory quiche Lorraine and brioche from France, leek tart from Germany, pizza from Italy.

Brioche, bread, and rolls are usually served with coffee or tea. The wholewheat versions in this chapter are brand new and really worth your while. They are wonderfully appetizing served with fresh butter, cheese, and ham. "Good gods, how many people does a single stomach keep on the move!" remarked Seneca, the rhetorician who lived at the turn of the millennium. This is still true—consider how many people work to supply us so that we can do our baking fresh at home. Here's a toast to them!

BRIOCHE, ROLLS, AND BREAD

Brioches are made from a yeast dough enriched with lots of butter and eggs. In France they are made in a variety of shapes and sizes—there's *brioche Nanterre*, for example, made from 4 balls of dough placed in a loaf pan. It rises for an hour and a half, is brushed with an egg glaze and cut along the top so it will split during baking, then baked in a 425°F (220°C) oven for 20 minutes. The small, individual brioches are the best known, however. They are baked in round molds with scalloped edges. Larger molds are available in the same shape, and they hold about one pound of dough. Bake these large brioches for 20 minutes, or until golden.

BRIOCHES

3³/₄ cups (500 g) flour
1 envelope dry yeast
¹/₄ cup (60 mL) lukewarm water
6 eggs
¹/₄ cup (50 g) sugar
2 teaspoons salt
1¹/₄ cups (300 g) butter, softened
3-inch (7-cm) round brioche molds

Prepare the dough in a mixer the night before. (You may double the recipe and freeze half of it for later use.) Cover the dough you plan to use and refrigerate for 2 hours; this slow rising process guarantees the best result. Knead dough briefly, roll into a ball, place in a large bowl, cover, and refrigerate overnight. The following day, knead again and continue as shown in photographs.

Preheat oven to 450°F (230°C), brush brioche with glaze, place on the center oven rack, and bake for 12 minutes, or until golden. Serve fresh!

1 **Yeast dough.** In a mixing bowl, combine flour, yeast, water, eggs, sugar, and salt and mix well. Knead dough in a mixer with dough hook on medium speed until it is light and comes away from the sides of the bowl.

2 **Soft butter.** Add softened butter in large pieces. Start on low speed and increase speed until dough is light and satiny.

3 **Shape balls of dough.** Weigh dough into 1-ounce pieces and shape them, using your hands, on a floured board.

4 **Brioches.** Roll a ball with the edge of your hand, separating ¹/₃ of the dough to form a smaller ball. Place the larger ball in the tin, then set the smaller ball on top and press it to adhere.

5 **Egg glaze.** Let brioche rise for 1¹/₂ hours, then brush with egg glaze.

6 **Brioches are done** when they are golden and shiny. They are very delicate and light because of the eggs and butter in the dough. The French love brioche with their morning *café au lait*!

194

Wholewheat rolls will bring a nice change to your breakfast table. If you have a grain mill you can make your own wholewheat flour, which will make your rolls especially nutritious. But be sure you buy the best wheat available from a reliable source, and store it in a dry place. Grind wheat, rye, millet, dark wheat (spelt), corn, and hulled barley on low speed, and rolled oats on high speed since they are softer. If you buy wholewheat flour to make rolls, be sure it is fresh. Wholegrain doughs need to rise longer than yeast doughs made with all white flour. You may add your favorite spices and flavorings to the dough, which, like brioches, can rise slowly in the refrigerator overnight.

WHOLE-GRAIN ROLLS

| 1½ cups (200 g) rye flour |
| 2 cups (300 g) wholewheat flour |
| 2 envelopes dry yeast |
| 1 cup (240 mL) lukewarm water |
| 1 teaspoon honey |
| 2 teaspoons sea salt |

Follow directions on page 194 to prepare the dough. Cover and let rise for at least 1 hour at room temperature (or overnight in the refrigerator). Punch down and let rise for an additional hour. Shape as for Wholewheat Rolls (see following recipe). Arrange on a floured baking sheet, cover, and let rise for 30 minutes. Slash tops of rolls with a knife, brush with water, place on the center oven rack, and bake at 425°F (220°C) for 25 minutes. Place a pan filled with water on the bottom of the oven during baking, because wholewheat doughs need moist heat to stay soft.

WHOLEWHEAT OR TRITICALE ROLLS

| 4½ cups (500 g) whole wheat or triticale (or 4½ cups wholewheat flour) |
| 2 envelopes dry yeast |
| 1 cup (240 mL) lukewarm milk |
| 1 teaspoon salt |
| 1 egg yolk, beaten |
| caraway and sesame seed |

Prepare the yeast dough according to the recipe on page 194. Shape into a long roll and cut into 10 to 12 equal pieces. Dust your hands with flour and roll the dough into balls. Arrange on a floured baking sheet, cover, and let rise for about 15 minutes. With a sharp knife, slash top of each with a cross. Brush with beaten egg yolk and sprinkle half the rolls with caraway seed, the other half with sesame. Cover and let rise again until doubled. Place rolls on the center oven rack and bake at 400°F (200°C) for 20 minutes. The rolls taste best while still warm, with butter. Use a serrated knife to cut them evenly.

TARTS AND PIZZAS

QUICHE LORRAINE

For the pastry:

2 cups (250 g) flour
½ teaspoon salt
6 tablespoons (90 g) lard
3 tablespoons water
For the filling:
4 ounces (100 g) lean bacon
1½ pounds (750 g) onions, sliced
6 tablespoons (80 mL) crème fraîche
2 tablespoons breadcrumbs
3 eggs
½ cup (125 mL) plain yogurt
2 tablespoons heavy cream
1 teaspoon flour
¼ teaspoon each salt and paprika
pinch of freshly grated nutmeg

Prepare pastry according to the recipe on page 164 for short pastry. Fit into a 10-inch (26-cm) pie plate or springform pan. Dice bacon and fry in a large skillet over low heat until fat turns transparent. Add onions and sauté for 5 minutes. Spread crème fraîche over pastry in pan and sprinkle evenly with breadcrumbs. Combine remaining ingredients and mix until blended. Spread onions evenly over crème fraîche and pour egg mixture over all, smoothing the surface. Place on the center oven rack and bake at 400°F (200°C) for 45 minutes; if quiche browns too quickly, cover with foil. Serve with red or white wine.

Savory tarts taste great any time. Make sure there are no cracks or breaks in the pastry so that egg mixture doesn't run out before it is baked.

LEEK TART

For the pastry:

1½ cups (200 g) flour
6 tablespoons (100 g) butter, softened
1 egg
¼ teaspoon salt
For the filling:
2 small onions
1¾ pounds (800 g) leeks
2 ounces (60 g) lean bacon
6 ounces (175 g) cooked ham
1 tablespoon oil
1 cup (240 mL) sour cream
2 eggs
3 ounces (100 g) grated Emmenthal cheese
¼ teaspoon curry powder
pinch of freshly grated nutmeg
salt and black pepper

Prepare the pastry dough as shown on page 164 and line a pie pan or springform pan. Cut onions and leeks as shown below. Dice bacon and ham.

In a large skillet sauté bacon in oil until fat is transparent, add ham and onions, and sauté for 1 minute. Add leeks and cook, stirring constantly, for 2 minutes. Transfer mixture to a plate to cool quickly, then spread evenly over dough in pan. Combine sour cream with remaining ingredients and mix well. Pour over leek mixture. Place tart on center oven rack and bake at 400°F (200°C) for 45 minutes. Serve hot.

Slicing onions won't make you cry if you use the processor. To slice leeks, hold several together upright so they fit tightly in the

feed tube. Feed them through with the pusher, to get neat ring slices.

Pizza has been introduced everywhere, and it's a universal favorite. It is made in a variety of sizes and shapes. At home, use a convenient rectangular baking sheet to make 4 generous servings. You may use wholewheat flour in the dough, if you wish. Then place tomato slices on dough or spread it with tomato sauce. You may add almost any type of fish, shellfish, meat, or vegetable—try shrimp or anchovies, sausage or ham, ground beef or meatballs, sliced bell peppers or mushrooms. Arrange ingredients on dough individually or in any combination, and always drip olive oil over the entire pizza before baking to prevent it from burning or drying out.

Place pizza on the bottom oven rack and bake for about 20 minutes, or until crisp. If you use cheese, choose mild varieties, which melt more easily. Try Italian mozzarella, finely diced and sprinkled over the dough, to make simple cheese pizza, or add some freshly grated Parmesan.

PIZZA DOUGH

| 2⅓ cups (300 g) flour |
| 2 envelopes dry yeast |
| ½ cup (125 mL) lukewarm water |
| ½ teaspoon salt |
| 2 tablespoons olive oil or 1½ tablespoons softened butter |

Sift flour into mixing bowl, make a well in center, and add yeast. Mix yeast with water and some of the flour to make a sponge. Dust with flour, cover, and set aside for 20 minutes, or until flour on top is cracked. Add salt and oil or butter and knead to make a smooth dough, as shown on page 194; dough should not be sticky. Cover and let rise for 30 minutes, or until doubled in size.

PIZZA MARGHERITA

| Pizza dough |
| 1 pound 10 ounces (800 g) canned tomatoes |
| 2 8-ounce mozzarella cheeses |
| salt and pepper |
| 16 fresh basil leaves |
| 3 ounces (90 g) freshly grated Parmesan cheese |
| ½ cup (125 mL) olive oil |

Roll out dough thinly on a floured board. Place on a greased baking sheet. Follow photographs and directions for pricking dough and garnishing pizza. Let rise, drizzle with olive oil, and bake until dough is golden.

1 **Prick dough with a fork** so air bubbles don't form during baking. Drain canned tomatoes.

2 **Arrange toppings on dough.** Mash tomatoes with a fork and spread evenly over dough. Top with thinly sliced cheese.

3 **Add basil, salt, pepper, and Parmesan** cheese, let rise for 15 minutes, drizzle olive oil over pizza, and bake in a preheated 425°F (220°C) oven for 18 to 22 minutes.

4 **The pizza is done** when dough is golden and crisp. Use a large knife or spatula to transfer pizza to a cutting board and cut into serving pieces.

Pizza with anchovies is a fabulous variation. If you have a convection oven you can bake several pizzas simultaneously, which is perfect for a large party.

TOMATO SAUCE
for pizza

2 tablespoons olive oil
2 onions, minced
1 teaspoon minced garlic
1 large can (26 ounces/780 g) peeled tomatoes
1 teaspoon oregano
1 teaspoon basil
1 bay leaf
1 teaspoon sugar
6 tablespoons (80 mL) tomato paste
salt and freshly ground pepper

In a deep skillet heat olive oil over low heat. Add onions and sauté for 5 minutes or until soft and transparent, being careful not to let them brown. Add garlic and sauté for 1 minute. Cut canned tomatoes into chunks and add to skillet with their juice. Add seasonings and sugar and simmer sauce over low heat for 20 minutes, or until thickened. Stir in tomato paste, remove bay leaf, and season sauce to taste with salt and pepper.

PIZZA WITH ANCHOVIES

Pizza dough (see box on page 198)
1 generous pound (500 g) tomatoes
2 small onions, sliced
½ cup (125 mL) olive oil
12 anchovies
15 black olives
2 8-ounce mozzarella cheeses
12 fresh basil leaves
salt and freshly ground pepper

Thinly roll out dough on a floured board. Place on an oiled baking sheet and prick with a fork. Cover with tomato slices. Sauté onions in olive oil until soft and transparent. Soak anchovies in cold water for 10 minutes, drain, and pat dry with a paper towel. Chop, if desired. Drain olives, slice mozzarella, and tear basil leaves into small pieces. Top pizza evenly with all ingredients, sprinkle with a small amount of salt and pepper, let rise for 10 minutes, and bake in a 425°F (220°C) oven for 20 minutes. Serve hot.

PUMPERNICKEL BREAD

1 generous pound (500 g) whole rye (or 6 cups rye flour)
1 teaspoon salt
1 teaspoon honey
2 cups (450 mL) lukewarm water
1 generous pound (500 g) whole wheat (or 6 cups wholewheat flour)
1 tablespoon coriander seed
4 envelopes dry yeast
1 tablespoon lukewarm water

To grind your own grains, see photos opposite. Remember that the finer you want the flour, the slower you must grind the grains; speed increases the heat, which will damage the grains. Make sure grains are very dry so they won't clog the mill.

Prepare the wholewheat bread as shown in photographs. If desired, grind the grains coarsely, but in this case increase the rising times. (Try adding hazelnuts and almonds, or sesame, flax, sunflower, or pumpkin seed. Add herbs and spices according to your taste—try caraway, fennel, anise, thyme, fresh herbs, or minced sautéed onions.) Brush bread with water before baking if you want a soft crust. Place pan of water on the bottom of the oven, to increase the bread's volume. Slice bread 3 to 4 hours after it comes out of the oven. Use bread within 2 days, or freeze it.

1 **Crush rye.** Use a grain mill to grind rye to a medium-fine flour.

2 **Add water.** Dissolve salt and honey in water, add to rye, mix, cover, and let ferment overnight at room temperature. It should smell sour the following day.

3 **Make a sponge.** Grind wheat and coriander to a fine flour. Make a well in the center, add yeast and lukewarm water, and mix well. Incorporate remaining flour into sponge.

4 **Add wheat flour mixture** to rye mixture. Combine doughs in a mixer with a dough hook.

5 **Knead dough.** Continue kneading dough on low speed for 15 minutes. Cover and let rise for 1 hour, or until doubled in size.

6 **Punch down.** First punch dough down with a dough hook, then remove from bowl, dust hands with flour, and knead dough on a floured board. Shape 2 loaves.

8 **Slash loaves.** Using a sharp knife, slash top of dough. Bake on the bottom oven rack at 425°F (220°C) for about 1 hour. Place a pan of water on the bottom of the oven during baking.

Homemade wholewheat bread requires time but not much work, especially if you have a heavy-duty mixer to do it for you. The bread is baked if it sounds hollow when you tap it.

7 **Place dough** in two buttered 9-inch (35-cm) loaf pans (pans should be ¾ full). Let rise for 40 minutes.

Conversion Tables

The following are conversion tables and other information applicable to those converting the recipes in this book for use in other English-speaking countries. The cup and spoon measures given in this book are U.S. Customary (1 cup = 236 mL; 1 tablespoon = 15 mL). Use these tables when working with British Imperial or Metric kitchen utensils.

Liquid Measures

The Imperial pint is larger than the U.S. pint; therefore note the following when measuring liquid ingredients.

U.S.	IMPERIAL
1 cup = 8 fluid ounces	1 cup = 10 fluid ounces
½ cup = 4 fluid ounces	½ cup = 5 fluid ounces
1 tablespoon = ¾ fluid ounce	1 tablespoon = 1 fluid ounce

U.S. MEASURE	METRIC*	IMPERIAL*
1 quart (4 cups)	950 mL	1½ pints + 4 tablespoons
1 pint (2 cups)	450 mL	¾ pint
1 cup	236 mL	¼ pint + 6 tablespoons
1 tablespoon	15 mL	1 + tablespoon
1 teaspoon	5 mL	1 teaspoon

*Note that exact quantities cannot always be given. Differences are more crucial when dealing with larger quantities. For teaspoon and tablespoon measures, simply use scant quantities, or for more accurate conversions rely upon metric measures.

Solid Measures

Outside the U.S., cooks measure more items by weight. Here are approximate equivalents for basic items in this book.*

	U.S. CUSTOMARY	METRIC	IMPERIAL
Apples (peeled and chopped)	2 cups	225 g	8 ounces
Beans (dried, raw)	1 cup	225 g	8 ounces
Butter	1 cup	225 g	8 ounces
	½ cup	115 g	4 ounces
	¼ cup	60 g	2 ounces
	1 tablespoon	15 g	½ ounce
Cheese (grated)	1 cup	115 g	4 ounces
Chocolate chips	½ cup	85 g	3 ounces
Coconut (shredded)	½ cup	60 g	2 ounces
Fruit (chopped)	1 cup	225 g	8 ounces
Herbs (chopped)	¼ cup	7 g	¼ ounce

	U.S. CUSTOMARY	METRIC	IMPERIAL
Meats/Chicken (chopped, cooked)	1 cup	175 g	6 ounces
Mushrooms (chopped)	1 cup	70 g	2½ ounces
Nut Meats (chopped)	1 cup	115 g	4 ounces
Pasta (dried; raw)	1 cup	225 g	8 ounces
Peas (shelled)	1 cup	225 g	8 ounces
Potatoes (mashed)	2 cups	450 g	1 pound
Raisins (and other dried fruits)	1 cup	175 g	6 ounces
Rice (uncooked)	1 cup	225 g	8 ounces
(cooked)	3 cups	225 g	8 ounces
Spinach (cooked)	½ cup	285 g	10 ounces
Vegetables (chopped, raw: onions, celery)	1 cup	115 g	4 ounces

*So as to avoid awkward measurements, some conversions are not exact.

Dry Measures

The following items are measured by weight outside of the U.S. These items are variable, especially the flour, depending on individual variety of flour and moisture. American cup measurements on the following items are loosely packed; flour is measured directly from package (presifted).

	U.S. CUSTOMARY	METRIC	IMPERIAL
Flour (all-purpose or plain)	1 cup	150 g	5 ounces
(bread or strong)	½ cup	70 g	2½ ounces
(cake)	1 cup	125 g	4¼ ounces
Cornmeal	1 cup	175 g	6 ounces
Bran	1 cup	60 g	2 ounces
Wheat Germ	1 cup	85 g	3 ounces
Rolled Oats (raw)	1 cup	115 g	4 ounces
Sugar (granulated or caster)	1 cup	190 g	6½ ounces
	½ cup	85 g	3 ounces
	¼ cup	40 g	1¾ ounces
(confectioners or icing)	1 cup	80 g	2⅔ ounces
	½ cup	40 g	1⅓ ounces
	¼ cup	20 g	¾ ounce
(soft brown)	1 cup	160 g	5⅓ ounces
	½ cup	80 g	2⅔ ounces
	¼ cup	40 g	1⅓ ounces

Oven Temperatures

Gas Mark	¼	2	4	6	8
Fahrenheit	225	300	350	400	450
Celsius	110	150	180	200	230